Do you not know that in a race the runners all compete, but only one receives the prize? Run in such a way that you may win it. Athletes exercise self-control in all things; they do it to receive a perishable wreath, but we an imperishable one. So I do not run aimlessly, nor do I box as though beating the air, so that I myself should not be disqualified.

St. Paul
1st letter to the Corinthians

The
SPIRITUAL
ATHLETE

a primer for the inner life

❖

compiled & edited by
RAY BERRY

illustrated by
NICLAS BERRY

Joshua Press
Olema, California

Publisher's Cataloging in Publication
(Prepared by Quality Books, Inc.)

The spiritual athlete : a primer for the inner life / compiled and edited
by Ray Berry ; illustrated by Niclas Berry.
p. cm.
Includes bibliographic references.
ISBN 0-9630839-0-2

1. Spiritual life. 2. Spirituality. 3. Mysticism.
I. Berry, Ray. II Berry, Niclas, ill.

BL625.S6 1992   291.422
QB192-10378

The
SPIRITUAL
ATHLETE

a primer for the inner life

Surely great words do not make a man holy
and just; but a virtuous life makes him dear to
God.

- Thomas à Kempis

It gives me genuine pleasure to be able to
dedicate this book to my Amish friends Joe and
Marie Delagrange. They *live* the life!

- RB

Contents

Foreward
Georg Feuerstein

Ever since my teens I have been intrigued with and challenged by the wisdom found in the spiritual traditions of the world.

The vistas and possibilities I saw opening up before me changed my life completely, I knew I could never live an ordinary, well-regulated life. I felt I had breathed a purer air, and I wanted to immerse myself in it wholeheartedly.

Little did I know then what such an avocation entails. The greatness of the people I was reading about did not come overnight, nor for the asking. Behind it lay incredible courage, persistence, and plain hard work over many years. But my youthful optimism knew no bounds and, to be sure, it carried me a long way. However, sooner or later it dawned on me that enthusiasm must be backed by appropriate self-discipline, and that on the spiritual path there is no simple forward progression.

There has always been the right person or the right book at critical moments in my life. More than anything, I have derived strength from hearing or reading about the struggles, experiences, and triumphs of the great masters of the inner life.

Thus I have quenched my thirst for higher knowledge as much on the dialogues of the saintly Sri Ramakrishna as on Kabir's and Mira Bai's poems, Lao Tzu's aphoristic sayings, and Meister Eckhart's talks.

These great men and women, as well as many

others, have been my most faithful friends for many years. I can vouch for their absolute fidelity and unfailing readiness to be helpful to spiritual seekers wherever they may be.

Enmeshed as we are in a culture largely devoid of profound wisdom and grand ideals, we need to seek out such steady friends as have been gathered in the present anthology. The twenty-two essays are brief portrayals, giving the reader valuable glimpses into the life and work of many beloved individuals from the East and the West, who have accomplished extraordinary things. As an added bonus, these exemplary men and women are quoted verbatim on the following pages. Ray Berry has done all pilgrims on the spiritual path a great service by putting together this volume, which cannot fail to inspire.

This book will educate as well as edify. Edification strengthens our essential purpose; it affirms our highest potential, which is our realization of the oneness of all beings and things.

Because the mass media, and everyone under their hypnotic spell, daily bombard us with a quite different message, we need to consciously cultivate that other perspective. I can think of no better way of doing this than by regularly refreshing oneself at the fountain of perennial wisdom springing from the great mystics, saints and sages of whatever culture and era.

Read on, then!

Lower Lake, California

SRI RAMAKRISHNA
and the Indian contribution to world harmony
Arnold Toynbee

Arnold Toynbee gave this talk at the Ramakrishna Vedanta Center in London on the occasion of the 1959 anniversary meeting in honor of Sri Ramakrishna.

I HAVE BEEN asked to speak, as well as to take the chair. I am much touched and honored. It is characteristic of the Indian spirit that an Indian religious order has invited an Englishman to speak at this anniversary meeting that is a memorial to Sri Ramakrishna.

I speak with diffidence, because I am an outsider. In a few minutes you will be hearing Swami Ghanananda, who will be speaking from inside. An outsider cannot say anything of much value. Still, I have several things in my mind which I should like to put before you: firstly, whether one is an insider or an outsider, one is deeply concerned, because religion is the most important concern of every human being who passes through this world. Secondly, religion knows no barriers of nationality. It may speak through a Hindu mouth or through a Christian one or through a Muslim one; but, if the message does truly come from the source of truth, it speaks to each one of us directly. Thirdly, this is the special insight of Hinduism, and the special gift that Indian religion has to give to the world.

Some of the religions that have arisen to the west of

India are inclined to say, "We have the truth." Hinduism would not dispute this, but it would go on to say: "Yes, you have the truth; we have it too, but neither of us has the *whole* truth or the same piece of it. No human being ever can have the *whole* truth, because truth has an infinite number of sides to it. One human being will get one glimpse. Truth is one, but there are many approaches to it. These different views do not conflict; they supplement each other."

This recognition of the many-sidedness of religious insight and experience was part of Sri Ramakrishna's message. It was also part of his life, because — if I am right — his life and his message cannot be distinguished from each other. He gave his message by living as he did.

The goal of Sri Ramakrishna's life was union with God. Having been born in India as a Hindu, he approached this goal first along the Hindu road. Later, he approached it along the Muslim road and then along the Christian road as well. But all the time he was also a Hindu.

A Muslim or a Christian might say: "You can't do that. You can't take our road unless you give up all others, because ours is the *only* right one." A Hindu will say: "I can take all these roads and many more, because they are not mutually exclusive."

On this point, I myself believe that Hinduism has seen further into the truth than the Western religions have. I also believe that this Indian understanding of the truth is of supreme significance and value for the human race today.

Of course, it always has been, and always will be, right and good that we should appreciate and value other people's glimpses of truth as well as our own; but this is particularly important today, when the peoples of the world are facing each other at close quarters, armed with fearful weapons. In this situation, the exclusive-minded, intolerant temper is not more wrong than it has been in the past; it has always been as wrong as it could be, but today it is more *dangerous* than it has ever been. The Hindu attitude is the opposite of exclusive-mindedness and this is India's contribution to world harmony.

Sri Ramakrishna was in this world for half a century: 1836-1886. Look up one of the conventional histories of India dealing with those years. You may not find the name Sri Ramakrishna in the index. You will find a lot about war and politics; the establishment of British rule over India; the Indian Mutiny. You will find something about economics; the digging of irrigation canals; the building of roads and railways.

Now open a life of Sri Ramakrishna. Fortunately he had a disciple who did for him what Boswell did for Dr. Johnson. This book is a very full record of his conversations, with a great deal too about his religious experiences, recorded at first-hand by an eye-witness. You will find that this book — it is called *The Gospel of Sri Ramakrishna* — mentions none of the things that fill the conventional history books about India in those same fifty years.

Sri Ramakrishna was born and brought up in a village in Bengal. He spent most of his life in a temple on the bank of the Ganges, only a few miles away from Calcutta. Outwardly, his life might seem uneventful. Yet in its own field — the field of religion — his life was more active, and more effective, than the lives of his contemporaries

— Indian and English — who were building the framework of modern India in Sri Ramakrishna's lifetime. Perhaps Sri Ramakrishna's life was even more *modern* than theirs, in the sense that his work may have a still greater future than their work may be going to have.

Sri Ramakrishna's action was communion with God. It drew to him people of all ages, and a group of his younger disciples, headed by Swami Vivekananda, became the first members of the religious order that is holding this meeting here tonight. If I am right, Sri Ramakrishna himself did not found his order in any formal way. You might say that it founded itself after his death through the continuing effect of his life on disciples who had lived with him during his later years.

There can be few people alive today who are old enough to have known Sri Ramakrishna personally. Most of us today can know him only at second hand, in the way we know, say, Socrates or the Buddha or Christ or Mohammed. But we can measure his spiritual power, like theirs, indirectly by seeing the force and impetus of the religious movement which he set in motion.

One last word: Indian ideals and Western ideals are not mutually exclusive. There is room for them both, and need for them both. Put them together, and they will be able, between them, to do great things for humanity.

SRI RAMAKRISHNA'S OWN WORDS

Some people insist that God is formless. Suppose they do. It is enough to call on Him with sincerity of heart. If the devotee is sincere, then God, who is the Inner Guide of all, will certainly reveal to the devotee

16

His true nature.

But it is not good to say that what we ourselves think of God is the only truth and what others think is false; that because we think of God as formless, therefore He is formless and cannot have any form; that because we think of God as having form, therefore He has form and cannot be formless. Can a man really fathom God's nature?

I see people who talk about religion constantly quarrelling with one another. Hindus, Mussalmans, Brahmos, Saktas, Vaishnavas, Saivas, all quarrel with one another. They haven't the intelligence to understand that He who is called Krishna is also Siva and the Primal Sakti, and that it is He, again, who is called Jesus and Allah. 'There is only one Rama and He has a thousand names.'

Truth is one; only It is called by different names. All people are seeking the same Truth; the variance is due to climate, temperament, and name. A lake has many ghats. From one ghat the Hindus take water in jars and call it 'jal'. From another ghat the Mussalmans take water in leather bags and call it 'pani'. From a third the Christians take the same thing and call it 'water'. Suppose someone says that the thing is not 'jal' but 'pani', or that it is not 'pani' but 'water', or that it is not 'water' but 'jal'. It would indeed be ridiculous. But this very thing is at the root of the friction among sects, their misunderstandings and quarrels. This is why people injure and kill one another, and shed blood, in the name of religion. But this is not good. Everyone is going toward God. They will all realize Him if they have sincerity and longing of heart.

SWAMI VIVEKANANDA
Swami Prabhavananda

 Before we can understand Swami Vivekananda —
or any other great spiritual leader or prophet— we must
understand the true spirit of religion. And by religion I
do not mean any particular faith, such as Hinduism, or
Christianity, or Mohammedanism, or Buddhism, but
what in India we call *Sanatana dharma,* the eternal
religion. In this eternal religion there is no dogma, no
creed, no doctrine, no theology. Three truths are pre-
served at the core of the eternal religion, and these may
be very simply expressed.

The first of these truths states that *God is.* This
proposition has been proclaimed by God-men in every
age, and in every age people have asked for proofs that it
is true. Many plausible arguments have been devised by
philosophers and theologians to establish the existence
of God. But every single argument substantiating His
actuality on the basis of logic and reason may be contra-
dicted by equally plausible arguments of opposing
philosophers. All attempts to prove the existence of God
through logic and reason are essentially futile. What,
after all, can the philosophers and theologians establish?
Only their particular idea of an absolute Reality, not the
Reality itself. And what guarantee is there that their idea
of God and the reality of God are one and the same?

The only proof of the existence of God is to be
found in the second proposition: *God can be realized.*
You can know Him, you can see Him, you can talk to
Him, and you can experience your oneness with Him—

in the transcendental state of consciousness.

And the third proposition is that *God-realization is the supreme goal of human existence.* We ask ourselves, Why am I here? What am I to achieve? The answer to these questions is, to find the abiding Reality in the midst of the transitory objects of life. Everything is ephemeral, everything passes away; except the truth of God, which is eternal.

When we come to the conclusion that these propositions are true, then we begin to understand that every being in the universe is divine. Divinity is our birthright. In the words of Vivekananda: "Each soul is potentially divine. The goal is to manifest this divine within . . ." Behind the sinner's sins, behind the saint's saintliness, behind all activities and desires in this world is that one goal — unconscious though it may be: to unfold the indwelling Godhead. Every human being wants to rid himself of his bondages and frailties, and overcome death. And after experiencing pleasure and pain, good and evil, in many lives, he finally learns this truth: Abiding peace and freedom can be found only in God-realization. And who realizes the eternal truth of God? *He who consciously directs his mind and life toward this attainment.*

Once we understand this message of *Sanatana dharma,* we can understand any great prophet or divine incarnation. And we can test whether a spiritual teacher is genuine or not. The criterion is: Does he give the message of eternal religion? Does he teach that God is, that He can be known, and that the purpose of life is to know Him?

IF a man becomes convinced that he should devote

himself to the attainment of God-realization, naturally he will ask: "Are there any exemplars of divine knowledge in this present age who can say: 'I have known the truth of God. I have reached immortal life. I have overcome the fear of death'?"

This question arose in the heart of young Naren, the future Swami Vivekananda. Naren was born with the ability to discriminate between the Eternal and the non-eternal. Sense pleasures and enjoyments did not attract him, knowing as he did that they are ephemeral. Philosophy and books did not satisfy him. He wanted to find the abiding Reality behind the fleeting things of life. He wanted to meet a man of enlightenment, a living example of religious truth. And so he went to various priests and preachers, asking each one: "Sir, have you seen God?" Not one of them could answer that he had.

At long last, Naren went to Sri Ramakrishna, who was serving as priest of the Divine Mother in the Kali temple at Dakshineswar. This meeting between Naren and Sri Ramakrishna has a great significance.The Master was living in the Dakshineswar temple garden as if on an island, far away from the noise of the world. He hardly knew how to read and write. He had no book learning. And he had no idea of Western culture, education, or politics.

Naren, on the other hand, was steeped in Western science and philosophy. And he approached religion with the Western spirit of rationalism and inquiry. As he had asked the others, so he asked Sri Ramakrishna: "Have you seen God, sir?" And the answer was: "Yes, I see Him, just as I see you here — only much more intensely."

From the very first, Sri Ramakrishna behaved with

Naren as if he had always known him. He said: "You have come so late! Why did you keep me waiting so long?" Then, with folded hands, the Master addressed the young man: "You are the ancient sage Nara, a part of Narayana [the Lord], born on earth to remove the sufferings of mankind." And Naren thought to himself: "Who is this man to whom I have come? He must be mad!" Yet the Master's behavior with others seemed perfectly normal, and Naren could not help but be impressed by his evident renunciation and saintliness.

After returning to Calcutta, Naren could not get Sri Ramakrishna out of his mind. And he began to visit the Master often, feeling the attraction of his magnetic personality.

Sri Ramakrishna, on his part, recognized Naren as his apostle at their first meeting. Furthermore, he knew his future disciple to be a *nityamukta,* an ever-free soul. An associate of God, the nityamukta incarnates on earth for the good of mankind. Sri Ramakrishna regarded six of his disciples as belonging to this category of perfect souls; and among these was Naren.

THE Master was very careful to train each of his disciples according to his own particular temperament and capacity. He considered Naren ready to follow the path of Advaita Vedanta, or nondualism, from the very beginning. In this path, the aspirant rejects all transitory phenomena, asserting that Brahman — the impersonal Existence behind name and form—alone is real.

In this connection, the following reminiscences, which I heard directly from Swami Turiyananda, may be of interest. This brother monk of Swamiji (Vivekananda's familiar name in later years) told me:

"At one time I was very interested in Advaita Vedanta. I spent much time reading Shankara and studying the scriptures, and therefore did not visit Sri Ramakrishna often. Later, one day, the Master said to me: 'Why did you not come to see me?' I explained to him that I had been studying Advaita Vedanta. So he asked me: 'Well, what is the truth of Vedanta? Isn't it that Brahman alone is real and that the world is unreal?' The Master added: 'You may say that the world is unreal, but if you put your hand on a thorn, the thorn will prick your hand. But there is one, Naren, if he says there is no thorn, there is no thorn.'"

When Naren first came to Sri Ramakrishna, he was imbued with the religious ideal of the Brahmo Samaj, a theistic movement whose members worshipped God as a Personal Being with attributes, but formless. Naren, in those days, therefore thought it blasphemy to say "I am Brahman." When Sri Ramakrishna wanted him to read the *Ashtavakra Samhita,* a treatise on extreme nondualism, Naren objected that the ideas expressed in the book were atheistic and sinful. The Master smiled and said: "Just read a little to me. You won't have to think that you are Brahman."

One day at Dakshineswar, Naren and a friend were smoking and making fun of Advaita Vedanta. Naren said: "How can it be that this jug is Brahman, this cup is Brahman, and we too are Brahman? Nothing could be more absurd!" Hearing them laugh, Sri Ramakrishna came out of his room and asked: "What are you talking about?" And he gave Naren a touch. As a result, Naren had an experience which he later described as follows:

That magic touch of the Master that day

immediately brought a complete revolution over my mind. I was amazed to find that there really was nothing in the universe but Brahman. . . . For the whole day I lived in that consciousness. I returned home, but there too everything I saw appeared to be Brahman. When I sat down to eat, I found that the food, the plate, the server, and I myself were nothing but Brahman. I took one or two morsels of food and again was absorbed in that consciousness . . . All the while, whether eating or lying down or going to college, I had the same experience. I was constantly overwhelmed with an indescribable intoxication. While walking in the streets, I noticed horse carriages go by, but I did not feel inclined to move out of the way. I felt that the carriages and I myself were made of the same substance . . . When this state abated a little, the world began to appear to me as a dream . . . When I returned to the normal plane, I realized that I had had a glimpse of the nondual consciousness . . . Since then I have never doubted the truth of nondualism.

SRI Ramakrishna did not want any of his disciples to be one-sided. Through the Master's grace, Naren had had a glimpse of the impersonal Reality. Now Sri Ramakrishna wanted to teach him that God can also have form. But Naren was firmly opposed to image worship, and used to call the Master's visions of the Divine Mother Kali hallucinations.

Meanwhile, Naren's father had died, leaving his family poverty-stricken. As the eldest boy, it was

Naren's duty to provide for his mother and two brothers. He looked for a job, but could not find one. Worried and sad, he came to Sri Ramakrishna and appealed to the Master to pray for the removal of his family's wants. Sri Ramakrishna said: "I can't make such demands! Why don't you go and ask the Divine Mother yourself? You don't accept Her; that's why you suffer so much." Then the Master told Naren to go to the Kali temple. On the way, Naren was filled with divine intoxication; and when he saw the image, the Divine Mother appeared to him living and full of consciousness. When he returned to Sri Ramakrishna, the Master asked him if he had prayed to the Mother on behalf of his family. But Naren had forgotten all about it; he had asked the Mother only for pure knowledge and pure devotion. Sri Ramakrishna sent him back to the temple to pray to Mother Kali to provide for his family's needs. At the sight of the Divine Mother, Naren again went into ecstasy. All his problems vanished in her presence. The Master sent Naren to the temple once more; and for the third time the young disciple could not pray for anything material. Then he understood the lesson the Master had wanted him to learn. He bowed before Mother Kali and Her power. After returning to the Master's room, he begged Sri Ramakrishna again to pray to the Divine Mother on behalf of his people. And now the Master agreed, saying: "All right, they will never be in want of plain food and clothing." This actually proved to be the case.

Naren had now realized God with form as well as without form. One day, he told Sri Ramakrishna that he wished to remain continually absorbed in the superconscious state, coming out of it only to eat a little in order to keep his body alive. The Master was displeased, and said: "Shame on you! . . . There is a higher state than that." Naren was born for the good of mankind. He was not meant to taste the bliss of God only for himself, sitting absorbed in meditation, but to share this bliss with others. And so the Master taught Naren the highest spiritual ideal: to realize God and live in the service of mankind.

How this service was to be performed, Naren learned in a unique manner. On one occasion Sri Ramakrishna was seated in his room, surrounded by his disciples. Naren was present. The Master was quoting the following teaching of a great saint: "Utmost compassion should be shown to all creatures." Sri Ramakrishna, in ecstasy, repeated the word compassion, and then remarked: "Who am I to show compassion to others? No, not compassion for man, but service to him as the manifestation of God." On coming out of the room, Naren said: "If the Lord grants me the opportunity, I will proclaim throughout the world the wonderful truth I have heard today."

And he did proclaim this truth: See God in every being, and serve — not as philanthropy, but as a spiritual practice, as worship.

After the passing away of Sri Ramakrishna, his monastic disciples plunged themselves into spiritual disciplines. Swamiji passed several years traveling through India as a wandering monk. He practiced meditation intensively and depended entirely on the Lord for food and shelter. Seeing his people's poverty and suffering, he realized that the economic and educational standards of the masses needed to be raised. How could they be taught religion when their stomachs were empty! He received the inspiration to plan a voyage to America, there to give the message of Vedanta and to raise funds for his needy countrymen. Money was collected for his passage to the United States, and Swamiji gave it away to the poor. Another fund was collected. But Swamiji wanted to know the Lord's will directly before undertaking the journey. After praying to Sri Ramakrishna he had a vision of the Master, walking on the ocean and beckoning him to follow.

VIVEKANANDA preached his first sermon in Chicago at the World's Parliament of Religions, where the Western intellectuals of his day had congregated. What was the substance of Vivekananda's message? It was the message of harmony and universality in religion. To quote from Vivekananda's Chicago Address:

> . . . if there is ever to be a universal religion, it must be one which will have no location in place or time; which will be infinite, like the God it will preach, and whose sun will shine upon the followers of Krishna and of Christ, on saints and sinners alike; which will not be Brahminic or Buddhistic, Christian or Mohammedan, but the sum total of all these, and still have infinite space for development; which in its catholicity will embrace in its infinite arms, and find a place for every human being, from the lowest groveling savage not far removed from the brute, to the highest man towering by the virtues of his head and heart almost above humanity, making society stand in awe of him and doubt his human nature. It will be a religion which will have no place for

persecution or intolerance in its polity, which will recognize divinity in every man and woman, and whose whole scope, whose whole force, will be centered in aiding humanity to realize its own true, divine nature.

This is, in short, the message of Vivekananda.

Now again, Vivekananda had a dream. And his dream was to harmonize the cultures of the East and the West.

If we go to the original teachings of Christianity, we find there the one eternal truth of all religions. And if we go to the original teachings of Hinduism, we find there that same eternal truth. But what is preached as Christianity today and what is preached as Hinduism, that is what we have to consider, and that is where harmony must be established between the Eastern and Western cultures.

What has been the emphasis in the West? Human-istic and scientific development. Yes, there are God-fearing people. But what is their objective? For the majority of them it is enrichment of their life on earth. The idea of contemplation also exists in the West, but, generally speaking, contemplation is considered to be a means for a temporal end. The religion taught by Christ — to know the truth, to pray unceasingly, to be perfect even as the Father in heaven is perfect — has become forgotten.

And what has been the emphasis in India? The spiritual life. Achievements in the external world were neglected because they were considered ephemeral. And what is the result? A few individuals devote themselves to God and become saints, and the masses fall into inertia and idleness because they are not ready to devote themselves to a meditative life. That of course is not the true religion of the Hindus, but that is how Hinduism has been preached and misunderstood.

And so the Western and the Eastern spirit, action and contemplation, are to be harmonized and combined. If external achievements are made the goal of life and God the means to reach that goal, there will continue to be suffering and misery. But if God is known to be the supreme purpose of existence, and activity and outward achievements are made the means to fulfill this purpose, then the divinity within man will become manifest, and he will see this divinity everywhere. This is the essence of religion, which Vivekananda summed up as follows:

> Do not depend on doctrines, do not depend on dogmas, or sects, or churches or temples; they count for little compared with the essence of existence in man, which is divine; and the more this is developed in a man, the more powerful is he for good. Earn that first, acquire that, and criticise no one, for all doctrines and creeds have some good in them. Show by your lives that religion does not mean words, or names, or sects, but that it means spiritual realization. Only those can understand who have experienced it. Only those who have attained to spirituality can communicate it to others, can be great teachers of mankind. They alone are the powers of light.

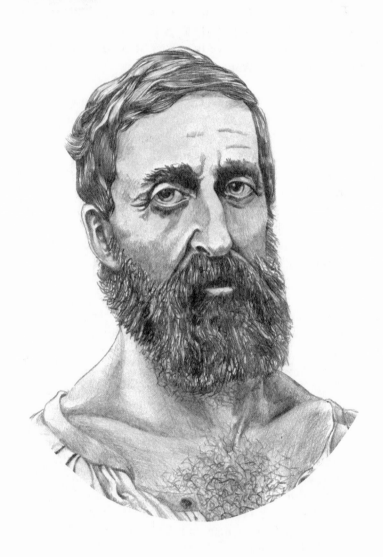

THE SPIRITUAL LIFE OF HENRY D. THOREAU

C. H. MacLachlan

In the summer of 1837, after his graduation from Harvard, Henry D. Thoreau, like many another bright young college graduate, was thinking about what he should do for a living. There were no corporation recruiters in those days, and no seductive baits offered by business and the professions. Thoreau would certainly have rejected them in any case, for he had already decided that he was going to live his life in his own way. But how? "How," he asked himself, "shall I get my living and still have time to live?"

His answer to this question must have seemed daring and unique at that time and would seem even more so to this prudent generation. For he had decided upon a reversal of tradition. "The seventh day," he said, "should be man's day of toil, and the other six his Sabbath of the affections of the soul." This was only seeming exaggeration. During the greater part of his life, he managed to live on only six weeks of gainful work a year. In New England such a thing was heresy. What good was a college education if one intended to do odd jobs for a living and spend most of his life in the woods? His fellow townsmen of Concord were nearly unanimous in their feeling about Henry Thoreau: he was lazy.

Henry was either too proud, too independent, or too much of a realist to offer any explanation. He revealed his aims mainly in his life and, when they were eventually published, in his books. "What I am, I am and say not. Being is the great explainer," he wrote. And in a letter to a friend he offered this bit more along the same line: "If you want to convince a man that he does wrong, do right. But do not care to convince him. Men will believe what they see. Let them see."

Emerson, his neighbor and good friend, understood. It was his touch that awakened Thoreau's genius, and the friendship begun in Thoreau's youth ended only with his death. Thoreau felt no shame in not studying for a profession, and Emerson approved. "My brave Henry," he commented in his journal, "does not postpone his life, but lives already."

For Henry, the ideal was all important and therefore not severe. He was a nonconformist by nature. He sternly disapproved of all frailty, especially his own. He was determined to live in as complete accord with his ideal as he could, and this was the central urge of his whole life. The intuitive awareness of an underlying reality often found in poets and men of genius was always strong in him. "Our whole life is startlingly moral," he wrote in *Walden.* "There is never an instant's truce between virtue and vice. Goodness is the only investment that never fails. Though the youth at last grows indifferent, the laws of the universe are not indifferent but are forever on the side of the most sensitive."

EMERSON greatly loved and admired his young friend and neighbor. "He was," he said, "a person of rare, tender, and absolute religion, a person incapable of any profanation, by act or thought." And in his funeral oration he submitted this explanation to the man who refused to explain himself:

I must add the cardinal fact that there was an excellent wisdom in him, proper to a rare class of men, which showed him the material world as a symbol. This discovery, which sometimes yields to poets a certain casual and interrupted light, serving for the ornament of their writing, was in him an unsleeping insight; and whatever faults or obstructions of temperament might cloud it, he was not disobedient to the heavenly vision. In his youth he said one day: "The other world is all my art: my pencils will draw no other; my jack-knife will cut nothing else; I do not use it as a means."

At what point in his life Thoreau became aware of "the material world as a symbol" is not precisely known. It has been suggested by more than one writer that he experienced some kind of spiritual rebirth, and that it took place soon after he joined the Emerson circle in 1841. As usual, Thoreau has given us no clue. Henry Seidel Canby, his biographer, indicates that Emerson discerned in Thoreau a genius that was not awake until he touched it, "that he felt an instant response of like-mindedness, and in his Olympian way overlooked the differences; that his magnanimity set about to create a poet and found unexpectedly an interpreter as Transcendental as himself and far more sensitive to the realities of the American fields and woods, which were the visible face of that nature which he worshipped in spiritual form."

Two verses from Thoreau's first book, *A Week on the Concord and Merrimack Rivers,* which date from this time, reflect some extraordinary experiences. They are animated by the thought which Emerson says "makes all his poetry a hymn to the Cause of causes, the Spirit which vivifies and controls his own."

> I hearing get, who had but ears,
> And sight, who had but eyes before;
> I moments live, who lived but years,
> And truth discern who knew but learning's lore.

And again in these lines:

> Now chiefly is my natal hour.
> And only now my prime of life;
> I will not doubt the love untold,
> Which not my worth or want has brought,
> Which wooed me young, and wooes me old,
> And to this evening hath me brought.

WHATEVER happened, Thoreau seems always to have been single-minded about purity. There was no apparent deviation throughout his life, no change off course; only an intensified experience. Emerson remarked while Henry was still young: "I can see, with his practical faculty, he has declined all the kingdoms of this world. Satan has no bribe for him."

It was at this time that Henry discovered *The Laws of Manu* in Emerson's well-stocked library. He reported the find in his journal with the excitement of one who has unexpectedly encountered a seminal mind:

> I cannot read a sentence in the book of the Hindoos without being elevated upon the table-land of the Ghauts . . . The page nods toward

the fact and is silent . . . The impression which
those sublime sentences made on me last night
has awakened me before any cockcrowing. . .
The simple life herein described confers on us a
degree of freedom even in perusal . . . Wants so
easily and gracefully satisfied that they seem
like a more refined repleteness.

When Thoreau read the *Bhagavad-Gita* some four
years later, the effect was even more significant. He read
it in the first English edition, the Charles Wilkins
translation of 1785, with a preface by Warren Hastings.
He quotes without comment in his Journal the paragraph
about action versus inaction. Arjuna is irresolute about
engaging in a battle in which he must meet and slay his
kinsmen and best friends. Is not understanding better
than action, he asks, which here leads to slaughter?
Krishna resolves these doubts, and Thoreau made
careful note of the answer:

A man's calling, with all its faults, ought
not to be forsaken . . . wherefore, O Arjoon, resolve to fight . . . Children only, and not the
learned, speak of the speculative and the
practical doctrines as two. They are but one. For
both obtain the self-same end, and the place
which is gained by the followers of the other . . .
No one ever resteth a moment inactive. Every
man is involuntarily urged to act by those
principles which are inherent in his nature . . .
So the man is praised who, having subdued all
his passions, performeth with his active
faculties all the functions of life, unconcerned

about the event . . . He who may behold as it were inaction in action, and action in inaction, is wise amongst mankind. He is the perfect performer of all duty.

Action and inaction, says Krishna, obtain the selfsame goal, since God is both and the issue is always in Him. A man must seek out "those principles which are inherent in his nature," and act accordingly. And this was the principal idea which Thoreau took from the *Gita,* that "the wise man . . . seeketh that which is homogeneous to his own nature." This struck a responsive chord in Thoreau, for years before he had expressed the same thought in different words in his journal, where he wrote: "We are constantly invited to be what we are."

THOREAU accepted the great religions, often with some expression of scorn for the narrow-minded. "I have no sympathy with the bigotry and ignorance which make transient and partial and puerile distinctions between one man's faith or form of faith and another's — as Christian and heathen," he wrote in his journal. "I pray to be delivered from narrowness, partiality, exaggeration, bigotry. I like Brahma, Hari, the Great Spirit as well as God."

Thoreau had read extensively in the Vedas and he had been profoundly influenced by what he had read. He believed in the practice of religion and not in religious attitudes. He excluded no religion and had even urged publishing together the collected scriptures of mankind: Hindu, Persian, Hebrew and many others. Many thought him arrogant, but he had depths of humility unsuspected by all but his close friends. He held the ordinary values of society in contempt.

Thoreau's interest in the *Gita* is reflected in the space he devoted to it in the *Week,* where among other comments he made this one:

> What after all does the practicalness of life amount to? The things immediate to be done are trivial. I could postpone them all to hear this locust sing. The most glorious fact of my experience is not anything I have done or may hope to do, but a transient thought, or vision, or dream, which I have had. I would give all the wealth of the world, and all the deeds of the heroes, for one true vision. But how can I communicate with the gods, who am a pencil-maker on the earth, and not be insane?

It would be interesting to know precisely when Thoreau read the *Gita.* His biographer says he probably read it in June 1845, after he had made his decision to go to Walden Pond. But this is only a guess, based on the probability that he had discovered the *Gita* through Emerson, who had just read it for the first time and was discussing it with enthusiasm in his correspondence. But it is challenging to speculate on the possibility that Thoreau had not decided to go to Walden prior to reading the *Gita.* There are no journal entries between April 1842 and July 5, 1845, the day after he went to live at the pond. Thoreau seldom acknowledged his indebtedness to persons or institutions, and he well understood the value of an epochal book.

"How many a man has dated a new era in his life

from the reading of a book!" he exclaims in *Walden*. What if the book behind *Walden* was that book of which Thoreau wrote in *Walden*:

> In the morning I bathe my intellect in the stupendous cosmogonal philosophy of the *Bhagvat-Geeta*, since whose composition years of the gods have elapsed, and in comparison with which our modern world and its literature seem puny and trivial; and I doubt if that philosophy is not to be referred to a previous state of existence, so remote is its sublimity from our conceptions.

It may well have been the *Gita* that sent Thoreau on the great adventure in simple living and high thinking, and one of the notable gestures of the human spirit.

Two days after he went to live at the pond, Thoreau gave his own reasons for the move: "I wish to meet the facts of life — the vital facts, which are the phenomena or actuality the gods meant to show us, face to face, and so I came down here. Life! who knows what it is, what it does? If I am not quite right here, I am less wrong than before and now let us see what they will have . . . Even time has a depth, and below its surface the waves do not lapse and roar."

The reason given in *Walden* when it was published nine years later differed only in its phrasing: "I went to the woods because I wished to live deliberately, to front only the essential facts of life, and see if I could not learn what it had to teach, and not, when I came to die, discover that I had not lived."

For Thoreau, living was the greatest art of all, the art for which he labored so hard on nature and his own thinking and for which he so eloquently opposed dishonesty, injustice, bigotry, and every device by which the spirit of man is enslaved. It was the art for which he cultivated so many arts, and in *Walden* he reveals how incessantly he worked at it. "Do not be among those who have eyes and see not and ears and hear not," he advised.

Was there folly in demanding too much of life? Not for Henry Thoreau. He was not afraid of exaggerating the value or significance of life, but only that he might not be up to its demands. In a letter to a friend, he revealed his eagerness to live. "I shall be sorry to remember," he said, "that I was there, but noticed nothing remarkable; not so much as a prince in disguise: lived in the golden age a hired man; visited Olympus even, but fell asleep after dinner and did not hear the conversation of the gods . . . lived in Judea eighteen hundred years ago, but never knew there was such a one as Christ among my contemporaries."

Lines from the journal of 1841 are a further avowal of his feeling. "My life has been the poem I would have writ, but I could not both live and live to utter it."

Like all great books, *Walden* is one that lingers in the mind and in the heart. It is a book for those who love all nature and wildness, and it is also a book for those who want to explore life, who want to live daringly and meaningfully. It is a book for those who have the courage to create for themselves the values they shall live by, and who reject all meanness and conformity. It is a book that is "solidly done," not "cursed with a style." It is a book to be read as it was written, in sentences and paragraphs, as a manual of devotion is read.

Thoreau had an original mind. He did not get his

ideas at second hand, not even from Emerson. He "filtered" them from himself. *Walden* is against the values which make "lives of quiet desperation" for the majority of men. Thoreau urged a life of principle dictated by conscience rather than a life of expediency dictated by society. He obeyed laws which he felt were more fundamental than those in force in the State. In *Walden*, he challenged the values of a society which refused to make an adequate return for a man's labor. And he offered a solution in simplified living and self-reliance, the deliberate reduction of one's wants to a level that could be easily satisfied, and still leave time to cultivate the garden of the soul.

"A man is rich in proportion to the number of things he can afford to let alone," Thoreau declared in *Walden,* and he noted in another place that "My greatest skill has been to want but little." But even Thoreau made allowance for exceptions to his rules. "I do not," he explained, "mean to prescribe rules to strong and valiant natures, who will mind their own affairs whether in heaven or hell, and perchance build more magnificently and spend more lavishly than the richest . . ."

"I do not speak to those who are well-employed, in whatever circumstances, and they know whether they are well-employed or not . . ." He spoke, he said, "mainly to the mass of men who are discontented, and idly complaining about the hardness of their lot, of the times, when they might improve them."

He was ashamed of time wasted in reading a novel or a newspaper. But he never felt ashamed of his rambles in the woods and along the streams of Concord, although his neighbors thought him lazy and a wastrel of time. "If a man does not keep pace with his companions," he said, "perhaps it is because he hears a different drummer." Living was the great art he wished to learn, and he felt that his neighbors who exchanged so much of life for property and respectability were the real wastrels. He was not thinking only of his neighbors in Concord or even in New England when he asked why men gave so poor an account of their time as if they had not been asleep. "The millions," he wrote, "are awake enough for physical labor; but only one in a million is awake enough for effective intellectual exertion, and only one in a hundred millions to a poetic or divine life." He had never, he said, met a man who was quite awake. "How could I have looked him in the face?"

PONDERING Thoreau's life after it was over, Emerson so much regretted the loss of his rare powers of action that he said he could not help counting it a fault in him that he had no ambition, that "instead of engineering for all America, he was the captain of a huckle-berry party." Few lives, he noted, contained so many renunciations. "Thoreau was trained for no profession. He never married. He never went to church. He never voted. He refused to pay his tax to the State. He never smoked tobacco, and although a naturalist, he used neither trap nor gun. He had no talent for wealth, and he knew how to be poor without the least hint of squalor or inelegance." Emerson said he had "no temptations to fight against — no appetites, no passions, no taste for elegant trifles."

Many of Thoreau's friends and acquaintances found him prickly, often blunt and even harsh.

His frankness could be painful to all he met. In his youth he was not fond of visiting, but could not bring himself to give the conventional reasons for declining invitations, such as that it was not convenient or that he was unable to go. Instead he spoke the truth: "I do not want to go."

There were thorny aspects of Thoreau that Emerson did not understand or that at least he found painful and limiting. "I think," he wrote after Thoreau's death, "the severity of his ideal interfered to deprive him of a healthy sufficiency of human society." Emerson found "something in his nature not to be subdued, always manly and able, but rarely tender, as if he did not feel himself except in opposition. He wanted a fallacy to expose, a blunder to pillory, I may say required a little sense of victory, a roll of the drum, to call his powers into full exercise.

"It cost him nothing to say No," Emerson wrote in a biographical sketch.

Indeed, he found it much easier than to say Yes. It seemed as though his first instinct in hearing a proposition was to controvert it, so impatient was he with the limitations of our daily thought. This habit, of course, is chilling to the social affections; and though the companion would in the end acquit him of malice or untruth, yet it mars conversation. Hence no equal companion stood in affectionate relations with one so pure and guileless.

Fine manners were an offense to him as was any affectation. "The finest manners in the world are awkwardness and fatuity when contrasted with a finer intelligence," he wrote.

They appear but as the fashions of past days, mere courtliness, small-clothes and kneebuckles . . . an attitude merely. The vice of manners is that they are continually deserted by the character; they are cast-off clothes or shells, claiming the respect of the living creature . . . The man who thrusts his manners upon me does as if he were to insist on introducing me to his cabinet of curiosities, when I wish to see himself. 'Manners are conscious; character is unconscious.'

Emerson had noted that the isolation which belonged to Thoreau's original thinking had detached him from the social religious forms. This, he said, was neither to be censured nor regretted. Aristotle had explained it long before when he said. "One who surpasses his fellow-citizens in virtue is no longer a part of the city. Their law is not for him, since he is a law to himself."

No college ever offered him a diploma or a professor's chair, Emerson observed, commenting that perhaps the learned bodies feared the satire of his presence. "Yet so much knowledge of Nature's secret and genius few others possessed, none in a more large and religious synthesis. For not a particle of respect had he to any man or body of men, but homage solely to the truth itself . . ."

WAS it strange that the man who had set for himself so high a standard should find himself so constantly disappointed in his relations with his friends? Thoreau's journal reveals an ambivalence about friendship that has baffled even his admirers. He had a passionate nature that longed for love and friendship, but if the journal is to be believed, he seldom, if ever, found a truly satisfying relationship.

"I find it wholesome to be alone the greater part of the time," he wrote in *Walden*. "To be in company, even with the best, is soon wearisome and dissipating. I love to be alone. I never found the companion that was so companionable as solitude. We are for the most part more lonely when we go abroad among men than when we stay in our chambers."

But in the journal he reveals a longing for friendship that he did not admit in *Walden*. "How happens it," he asks, "that I find myself making such an enormous demand on men and so constantly disappointed? Are my friends aware how disappointed I am? Is it all my fault? Am I incapable of expansion and generosity? I shall accuse myself of anything else sooner."

It was his greatest wretchedness to be loneliest when he was in the company of his closest friends, and Emerson was no exception. He is invited to see them, and "they do not show themselves." He feels "a thousand miles off." "I leave my friends early. I go away to cherish my ideas of friendship." "No fields are so barren to me as the men of whom I expect everything, and get nothing. In their neighborhood I experience a painful yearning for society."

Friendship for Thoreau was an ideal state, and he demanded much of it. There must be a sacramental quality about a meeting with a friend. "Unless we meet religiously we profane one another." "Our friend's is as holy a shrine as any God's, to be approached with sacred love and awe." And again: "Some men may be my acquaintances merely, but one whom I have been accustomed to regard, and mix up intimately with myself, can never degenerate into an acquaintance. I must know him on that higher ground or not know him at all." Friends need not confess and explain, but must be so intimately related as to understand each other without speech.

Sensibilities as fine as Thoreau's could seldom have found matching sensibilities in others. His noblest and truest thoughts on friends and friendship were communicated to the journal. There is much evidence there that he loved his friends, but with his New England reticence he never told them so. "Praise," he once wrote, "should be spoken as simply and naturally as a flower emits its fragrance."

THOREAU attracted admirers to whom he was, as Emerson said, "confessor and prophet." It was the praise of one of these followers that he disowned in this note of disparagement: "Do not waste your reverence on my attitude. I merely manage to sit where I have dropped. I am sure that my acquaintances mistake me. They ask for my advice on high matters, but they do not know how poorly I am now for hats and shoes. Just as shabby as I am in my outward apparel, aye, and more lamentably shabby, am I in my inward substance. If I should turn myself inside out, my rags and meanness would indeed appear. I am something to Him that made me, undoubtedly, but not to any other that He has made."

He lived steadfastly by truth. "Rather than love, than money, than fame, give me truth," Thoreau wrote in Walden, and nothing is more certain than the fact that he practiced it throughout his life. When he was a boy he was accused of taking a knife belonging to another boy.

"I did not take it," Henry said, and he was believed. Later the real culprit was found, and Henry then acknowledged that he had known at the time who had taken the knife. But when asked why he had not said so at the time, his reply was still the same: "I did not take it."

His character seems to have been formed from the beginning and was undeviating throughout his life. In 1851 he noted his resolve "to read no book, take no walk, undertake no enterprise, but such as he could endure to give an account of to himself and to live thus deliberately for the most part."

He was impressed by virtue rather than by mere professions of virtue. Actions not words. Thoreau found men talking a great deal about *doing good*, and he said he had tried it fairly and found that it didn't agree with his constitution. "If I were to preach at all in this strain," he said, "I should say, rather, set about being good."

"Do what you ought to do," he wrote in his journal in 1854. "Why should we ever go abroad, even across the way, to ask a neighbor's advice? There is a nearer neighbor within us incessantly telling us how we should behave. But we wait for the neighbor without to tell us of some false, easier way."

He did not believe in the ordinary values of society. One of his most quoted comments from *Walden* concerned this. "The mass of men lead lives of quiet desperation," he wrote. And again: "Most men, even in this comparatively free country, through mere ignorance and mistake, are so occupied with the factitious cares and superfluously coarse labors of life that its finer fruits cannot be plucked by them. Their fingers from excessive toil, are too clumsy and tremble too much for that. Actually, the laboring man has not leisure for a true integrity day by day . . . He has no time to be anything but a machine."

In earlier days when Thoreau was deciding what he should do for a living, he had considered trade, but soon decided against it, because he found that it would take ten years to get under way, and he was afraid by then that he might be doing "what is called a good business." For he was genuinely shocked to find men spending so much of their lives getting a living and so little in fulfilling the higher purpose for which he believed man was created. He believed that "trade cursed everything it handles."

That was why in 1854 he prepared another lecture which has come to us as the essay "Life without Principle." He felt that if he were to sell his forenoons and afternoons to society, as most other men did, there would be nothing left worth living for. A man might be very industrious and yet not spend his time well. "It is remarkable," he noted, "that there is little or nothing to be remembered on the subject of getting a living not merely honest and honorable but altogether inviting and glorious; for if *getting* a living is not so, then living is not."

This essay is not the work of a professional agitator or reformer, but of an upright man, a man who throughout his life was moved solely by principle. "The community," he said, "has no bribe that will tempt a wise man . . . An efficient and valuable man does what he can, whether the community pay him for it or not." He found it so difficult to dispose of the few facts which were significant to him that he hesitated to burden his attention with those that were insignificant. It was important to him to preserve the mind's chastity and not "to make a very bar-room of the mind's inmost apartment, as if for so long the dust of the street occupied us." "We quarter our gross bodies on our poor souls, till the former eat up all the latter's substance."

Thoreau also believed every man should perform his own duty. "Be resolutely and faithfully what you are," he wrote in his journal; "be humbly what you aspire to be. Be sure you give men the best of your wares, though they be poor enough, and the gods will help you lay up a better store for the future. Man's noblest gift to man is his sincerity, for it embraces his integrity also . . ." And on another day he wrote: "We are constantly invited to be what we are, as to something worthy and noble. I never waited but for myself to come round; none ever detained me, but I lagged and tagged after myself."

Thoreau was plain in feature and dress, and only five feet seven inches tall. William Dean Howells described him as a "quaint stump figure of a man," who habitually dressed more like a laboring man than a scholar. It was the eyes that enlivened the face. They were blue, deep-set and probing. We have Emerson's word for it that he was a penetrating judge of men. "At one glance," he wrote, "he measured his companion . . . and saw the limitation and poverty of those he talked with, so that nothing seemed concealed from such terrible eyes." He could detect hypocrisy in dignified and prosperous persons as readily as in beggars, and with equal scorn. In his youth and young manhood he must often have been an uncomfortable companion, but in his later years he mellowed so that Emerson found that "his foibles, real or apparent, were fast vanishing in the incessant growth of a spirit so robust and wise, and which effaced its defects with new triumphs."

Henry Thoreau called himself "a mystic, a transcendentalist and a natural philosopher to boot." Nature was a great passion with him, but his greatest skill was not as a naturalist. John Burroughs, the famous American naturalist, discovered an idiosyncrasy in Thoreau. "He was too intent upon the bird behind the bird always to take careful note of the bird itself," he said. But he added that, "All other nature writers seem tame and insipid beside Thoreau." And it is fundamental to Thoreau to be deeply concerned with the spirit manifest in form — the bird behind the bird. There was some strange, mystic, deeper meaning always struggling to the light. "At one leap," he said, "I can go from the buttercup to the life everlasting."

"Man," he explained, "cannot afford to be a naturalist, to look at nature directly, but only with the side of his eye. He must look through and beyond her. To look at her is as fatal as to look at the head of Medusa." What Thoreau was finally after in nature was something ulterior to poetry or science or philosophy. "It was," Burroughs said,

> that vague something which he calls the higher law and which eludes all direct statement. He went to nature as to an oracle; and though he sometimes, indeed very often, questioned her as a naturalist and a poet, yet there was always another question in his mind. He brought home many a fresh bit of natural history; but he was always searching for something he did not find . . . for the transcendental, the unfindable, the wild that will not be caught.

He saw architecture in the trees of the forest, the plumage of birds in the ripples of the Merrimack River, and man himself as only a part of nature's scheme, although sometimes a superior part. ("Shall I not have intelligence with the earth? Am I not partly leaves and vegetable mould myself?") He describes the formation of a small island at the confluence of two rivers as one who has been present at the creation of the world. He seems to see the earth in all of its ages. No beauty escapes his eye, and he has a name for everything. But he sees with the eyes of the soul. The society he loved best he found in the woods and along the streams or on the banks of ponds. There, in solitude, he felt his kinship with "the Spirit which vivified and controlled his own." And there in the cool of a summer morning, with the wind in the trees and the sound of crickets in the air, the man who had been called too cold for friendship could give expression to psalm-like utterances like this:

> My heart leaps out of my mouth at the sound of the wind in the woods. I, whose life was but yesterday so desultory and shallow, suddenly recover my spirits, my spirituality, through my hearing . . . Ah! if I could so live that there would be no desultory moments . . . I would walk, I would sit and sleep, with natural piety. What if I could pray aloud, or to myself, as I went along by the brookside, a cheerful prayer, like the birds! And then, to think of those I love among men, who will know that I love them, though I tell them not . . . I thank you, God. I do not deserve anything; I am unworthy of the least regard; and yet the world

is gilded for my delight, and holidays are prepared for me, and my path is strewn with flowers . . . O keep my senses pure!

Towards the end of *Walden* Thoreau summed up what he had gained from his sojourn at Walden Pond:

I learned this, at least, by my experiment: that if one advances confidently in the direction of his dreams, and endeavours to live the life which he had imagined, he will meet with success unexpected in common hours. He will put some things behind, will pass an invisible boundary; new, universal, and more liberal laws will begin to establish themselves around and within him; or the old laws will be expanded, and interpreted in his favor in a more liberal sense and he will live with the license of a higher order of beings. In proportion as he simplifies his life, the laws of the universe will appear less complex, and solitude will not be solitude, nor poverty poverty, nor weakness weakness. If you have built castles in the air your work need not be lost; that is where they should be. Now put the foundations under them.

ILL health clouded the last days of his comparatively short life. But as he grew older, he mellowed. His earlier strictures on friend and friendship no longer occupied a place in the journal. Emerson reported that "he grew to be revered and admired by his townsmen, who had at first known him only as an oddity." Over the years, he had attracted as admirers a number of men of like mind with whom he carried on a considerable correspondence, and who became very much like disciples. In 1850, he had written in a journal entry that "we inspire friendship in men when we have contracted friendship with the gods," but on the same day he had characteristically warned of the weakness of needing others: "Woe to him who wants a companion, for he is unfit to be a companion even of himself."

The last months of his life were peaceful. "There can have been few deaths more enviable," Mr. Canby writes, comparing Thoreau's passing with accounts of Northumbrian saints and holy men in Bede's *Ecclesiastical History*. He had begun to enjoy an entirely unsuspected popularity. Strangers sent grateful messages; children called on him; and boys of the neighborhood brought him game to eat.

Thoreau had confined his expressions of disappointment with his friends to the journal, and of these his friends were unaware. Emerson referred to him as "a friend, knowing not only the secret of friendship, but almost worshipped by those few persons who resorted to him as their confessor and prophet, and knew the deep value of his mind and great heart." And Bronson Alcott paid him a similar tribute in an article in the *Atlantic Monthly* a month before his death:

> I know of nothing more creditable to his greatness than the thoughtful regard, approaching to reverence, by which he has held for many years some of the best persons of his time, living at a distance, and wont to make their annual pilgrimage, usually on foot, to the

master — a devotion very rare in these times of confessed un-belief in persons and ideas.

A neighbor reported that Henry was deeply touched by the solicitude of his friends and neighbors and said that if he had known how people felt about him he would not have been so "offish." A friend, knowing that death was near, wondered "how the opposite shore may appear to you," but Thoreau replied, "One world at a time." And when his aunt asked him if he had made his peace with God, he said, "I did not know we had ever quarrelled."

Thoreau died quietly on the morning of May 6, 1862. Funeral services were conducted in the parish church where Emerson, "with broken, tender voice," read a eulogy of his departed friend, in which were included these words:

> The country knows not yet, or in the least part, how great a son it has lost. It seems an injury that he should leave in the midst his broken task, which none else can finish . . . But he, at least, is content. His soul was made for the noblest society; he had in a short life exhausted the capabilities of this world; wherever there is knowledge, wherever there is virtue, wherever there is beauty, he will find a home.

RABI'A

Ray Berry

THERE WAS A FIRE in the desert at Basra in the eighth century. This fire burned with a cool blue flame piercing everyone it touched.

This fire was a woman, Rabi'a al-'Adawiyya.

Of all things in that world— a woman who had burst into flame. A woman whose burning renunciation and fearless faith in God and steadfastness to the ideal left the ashes of the world behind as she carried many beyond the apparent to Al Haqq, the Real.

Rabi'a; Rabi'a, "the fourth" (that is what her name signified being the fourth child of her parents) would in truth become Rabia the first— God's first.

Rabi'a was born into a poor family living in a slum of Basra. But though poor they had firm faith in the will of the Lord. There was no cloth with which to wrap the newborn child, nor was there oil to light the lamp. The mother asked her husband to borrow oil from a neighbor, but he lived under a vow to never ask for anything from anyone, to only accept that which he felt came unasked from God.

The story is told that he had a dream of the Prophet that night which soothed his aching heart. Muhammad appeared to him and said:

"Do not worry, my son, your newborn daughter will be a great saint; she will inspire and be revered by thousands of my followers. Tomorrow you write a letter to the Amir and remind him that he is in the habit of

55

saying a hundred prayers to me every night and four hundred on Friday. Since he missed last Friday's prayers, tell him his penance is to send you four hundred dinars that were acquired honestly."

Rabi'a's father woke in great joy, full of tears, his heart overflowing. He wrote the letter that very day.

The Amir, when he read the letter, was thankful for the Prophet's remembrance. He commanded two thousand dinars be given to the poor and the four hundred dinars to Rabia's father with the message, "I would like you to come to me so that I can see you, but it is not proper for a man like you to come to me. I would prefer to come and rub my beard in the dust of your doorway. Please, whatever be your need, let me know."

However, in spite of this good fortune, hard times once more fell upon the family. Rabi'a's parents died and the ties with her three sisters were severed during a famine. All alone and helpless, her difficulties were compounded when she was abducted by a stranger and sold into slavery. One day in trying to escape from her master's clutches, she fell and broke her wrist. She cried out in despair, "O Lord, I am an orphan, a slave. My hand is broken. I feel I am a stranger in a strange land. I am not sorry for all this, but I would like to know is this your will, are you well-pleased or not?" Then she heard a voice say, "You must accept what I have to offer to you. You cannot dictate terms to me. My daughter do not grieve. Soon you will be the envy of the saints in heaven."

From this experience Rabi'a submitted to the will of the Lord and began her life of intense spiritual practice: prayer, fasting, and the performance of her duties as a slave in the service of God.

One night her master woke up and looked out the

window down into the courtyard. There he saw Rabi'a absorbed in her all-night prayer vigil. Suddenly to his eyes she became illumined, her body engulfed in a radiance which lit up the whole house. Of course the man was terrified and astonished. He crept back into bed and thought about this strange experience till dawn broke. Then he went to Rabi'a, told her what he had seen, and offered her her freedom or protection under his care. Rabi'a choose her freedom and with his blessing left Basra and went into the desert to continue her search for God-realization.

During this reclusive period in the desert, she had a desire to make a pilgrimage to the Ka'ba. On her way to Mecca, travelling the dry, hot, dusty road for days on end, she stopped exhausted and cried out, "O God, my heart is weary. Where am I going? I am a lump of clay, and your house is a stone! I need you here, the Lord of the house. What have I to do with only the house?"

God spoke in her heart, "Be content here with My name!"

Returning to her hermitage she applied herself ever more diligently to her prayer, meditation, and repetition of the name of Allah.

Even after she returned to Basra she lived apart from the world as much as her disciples and constant visitors would allow. She followed the path of poverty and self-denial with unwavering steps to her last days. Many well-meaning friends would have been honored to alleviate her poverty with gifts of money and provisions. She answered them, "I should be ashamed to ask for worldly things from Him to whom the world belongs. How should I ask for them from those to whom it does not belong?"

Once when she had fasted and gone without sleep, praying for seven days and nights, she became extremely hungry. A friend brought her food which a cat promptly ate. As she went to get a drink of water, the jug slipped and broke to pieces. In frustration she called out, "O Lord, what are you doing to me?" And she was answered, "Be careful, if you really desire it, I will give you all the pleasures of this world, but I will remove Myself from your heart, for your love for Me and the pleasures of this world cannot dwell together in one heart. Rabi'a, you have a desire, and I have a desire. I cannot combine the two."

When she heard this warning, she made up her mind to sever all worldly desires and hopes from her heart.

A friend of hers, one Malik Dinar, once found her lying on a tattered rush mat, with a stone for a pillow and his heart was torn at this sight. He said to Rabi'a, "I have rich friends and if you wish, I will take something from them for you."

"Malik," she said, "you have made a great mistake. Is it not the same One Who gives daily bread to me and to your friends?"

Malik replied, "It is."

She said, "Will He forget the poor because of their poverty, or remember the rich because of their riches?" Malik answered, "No."

Then she said, "Since He knows my state, what have I to remind Him of? What He wills, we should also will."

In the Sufi tradition it is prayer — inner prayer — the loving converse with God when the mystic speaks out of the depths of his heart, which gives the true measure of a man. Rabi'a's prayers reveal her depth more clearly than anything else.

At night she used to go up to her roof and pray:

"O My Lord, the stars are shining, and the eyes of men are closed. Kings have shut their doors and every lover is alone with his beloved, and here am I alone with Thee."

With this she began her all night vigil. When she saw the dawn break, she would pray:

"O Lord, the night has passed and the day is approaching. How I long to know if you have accepted my prayers. Please console me in this state of mine. You have given me life and cared for me. If You were to drive me from Your door, I could not forget You because of that love that You have instilled in my heart for You."

At one time Rabi'a lay sick in bed, and in the weakness which followed, she gave up her night prayer. However, even after regaining her health, she failed to resume her night vigils. One night, after some time had passed, she had a vivid dream. A beautiful maiden appeared to her and said:

Your prayers were light and your worship rest,
Your sleep was ever a foe to prayer,
Your life was an opportunity which you
    neglected,
It passes on and vanishes slowly and perishes.

When Rabi'a related her dream that next morning, she fell unconscious. Her attendant said that after this vision she never slept at night for the remainder of her life. When the day dawned she would allow herself a light sleep in her place of prayer. Yet waking with a start from this sleep she would exclaim, "O self, how long will you sleep and how often will you wake? Soon you will sleep a sleep from which you will not wake again until the Day of Awakening."

Prayer to Rabi'a was loving converse and total absorption with her Lord. There was no supplication for herself or for others. It was simply communion with the Divine Friend and perfect satisfaction in His presence.

> O Lord, whatever share of this world you could give to me, give it to Your enemies, and whatever share of the next world You would give to me, give it to Your friends. You are enough for me.

> O Lord, if I worship you from fear of Hell, burn me in Hell, and if I worship you from hope of Paradise, exclude me from Paradise. But if I worship You for Your own sake then do not withhold from me your Eternal Form.

> O God, my concern and my desire in this world, is that I should remember You above all the things of this world, and in the next I should meet with You alone. This is what I would say, 'Thy will be done.'

Miracles, physic phenomena, and occult powers (*karamat*, lit. "favors from God") can come to the spiritual aspirant during his advance along the path. This cannot be denied. They are a test, a supreme test. Sri Ramakrishna said that they should be shunned like filth as they are only serious distractions and obstacles on the way to the goal of union with the Divine.

The Sufis themselves set little value upon the exercise of such miraculous powers.

Abu Yazid al Bistami said, "The saints do not rejoice at the answers to prayers which are the essence of miracles, such as walking on water, and moving in the air and traversing the earth. Let not anyone who is perplexed by such things, put any faith in this trickery."

A man came to Abu Yazid and said, "I heard that you could pass through the air." He answered, "And what is there so wonderful in this? A bird which eats the dead passes through the air. A believer is more honorable than a bird."

Although there were instances of these powers manifested in Rabi'a's life, she turned from them deliberately, not by denying them, but by refusing to make a display of them and belittling their use by others.

Hasan of Basra, a notable figure in Sufi circles and friend and confidant of Rabi'a was given to extreme asceticism. As a result of his austerities, he developed some occult powers which he took great pride in displaying.

One day he saw Rabi'a on the bank of the river. Casting his prayer rug onto the water he called out, "Rabi'a, come! Let us pray two *rak'as* together."

Rabi'a retorted, "O Hasan, is it necessary to sell yourself in the bazaar of this world. This is necessary for people of your kind, because of your weakness."

Then Rabi'a rode her prayer rug up into the air and called down, "Hasan, come up here that people may see us." But Hasan, who had not attained that station, remained silent.

Rabi'a said to him in consoling tones, "What you did a fish can do. What I did a fly can do. The real work is beyond both of these tricks, and it is necessary to occupy ourselves with the real work."

Not only did Rabi'a disdain this miracle mongering, but she also had no taste for pious displays of religious emotion. One day she was passing by Hasan's house. He had his head on the window sill. He was weeping, and his tears fell on Rabi'a. She thought at first that it was raining, but looking up saw that it was Hasan's tears streaming down. She called up to him, "Hasan, this weeping is a sign of spiritual weakness. Guard your tears and hold your emotions in check so that you may build up the capacity of your inner life. Then there may surge within you such a wave of grace that you will have the strength to hold onto God's gift."

These words distressed Hasan, but he kept his peace.

It's not hard to imagine the condition of women in this place at this time. In many instances, women were treated no better than donkeys or goats, traded by fathers or brothers into marriage or slavery!

However, women in the Sufi tradition, women of distinct spiritual attainment, were looked upon as equals by their male counterparts. In Rabi'a's case, she held an exalted position among spiritual masters or adepts, surpassing the men in her understanding and realizations. It is to their credit that these men could accept her as one of their teachers.

Rabi'a had several proposals of marriage from both rulers and sheikhs, but she rejected them all, feeling that only by living a celibate life could she pursue her goal unhindered.

Abd al-Wahid ibn Zayd, a saintly man and founder of one of the first monastic communities near Basra, sought her hand. Rabi'a despised his offer and shunned him with the greatest loathing. She said to him "O sensual one, seek another sensual like yourself. Have you seen any sign of desire in me?"

The Amir of Basra offered her a dowry of a hundred thousand dinars plus ten thousand dinars every month. She countered:

It does not please me that you should be my slave and that all you possess should be mine, or that you should distract me from God for a single moment. Renunciation of this world means peace, while desire for it brings sorrow. Curb your desires and control yourself and do not let others control you. As for yourself, give your mind to the day of death; but as for me, God can give me all you offer and even double it. It does not please me to be distracted from Him for a single moment. So farewell.

Hasan of Basra also proposed that they should marry. Rabi'a replied, "The contract of marriage is for those who have a phenomenal existence. Here existence has ceased, since I have ceased to exist and have passed out of Self. My existence is in Him, and I am altogether His. I am in the shadow of his command. The marriage contract must be asked for from Him, not from me."

This same Hasan is noted as being a follower and disciple of Rabi'a. He was a learned man and a preacher, a noted theologian whose opinions on Sufi doctrine were held in great esteem. Yet if Rabi'a were not present in Hasan's assembly, he left the meeting at once. Hasan said about his relationship with Rabi'a, "I passed one whole night and day with Rabi'a speaking of the Way and the Truth, and it never passed through my mind that I was a man nor she a woman, and when I looked at her, I saw myself bankrupt, spiritually worthless, and Rabi'a as truly sincere."

YES, there was a fire in the desert at Basra, and after almost ninety years, it burned stronger and brighter and illumined the way for many others.

Attar speaks of Rabi'a as "that woman on fire with love." Another said, "She who is on fire with love of God, what fear has she of judgement." And another, "the fire of God which He has kindled in the hearts of His saints to burn away what exists in them of vain fancies, desires, purposes and needs." And hear these words of St John of the Cross: "Love has set the soul on fire and transmuted it into love, has annihilated it and destroyed it as to all that is not love."

IN old age Rabi'a was feeble in body yet so clear in mind that many disciples continued to come and seek her counsel right up to her last days.

There could be no fear of death for her. She knew that death was the permanent Union with her Beloved, above and beyond the temporary experience of union that could be attained in this life. The mention of death made her tremble not with apprehension but with infinite joy. She would have agreed with Abd al-Aziz who said, "Death is a bridge whereby the lover is joined to the Beloved."

IT seems appropriate to end this account of Rabi'a with a poem by Shams of Tabriz that captures the

essence of Rabi'a's life, the Sufi path, and the way of all
true mystics through the ages.

> I am not of this world, nor of the next,
> Nor of Paradise, nor of Hell;
> My place is the Placeless, my trace is the
> Traceless;
> 'Tis neither body nor soul,
> For I belong to the soul of the Beloved.

> I have put away duality,
> I have seen that the two worlds are one;
> One I seek, One I know, One I see, One I call.
> I am mad with Love's cup,
> The two worlds have passed out of my ken.
> For I belong to the soul of the Beloved.
> He is the first, He is the last
> He is the outward, He is the inward.

> If once in my life I spent a moment without Thee
> From that time and from that hour I repent of
>   my life.
> If once in this world I win a moment with Thee
> I will trample on both worlds, I will dance in
>   triumph forever.

> For I am not of this world, nor of the next,
> Nor of Paradise, nor of Hell;
> My place is the Placeless, my trace is the
>   Traceless
> 'Tis neither body nor soul,
> For I belong to the soul of the Beloved.

GERHART TERSTEEGEN
The Quiet Way
Nancy Pope Mayorga

GERHART TERSTEEGEN (1697-1769), a ribbon
weaver living during the eighteenth century in the
middle of a remote woods outside of Mulheim,
Germany, was chosen by God. He talked with God and
he talked of God, and people came from as far away as
England to hear him. They came by the hundreds to his
cottage in the woods, and when they could not all crowd
in, they used to bring ladders and boxes and sit on the
tops of them to look in at him and listen through the
windows.

What is it that calls forth a saint? Perhaps suffering
refines the soul, or difficulties challenge the man, or the
misery of others summons him. Or perhaps, more
simply, God sends the saints at certain times to give
comfort and courage to men. But the fact is that saints
do rise to meet hard times. Gerhart Tersteegen, for example, appeared at one of the most difficult periods of
Germany's history. For three decades the country had
been torn and strafed by a Catholic-Protestant war. In
other countries where this same struggle was going on,
in England or France, one or the other factions had been
stronger and a quick conquest was made. But in
Germany, Protestant and Catholic were evenly matched,
and the bitter religious conflict swept unresolved back
and forth across the country for thirty terrible years. The
people lived in poverty, terror, and oppression; and at

the end, society was so prostrate that it took almost two hundred years for recovery. It was shortly after the Thirty Year's War, at the depth of this awful depression, that Tersteegen was born.

As a young child he had wanted to be a minister. His mother, however, was left a widow early in his life and there was no money to pay for a university education for him. He was an introverted boy, delicate in health. Apprenticed to a linen weaver in Mulheim, he found the work too taxing for his strength and town life unsuited to his temperament. Fortunately, about this time, he met a devout merchant who took an interest in him and pointed out to him that he need not necessarily be a minister of the church to be a man of God. So as soon as he was finished with his apprenticeship, he moved to a cottage in the woods, took up the less taxing work of ribbon weaving and the supremely taxing work of self-purification.

For five years he was in what he called a "state of darkness." He admitted that there were times when he began to doubt there was a God at all. But then one day, according to him, he received "such an internal manifestation of the goodness of God" that all his doubts vanished. At this time he wrote and signed in his own blood a covenant with God, (reminiscent of Pascal's amulet), a strange document which was a kind of self-dedication and which seemed to have brought him much peace and joy. From then on, he always had an intense feeling of the presence of God, together with a divine ability for reaching, comforting, and inspiring other hearts.

His life in the woods was very simple. He took only

milk, water, and cereal, never coffee or tea, and he gave
away to the poor what money he did not need. His
schedule started out to be ten hours at the loom, two
hours of prayer, with the rest of the time devoted to
composing hymns, translating the mystics, writing
letters of comfort and advice, and speaking informally to
groups of friends on devotional matters. These friends
became his steadfast disciples and, because of their
meditative ways, were known through the countryside
as *"The Quiet Ones."*

This last occupation, which he had begun humbly
and reluctantly, began to take more and more of his time
as people came from afar to hear and question him, and
he had not the heart to turn them away. There were
frequently twenty or thirty persons waiting for a chance
to speak to him. Sick people sent for him and he spent
many a night at their bedsides. He finally had to give up
weaving altogether and, perforce, to accept small dona-
tions from friends and disciples to keep himself going.

The last twenty-five years of his life, though he was
plagued with ill health and neuralgic pain, were nevertheless given entirely to the welfare of others. In answer
to a need, he opened a small medical dispensary in his
home. He became known as "the physician of the poor
and the forsaken." He hardly had a moment to himself.
If he decided just to take a little walk in the country, he
was pounced upon, carried off to the nearest barn or
shed where a crowd would immediately gather. What
bothered him most was this absence of solitude, but he
accepted it cheerfully as the task God had imposed upon
him. Those who knew him spoke of his gentle character,
his affection, his insight into people, and his holy
anxiety to fan even the faintest spark of spirituality.

Tersteegen's teaching was as simple as his life, his relationship with God so childlike and unaffected as to be touching. "It is as if there were a little secret room in your heart where your best friend lives and waits for you. And so your love must urge you now and then to purchase some time, and if possible some outward loneliness, so that you can go to your friend in the little room and talk to him privately, and tell him how you are and that you want to love him truly. And when you go back again to your business, let it be as if you took your friend by the hand and begged him to come with you and keep you company while you work and take care of you. And that he will do most willingly."

He was a mystic of the purest type. The key to spiritual life, he taught, is surrender. "Renew in your spirit that complete surrender to God by a gentle but inward act of presenting your whole self to God. Aim at remaining privately there." He constantly urged a childlike attitude. "Do all your work in God's sight and in God, in as simple and childlike a spirit as you can." The titles of his hymns and poems often contain the word 'child.' "Dear soul," he sang, "couldst thou become a child!"

WHEN it came to the practice of meditation, Tersteegen had endless pieces of advice, in every letter, in every sermon. He never tired of encouraging and urging, and though his advice is informal, there gradually grows a formula in the mind of the one who reads him.

The formula is this— look at God and let Him look at you. In his own words:

"Prayer is looking at God and letting Him look on

us. You must withdraw into yourself a little and keep quiet before the face of God, then look gently and perfectly frankly at God who is so near to us, to let Him see if there is anything in us or near us which must be handed over, and assure Him of our hearty consent to give up everything to Him. Remain exposed to Him in the light of truth simply". And again, "We should try to keep close in front of Him so that He may have a good look at us and cure us."

What it amounts to, this formula, is a subtle, mystical exercise, the practice of simultaneous concentration and self-surrender, both simple and difficult. He has given us the fruit of his years of struggle.

In his sixtieth year, Tersteegen's health broke down from overwork. Nevertheless, he rallied and lived for another twelve years, and though he looked, it is said, like a corpse, he continued to work for God, never slackening in his constant zeal to encourage the least trace of spirituality wherever he found it. In these last years he collected his sermons and letters into a book entitled *Spiritual Crumbs,* and his hymns and poems into another called *The Spiritual Flower Garden.* In this flower garden he showed himself to be truly a gentle spring of God's love, gushing forth hymn after hymn of childlike adoration. Many of these hymns are in our present-day hymnals, still inspiring and teaching.

At last he wrote to a group of disciples, "My head is very weak and my body weary, but I must not think about that; there are various people here much more ill than I who think my visits useful or stimulating, and therefore I am not free to keep away from them. Dear children, do pray to God for me that He may make the short remainder of my days fruitful to His glory!"

FROM THE LETTERS OF TERSTEEGEN

We are conscious these days of a deep-seated hunger, a secret need in our heart's core, to be set free from the world and from self-centeredness and so to be reunited with our source. We must only be in earnest about it. The power is close at hand.

Truly spiritual souls have no special sect of their own. I extol the holiness of these souls, not the name of their religion.

The true inner life is no strange or new thing; it is the ancient and true worship of God, the Christian life in its beauty and in its own peculiar form. Truly inward souls make no particular sects; if each one followed the teaching and life of Jesus by His Spirit, then, without any doubt, everyone would live the inner life and the world would be full of mystics.

You don't need to search for God; you have only to realize Him.

The inner life is much less known than one would imagine, even among those who have been called. The urge to the inner life is an urge to be hid with Him.

Outwardly narrow, inwardly wide, is my old rule.

We must speak with God in prayer, whether verbally or with our hearts; but we must not only pray, for we must also be silent before God, so that He may speak a little word unto our hearts.

We come now to what makes us men happy: and when I do speak of happiness, I do mean holy-making; for the holier we become, the happier do we become; and as soon as Christ does make us holy, then does He make us happy also.

Reason is, in itself, a noble faculty, so long as it is subservient to the mind; but it is a most harmful thing when it rules the mind. Oh, Reason, be still! The sea is all too wide and all too deep; here is no soil for thy wisdom and thy speculation. The evil neighbor, one's own mocking, sly reason, is a false advocate which crams men's heads with all manner of sham reasons for everything.

From the head into the heart, for not in the head but in the heart is there revealed that pure and true understanding whereby we may know God and the things of God; for the heart is the eye of the understanding, which must be opened for us by God. We can never find God and truth through the activity of the mind, but through the heart and through love.

We see, we admire, we bury ourselves in things which are not, and Him who *is*, we leave out of consideration.

In your conduct, try always to move forward without undue deliberation, in simplicity and innocence, like a speechless child. Do not think ahead and do not look back! Both bring unrest and are harmful to you in your present condition. The present moment must be your dwelling-place. There only can we find God and His will.

To pick up a straw with loving intention is more to God than to remove mountains without love.

A certain amount of movement and external affairs are good from time to time. It is not work which brings harm so long as the work goes no farther than your hands and the outer man; but your heart stays with God.

Let our real work be apart from us and everything. All else, even the edification of our neighbor, must only be in passing and with great moderation.

Accept everything then as from the hand of God; do all your work as in God's sight and in God, in as simple and childlike a spirit as you can. And just as we are glad when the sun shines, so that we can do our work, be glad inwardly that you have God as a close friend in whom everywhere and at all times, outwardly and inwardly, you can work, live, move, die, and love. Now God is, as

I have just said, really present everywhere, but, because He is a spirit, He is present in quite a special and more blessed way to our spirit. God is more inward than our most intimate thought. There He calls us, there He waits for us. He wants to impart Himself to us and make us blessed. This presence, too, we must believe in simply, without understanding it, yes, even without wanting to be always conscious of it.

As far as I am concerned, I would lead a completely different kind of life if I had the choice. I have to read, and write, and have intercourse with men, when I would much rather, according to my own wishes, remain almost completely silent, hide myself away, and think only of God.

Whosoever says solitude with God, says also: fundamental withdrawal from oneself and from one's fellow men. Solitude is the school of godliness; for this reason you must wholly shun needless intercourse with men.

One is too naive, if one thinks that, by conversion, one is completely ready in a few hours or days. It is wrong, however, to speak of an early conversion in which the religious character was wanting and then of a second change, which occurred some years later. Religious development is a constantly deeper submersion into the Divine.

All things can be a help to us, and all things can assist us on our way, yet if everything outside us, not only the good things of our life but all the outward things, cannot conform to the nature of our soul, then can our soul find no peace and no life in them. Oh how often must one grieve to see that so many of us in our exodus from spiritual Egypt take with us such a quantity of large bundles and of packages! Do but see! This can lead but to a most onerous journey; we must go out like pilgrims, free, simple, and truly empty-handed. All this collecting of things together and keeping them only makes our going hard. Whoever does earnestly seek peace for his soul must strive to make his pack as small as possible, so that he will fare even as a pilgrim.

The Lord gives a cross according to strength — or strength according to the cross.

Think and care in no wise about what is to come. Love and suffer in the present moment, thinking more about God and His strength than of yourself and your weakness. If increase of suffering comes, increase of grace will come also.

It is a little thing for Him to let us find in our souls in one moment, without any trouble, what we may have been seeking for years with much trouble outside ourselves.

Just stay where you are and unite yourselves with God as with something there already that you do not need to seek! For God is certainly with you and in you.

Drink then to the very dregs the cup handed to you by no enemy and no stranger, but by your Father.

I do not as yet desire the death of the body, but that death I do desire where I can neither find nor see myself any more.

Death releases God's children from this anxious world, from the narrow prison of this body of humiliations, from all spiritual perils, when it joyfully moves into the boundlessness of loving, sweet eternity. And indeed, this last birth is often sorely distressing so that the child must moan and weep until it is ended, but it is all for his best.

The storm and tempest of the sufferings of our time rush past us like a short, troubled dream, and then we will rest in God for ever.

Don't worry if you cannot understand everything I write. You don't need it all: take a little crumb from the dish for yourself, and let your friends take some too.

HYMNS BY TERSTEEGEN

The Tired Child

Ah God! the world hath nought to please;
One loses strength and light and peace
In needful toil of sense and brain;
Would I might here with Thee remain!
I am sated with these things of nought,
Wearied with hearing, sight, and thought;
O Mother-Heart to Thee I turn,
Comfort Thy child, for Thee I yearn;
Thy love, most gentle-innocent!
Would that each hour might there be spent,
That I absorbed in Thee might live,
And childlike to my Father cleave.
Like a parched field my soul doth lie
Pining beneath a sultry sky;
O Heavenly Dew, O gentle Rain,
Descend and bid it bloom again.

The Task

To learn, and yet to learn, whilst life goes by,
So pass the student's days;
And thus be great, and do great things, and die,
And lie embalmed with praise.

My work is but to lose and to forget,
Thus small, despised to be;
All to unlearn—this task before me set;
Unlearn all else but Thee.

The Mote in the Sunbeam

I lose me in the thought!
How great is God— and I how merely nought!
What doth that Sun whence clearest splendors stream
Know of the mote that dances in his beam?
Nay, if I may but ever live and move
In the One Being who is perfect Love,
Th' Eternal and the Infinite alone,
Let me forget all else, and all I deemed my own!
Closer than my own self art Thou to me,
So let me wholly yield myself to Thee;
Be Thou my sun, my selfishness destroy,
Thy atmosphere of Love be all my joy,
Thy presence be my sunshine ever bright,
My soul the little mote that lives but in Thy light!

Within

Within, within, O turn
Thy spirit's eyes, and learn
Thy wandering senses gently to control;
Thy dearest Friend dwells deep within thy soul,
And asks thyself of thee
That heart and mind and sense He may make whole
In perfect harmony.
Doth not thy inmost spirit yield
And sink where love stands thus revealed?
Be still and veil thy face,
The Lord is here, this is His holy place!
Then back to earth, and 'mid its toil and throng
One glance within will keep thee calm and strong;
And when the toil is o'er, O God, to flee
Within, to Thee.

MASTER OF THE NAME
The Baal Shem Tov
A Jewish Saint
Rabbi Asher Block

JEWISH HISTORY ENCOMPASSES more than forty centuries of a people's experience. During that span there were — not counting current life — eight important eras, each lasting about five hundred years. What is remarkably significant is that in each of these distinctive periods there was at least one towering religious figure who specially endowed it with its cultural or spiritual character. Those illuminating personalities, for the successive epochs they represented, were: Abraham (for the Patriarchal stage), Moses (for the Foundation-setting), Isaiah (for the Prophetic era), Mattattias (for the Priestly), Akiba (for the Rabbinic), Saadia (for the Gaonic), Maimonides (for the Philosophic), and Baal Shem Tov (for the Kabalist-Hasidic).

RABBI Israel *Baal Shem Tov* — sage and saint of our own times — is generally identified as the founder of the Hasidic movement. The term Hasidism derives from the Hebrew *hasid*, usually translated as 'pious' or 'saintly'. But what constitutes saintliness? At the risk of oversimplifying a profound matter, one might suggest that the root of that word itself — *hesed*, 'kindness' or 'love'— holds the clue to an answer. Pure, unselfish, all-inclusive love has been the hallmark of the great saints of all faiths—and such was also the case with Rabbi Israel.

The cognomen *Baal Shem*. 'Possessor or Master of The [God's] Name', which contemporaries and subsequent generations conferred upon him, was not new, but the connotations now were fundamentally different. Previously one so entitled was presumed to possess occult powers, whereas now with the addition of the adjective *Tov* — (good or kindly) it signified one who lives with and for his fellowmen, gaining their confidence, because he was steadfast in his relationship with the Divine.

Folk tradition relates that to his exceptionally upright and pious parents, in their advanced age, it was announced in a vision that they would have a son, to be named Israel, who was destined to enlighten his people in Godliness. Shortly after his birth, in 1700, his mother died, and before very long his father as well, yet he was carefully tended in the community throughout his early youth.

Subsequently he embarked on his own, conscientiously immersing himself in the building of his spiritual life from within, while outwardly performing semi-public religious services as tutor, sexton, and the like. His wife, whom he felt he met in a predestined way, was a true helpmate. She shared in the struggles during times of privation, and provided understanding support during his prolonged and profound contemplative moods. Indeed, he reverenced her as a saint. This rigorous pattern of seeking and training was pursued well into middle age, until about his fortieth year.

That which sparked this extraordinary devotional effort, according to his own account, was the final verbal legacy to him of his revered father, his first teacher.

> Before his passing, my father instructed me in these words: "My son, be sure to remember always that God is with you! Do not ever allow your mind to digress from this awareness" . . . These words were carefully treasured in my heart, and it became my deliberate practice to strengthen within myself the holy conviction that 'the whole earth is filled with God's glory' and that He is really with me at every step.

This is truly a precious testimony, for it affords us a glimpse into the inner life of a saint, and into what is prerequisite for a genuine spirituality and a comprehensive morality. Baal Shem was not content with abstractions or a formal creed; he strove and strove zealously until he actually realized the Spiritual-Universal God as a continuing Presence in his life.

In the last fifteen or twenty years of his earthly career, until his passing in 1760, while serving principally as a Rabbi in Medziboz and its environs, the province of Podolia in Eastern Europe, he gathered around him and trained a group of dedicated disciples, and simultaneously inspired a wider circle of devotees, numbering perhaps several thousand. These in turn, in later years, were multiplied into scores of thousands, thus deeply affecting the course of Jewish life in the last two hundred years.

THE Baal Shem's teachings, through example and precept, are many faceted, and can be highlighted and condensed into five major categories. First is God's Omnipresence. Time and again did he declare: "There is no spot where God is not." Of course not everyone 'sees' Him, because the physical creation is a 'garment' the Lord has put on, whereby— in a wondrously subtle manner— He is both revealed and concealed.

"But why," the Baal Shem was once pressed, "should God wish at all to hide from us?" To which he replied: "Observe well how a devoted father when teaching his young son to walk, stands in front of him, speaks encouragingly and holds his two hands on either side of the child. The boy goes toward his father with outstretched arms, but the moment he comes close to him the father moves away a little and holds his hands farther apart. He does this over and over so that the child may learn to walk."

According to an earlier mystical doctrine of Kabalah, which the Baal Shem largely accepted, there are 'holy sparks' in every nook and corner of creation. Through awareness of them, we are all one in God.

The 'need to be aware' brings us to the second category, that of *Intensive Worship*. Revelation, the communion between God and man, is potentially continuous, but we must yearn to experience it. When eating, drinking, working, the Baal Shem directed, take care that all should be 'for the sake of God'. Even if wrong was done, the possibility of 'return' is ever present. "No one has fallen so low as to be unable to raise himself to God"— was a favorite saying of his.

And he was eminently practical: he aimed at being as precise in his dealing with Faith and Prayer as others are in dealing with law and ritual. To illustrate:

> We are bid in the Bible 'to cleave to the Lord.' How to do that? Well, the Baal Shem taught to cleave to the Divine that is within you.

> Man is where his mind is! In man there is a
> divine soul whereby he rises above his corpore-
> al and mundane existence, above his sufferings
> and ills . . . 'Forgetfulness of God is exile,
> remembrance is Redemption.'

> 'The object of the whole Torah is that man
> should become a Torah himself,' and a most
> effective way of attaining this Goal is through
> clinging to the words of Torah whose essence is
> the Name of God. This is done through prayer,
> meditation, or spiritual study.

Here is practical wisdom for penetrating the secret
of *Mastering the Lord's Name*. It is in substance what
the Decalogue enjoins upon us when it prescribes, 'Take
not God's Name in vain'— but rather in conviction and
earnestness. Zeal and sincerity are the key to man's
relation to God. *Rachmana libba ba'ay* — 'God, the
Merciful, desires the devotee's heart'. There are numerous Hasidic tales, of shepherds in the fields or workers
at their jobs, who in their own unique ways succeeded in
true worship, because they were diligent and sincere.

A memorable anecdote among Hasidim recalls that
the Baal Shem once stood watching a tightrope walker
cross a dangerous ravine. Some followers were curious
as to why he should spend time on this 'secular' event.
Whereupon the Master explained that there is a lesson to
be learned:

> What enables the acrobat to do what he
> does? Do not most humans have physical and
> mental capacities as he? Ah, but one thing they

85

lack: his *confidence* to do it, based upon repeated practices and experience. Just think how
many chasms in life we could safely cross, if
only we built our faith through practice!

The third and fourth categories in the total teaching
are *Help of a Teacher* and *Removal of Obstacles.* These
are highly valuable in the process of implementing God-
consciousness through spiritual practice. A qualified
guide, who himself has blazed a path in spirituality, can
assist others tremendously in inspiration and methods.
The Baal Shem himself, in his teaching approach,
generally stressed the following priorities: the individual
over the mass, internal values versus externals, specific
techniques rather than vague ones, the positive (where
possible) instead of the negative, the promise of
redemption above preoccupation with sin, a cheerful,
not gloomy disposition, and the 'heart' in preference to
the 'brain'. It is told that when a perplexed father came
seeking some light on how to handle his son who was
not responding to lecturing and disciplines, this
exemplar-teacher simply and characteristically advised,
'Love Him more'.

As for the Removal of Obstacles here too the
agenda is quite explicit and clear. 'Before you can find
God you must lose yourself.' 'To rise to holiness,
worldly cravings must be subdued.' Coveting and mate-
rialism, sensuality and pride — these negate, and hence
obstruct, our quest for the Divine.

The fifth category pertains to *Interhuman Relations.*
'Love of neighbor', the Baal Shem insisted, is integral to
'Love of God'. Can one truly love the parent without
loving the children? 'Let no one think oneself superior

to others, for in each is embedded some God-given quality.' Judaism, for this saintly mentor, was a religion of respect for all — the prominent and the lowly, the rich and the poor, the learned and the unlearned, men and women, young and old. He ministered to them in temples, in the alleyways, at the market, in taverns, day or night. He reached out to as many people as possible, no place too distant and no man not worthy of his love. He said, "To pull another out of the mud a man must wade into the mud himself."

He pulled many out of the mud. He did not judge others.

His deep spiritual tendency developed in him a high regard for the common folk. He was a man of the people in the true sense of the word.

TALES IN THE TRADITION OF THE BAAL SHEM TOV

"Do you want to know what *Hasidism* is? Do you know the story of the ironmonger who wanted to become independent? He bought an anvil, a hammer and bellows and went to work. Nothing happened — the forge remained inert. Then an old ironmonger, whose advice he sought, told him: 'You have everything you need except the spark!' That is what Hasidism is: the spark."

The Baal Shem considered it an art and virtue to listen to others.

One day he saw a man who had had too much to

drink; he was stammering and singing sad songs. The Baal Shem listened attentively, and remarked: "When a man confesses himself, the way he chooses to do it doesn't matter. One may not turn away."

"Small Tzaddikim like small sinners, a great Tzaddik likes a great sinner."

He warned people to be suspicious of anyone claiming to have all the answers: "You want to know if a particular Rebbe is genuine? Ask him if he knows a way to chase impure thoughts from your mind; if he says yes, you'll know he is a fake."

"As long as the branch is not cut from the tree every hope is justified."

Said the Baal Shem, "I was riding in a coach drawn by three horses, and not one of them was neighing. I could not understand why. Until the day we came across a peasant on the road who shouted at me to loosen the reins. All at once, the three horses began to neigh.

"For the soul to vibrate and cry out, it must be freed; too many restrictions will stifle it."

Rebbe Mikhal of Zlotchev was asked an embarrassing question: "You are poor, Rebbe. And yet everyday you thank God for taking care of your needs. Isn't that a lie?"

"Not at all. You see, for me poverty is a need."

One of Rebbe Mikhal's prayers: "I have but one request. May I never use my reason against truth."

Rebbe Barukh, grandson of the Baal Shem said, "This world is filled with light for whoever knows it, and covered with darkness for whoever loses his way . . . As for myself, I live in it as a stranger. So does God. Thus our relationship is that of two strangers in a hostile land."

And another time: "Imagine two children playing hide-and-seek; one hides but the other does not look for him. God is hiding and man is not seeking. Imagine His distress."

Rebbe Wolfe of Zhitomir: "I fail to understand the so-called enlightened people who demand answers, endless answers in matters of faith. For the believer, there is no question; for the non-believer, there is no answer."

The Seer of Lublin, demanding of man that he assume his own condition and not till his neighbor's field, said: "There are many paths leading to perfection; it is given to each of us to choose our own, and by following it with great dedication, we can make it become truth, our only truth."

Rebbe Bunim of Pshiske said: "Know that there is more than one path leading to God, but that the surest goes through joy and not through tears. God is not that complicated; He is not jealous of your happiness nor of the kindness you show to others. The road to God goes through man. The sleeping child, the mother caressing him, the old man listening to the rustling of the leaves: God is close to each of them, in each of them God is present."

The Great Maggid Dov Baer of Mezritch a disciple of the Baal Shem: "Every lock has its key. But there are strong thieves who don't bother with keys — they break the lock. God loves the thief who breaks his heart for God."

Rabbi Pinhas used to say: "What you pursue, you don't get. But what you allow to grow slowly in its own way, comes to you."

Rabbi Rafael: "It is a curse when a man measures his behavior to his fellow-men. It is as if he were always manipulating weights and measures."

Rabbi Wolf would not allow his horses to be whipped. "You don't even have to yell at them. You only have to know how to talk to them."

When his son had died, Rabbi Levi Yitzhak danced as he followed the bier. Some of his hasidim could not refrain from expressing their astonishment. "A pure soul," said he, "was given to me. A pure soul I render back."

Rabbi Zalman, interrupting his prayers said: "I do not want your paradise. I do not want your coming. I want You, and You only."

The Seer of Lublin on the way: "It is not possible to tell men what way they should take. Through study, through prayer, through work. Everyone should carefully observe what way his heart draws him to, and then follow this way with all his strength."

Rabbi Nahum of Stepinesht said to the hasidim gathered around him: "If we could hang all our troubles on pegs and were allowed to choose those we liked best, every one of us would take back his own, for all the rest would seem even more difficult to bear."

Rabbi Moshe Leib said: "A human being who has not a single hour for his own every day is no human being."

And: "How easy it is for a poor man to depend on God! What else has he to depend on? And how hard it is for a rich man to depend on God! All his possessions call out to him: 'Depend on us!'"

Rabbi Heshel said: "A man should be like a vessel that willingly receives what its owner pours into it, whether it be wine or vinegar."

During a period when the cost of living was very high, Rabbi Mendel noticed that the many needy people who were his guests received smaller loaves than before. He gave orders to make the loaves larger than before, since loaves were intended to adjust to hunger and not to the price.

A learned but ungenerous man said to Rabbi Abraham of Stretyn: "They say that you give people mysterious drugs and that your drugs are effective. Give me one that I may attain to the fear of God."

"I don't know any drug for the fear of God," said the Rabbi, "but if you like I can give you one for the love of God."

"That's even better!" cried the other. "Just you give it to me."

"It is the love of one's fellow men," answered the Tzaddik.

Rabbi Moshe of Kobryn: "In this day and age, the greatest devotion, greater than learning and praying, consists in accepting the world exactly as it happens to be."

After the death of Rabbi Moshe, Rabbi Mendel of Kotzk asked one of his disciples: "What was most important to your teacher?"

The disciple replied: "Whatever he happened to be doing at the moment."

When Rabbi Yitzhak Meir was a little boy someone said to him: "Yitzhak Meir, I'll give you a gulden if you tell me where God lives!" He replied: "And I'll give you two gulden if you tell me where he doesn't!"

KABIR

Nancy Pope Mayorga

For over four centuries there has survived in India a group of religious men and women called the Kabirpanthis — followers of the path of Kabir. They are quiet, truth-loving, nonviolent, unobtrusive house-holders, somewhat like Quakers, refusing to recognize caste, seeing God in all men, seeing the same God behind all names of God. They are aspiring devotees of their great master, the fruit of his teaching. They are the molds into which the white-hot mystical love of Kabir was poured.

In the fifteenth century, Mohammedan invaders were ruling north India and trying to impose Islam upon the people. If reason and persuasion did not work to make converts, the Moslem rulers were not averse to using a ruthless, ferocious persecution. The Hindus lived in constant fear of the Moslem sword and resented the tax exemptions and other favors which the Mohammedans enjoyed. But, strangely enough, the Moslems disliked and distrusted the Hindus simply because of their philosophy of bhakti which turned out, in the face of all persecution, to be not only firm but contagious.

When Kabir was born in 1440, life was religiously intolerant and socially insecure. There was need for a powerful religious movement, a resurgence of faith to reassure the troubled hearts of men and remind them of tolerance and mutual respect. What kind of a giant could start such a movement? The answer: a gentle little

Moslem householder, a weaver by trade, with a heart full of love for God.

This remarkable man began by proclaiming himself a child of both Rama and Allah. He said, "Hari is in the East, Allah is in the West. Look within your heart, for there you will find both Karim and Ram." And surprisingly, in that bitterly divided society, he eventually was to be claimed by both Hindus and Moslems as their own. It is said that at his funeral, the Hindus wanted to burn the body, the Moslems to bury it. Then Kabir appeared to them in a vision and motioned them to lift the cover of the bier. When they did, they found not his body but a large mound of flowers, which they joyfully divided between them. This pleasant legend is not illogical. All the activity of Kabir's life moved in the direction of compromise between the Hindu and Islamic faiths.

In spite of the attempt of Hindus of later times to ascribe a miraculous quality to his birth to explain away his Mohammedanism, it seems irrefutable that Kabir was born a Moslem, son of a weaver, and, from the Hindu point of view, a person of a low caste. But he was a bright child with spiritual hunger in his soul. And he had the good fortune to live in the holy city of Benares, a city whose atmosphere was charged with devotion. There was also a great influence at work in Benares— the Hindu Saint Ramananda was there, teaching with divine authority the way to union with God. The boy Kabir, wandering through the templed city in search of something to satisfy his heart, came finally, with the sure instinct of a true mystic, to the feet of that great teacher. How Ramananda's clear message must have thundered in Kabir's soul!

But to receive a mantram and instructions, to be the

disciple of Ramananda, was not only difficult for Kabir but almost an impossibility. So great was the prejudice and rigidity of both faiths that even Ramananda, who preached the foolishness of caste, was unwilling to accept a Moslem as disciple. He turned the boy away many times. Then Kabir resorted to a trick. This is the classic story of his initiation.

Kabir knew where and at what time, before dawn, Ramananda was accustomed to bathe in the Ganges. One dark morning he went to the bathing ghat and lay down across the steps where the teacher would walk. When Ramananda, descending the steps, felt his foot on some-one's body, he was startled and exclaimed, "Rama! Rama!" Whereupon Kabir jumped to his feet and asked, "Master, may I say Rama, Rama?" Ramananda answered, "Yes, say Rama, Rama." That Kabir actually did become the disciple of the great Hindu teacher is substantiated in one of his own poems in which he says, "I became suddenly revealed in Benares, and Ramananda illumined me."

The same strong, one-pointed will is shown in Kabir's whole life. He challenged the narrow traditions of both religions. He was not afraid to speak out against violence, against caste, purdah, sati, and formal rituals. He had no use for philosophers whose hearts, he said, were bricks with no place for a drop of love. "Reading and reading, they have become stone." "Pandits have gone astray reading and studying the Vedas, because they do not know the secret of their own selves. I know that reading is good, but better than reading is meditation."

Kabir disparaged the life of ascetic withdrawal and preached the honest, useful, devout life of the householder. "In the home is the true union, in the home is the enjoyment of life; why should I forsake my home and wander in the forest? The home helps to attain Him who is real. So stay where you are and all things shall come to you in time." All his life he pursued his plain vocation of weaver, side by side with his holy mission. He made no pretense of being educated or literary, but his simple, warm, and loving songs penetrate the soul in a most affecting way. "Put thy cleverness away," he says simply. "Love is something other than this." Devotion is his keynote. "Open the gate with the key of love. By opening the door, thou shalt wake the Beloved." The love of God wells endlessly from his heart. "From the beginning until the end of time, there is love between me and Thee; and how shall such love be extinguished?"

Society is always shaken when God lets loose a great mystic in the world. And anyone who shakes the social structure makes enemies. Kabir made them on all sides. The Moslems resented his conversion to Hinduism. He was unpopular with the brahmins because he was of low caste and a Moslem, and because he rejected their formal ceremonials. The ascetics despised him as a householder who insisted that asceticism was not necessary. The scholars looked down upon him and resented his outspoken rebukes of their dry scholarship. And the priests feared him because he called images dead things, temples unnecessary, and both the puranas and the Koran mere words.

The furor of the small people grew, and finally in the interests of peace, this man, who preached only harmony and brotherliness, was banished from his home in Benares. But God was his mainstay, God was his home. He had long since taken his own advice: "When you have found Him, give yourself to Him utterly." In exile, with a small group of disciples, he continued to preach and sing the love of God for the remainder of his life. He died in 1518 in Maghar, not far from Benares.

MORE than five thousand stanzas are attributed to Kabir, many of them found in the Guru Granth, the basic scripture of the Sikhs. For, besides his own followers, the Kabirpanthis, the Sikhs are also Kabir's spiritual descendants, and their scripture is largely stocked with texts drawn from his compositions. Evelyn Underhill describes his work as "love-poetry which is often written with a missionary intention." This is true, but many of his poems are simply joyous outbursts in the spirit of "Behold how great is my good fortune! I have received the unending caress of my Beloved!"

There is no overlooking the fact, however, that for the aspirant in mysticism, Kabir's poems are an invaluable help. There is a hint on every page. He says, "The man who is kind and who practices righteousness, who remains passive amidst the affairs of the world, who considers all creatures on earth as his own self, he attains the Immortal Being." He says, "So long as man clamors for the I and the mine, his works are as naught. When all love of the I and the mine is dead, then the work of the Lord is done."

Kabir gives a beautiful picture of the perfect teacher, "who teaches the simple way, other than rites or ceremonies, who does not make you close the door and hold the breath and renounce the world, who makes you perceive the Supreme Spirit wherever the mind attaches itself, who teaches you to be still in the midst of all activities." And he, who was a perfect teacher, advises:

Know yourself, then, for He is within you
    from head to foot.
Sing with gladness, and keep your seat
    within your heart.

He did not make pilgrimages, he did not practice austerity or celibacy, he did not study. His one spiritual discipline was loving God with all his heart. He was not Hindu; he was not a Moslem; he belonged to both, and to all. In his ecstatic poems in praise of God, Kabir has left to us an exquisite mound of flowers to be divided infinitely among all, to instruct and comfort and inspire.

SONGS OF KABIR

Between the poles of the conscious and the unconscious,
    there has the mind made a swing:
Thereon hang all beings and all worlds, and that swing
    never ceases its sway.
Millions of beings are there: the sun and the moon in
    their courses are there:
Millions of ages pass, and the swing goes on.
All swing! the sky and the earth and the air and the
    water; and the Lord Himself taking form:
And the sight of this has made Kabir a servant.

My body and my mind are grieved for the want of Thee;
    O my Beloved! Come to my house.
When people say I am Thy bride, I am ashamed; for I
    have not touched Thy heart with my heart.

Then what is this love of mine? I have no taste for food,
    I have no sleep; my heart is ever restless within
    doors and without.
As water is to the thirsty, so is the lover to the bride.
    Who is there that will carry my news to my
    Beloved?
Kabir is restless: he is dying for sight of Him.

O Friend, awake and sleep no more!
The night is over and gone, would you lose your day
    also?
Others, who have wakened, have received jewels;
O foolish woman! you have lost all whilst you slept.
Your lover is wise, and you are foolish, O woman!
You never prepared the bed of your husband:
O mad one! you passed your time in silly play.
Your youth was passed in vain, for you did not know
    your Lord;
Wake, wake! See! your bed is empty: He left you in the
    night.
Kabir says: "Only she wakes, whose heart is pierced
    with the arrow of His music.

Where is the night, when the sun is shining? If it is
    night, then the sun withdraws its light.
Where knowledge is, can ignorance endure? If there be
    ignorance, then knowledge must die.
If there be lust, how can love be there? Where there is
    love, there is no lust.

Lay hold on your sword, and join in the fight, O my
    brother, so long as life lasts.
Strike off your enemy's head, and there make an end of
    him quickly: then come, and bow your head at your
    King's Durbar.
He who is brave, never forsakes the battle: he who flies
    from it is no true fighter.
In the field of this body a great war goes forward,
    against passion, anger, pride and greed:
It is in the kingdom of truth, contentment and purity, that
    this battle is raging; and the sword that rings forth
    most loudly is the sword of His Name.
Kabir says: "When a brave knight takes the field, a host
    of cowards is put to flight.
It is a hard fight and a weary one, this fight of the
    truth-seeker: for the vow of the truth-seeker is more
    hard than that of the warrior, or of the widowed wife
    who would follow her husband.
For the warrior fights for a few hours, and the widow's
    struggle with death is soon ended:
But the truth-seeker's battle goes on day and night, as
    long as life lasts it never ceases."

The lock of error shuts the gate, open it with the key of
    love:
Thus, by opening the door, thou shalt wake the Beloved.
Kabir says: "O brother! do not pass by such good fortune
    as this."

O friend! this body is His lyre; He tightens its strings
    and draws from it the melody of the Lord.

If the strings snap and the keys slacken, then to dust
    must this instrument of dust return:
Kabir says: "None but the Lord can evoke its melodies."

He is dear to me indeed who can call back the wanderer
    to his home. In the home is the true union, in the
    home is enjoyment of life: why should I forsake my
    home and wander in the forest? If the Lord helps me
    to realize truth, verily I will find both bondage and
    deliverance at home.
He is dear to me indeed who has power to dive deep into
    the Lord; whose mind loses itself with ease in His
    contemplation.
He is dear to me who knows the Lord and can dwell on
    His supreme truth in meditation; and who can play
    the melody of the Infinite by uniting love and
    renunciation in life.
Kabir says: "The home is the abiding place; in the home
    is reality; the home helps to attain Him Who is real.
    So say where you are, and all things shall come to
    you in time."

O Sadhu! The simple union is the best.
Since the day when I met with my Lord, there has been
    no end to the sport of our love.
I shut not my eyes, I close not my ears, I do not mortify
    my body;
I see with eyes open and smile, and behold His beauty
    everywhere:
I utter His name, and whatever I see, it reminds me of
    Him; whatever I do, it becomes His worship.

The rising and the setting are one to me; all
    contradictions are solved.
Wherever I go, I move round Him,
All I achieve is His service:
When I lie down, I lie prostrate at His feet.

He is the only adorable one to me: I have none other.
My tongue has left off impure words, it sings His glory
    day and night:
Whether I rise or sit down, I can never forget Him; for
    the rhythm of His music beats in my ears.
Kabir says: "My heart is frenzied, and I disclose in my
    soul what is hidden. I am immersed in that one great
    bliss which transcends all pleasure and pain."

There is nothing but water at the holy bathing places;
    and I know that they are useless, for I have bathed
    in them.
The images are all lifeless, they cannot speak; I know,
    for I have cried aloud to them.
The Purana and the Koran are mere words; lifting up the
    curtain, I have seen,
Kabir gives utterance to the words of experience; and he
    knows very well that all other things are untrue.

I have stilled my restless mind, and my heart is radiant:
    for in Thatness I have seen beyond That-ness, in
    company I have seen the Comrade Himself.
Living in bondage, I have set myself free: I have broken
    away from the clutch of narrowness.
Kabir says, "I have attained the unattainable, and my
    heart is colored with the color of love."

That which you see is not: and for that which is, you
   have no words.
Unless you see, you believe not: what is told you you
   cannot accept.
He who is discerning knows by the word; and the
   ignorant stands gaping.
Some contemplate the Formless, and others meditate on
   form: but the wise man knows that the Lord is
   beyond both.
That beauty of His is not seen of the eye: that meter of
   His is not heard of the ear.
Kabir says: "He who has found both love and
   renunciation never descends to death."

The flute of the Infinite is played without ceasing, and
   its sound is love:
When love renounces all limits, it reaches truth.
How widely the fragrance spreads! It has no end,
   nothing stands in its way.
The form of this melody is bright like a million suns:
   incomparably sounds the vina, the vina of the notes
   of truth.

Dear friend, I am eager to meet my Beloved! My youth
   has flowered, and the pain of separation from Him
   troubles my breast.
I am wandering yet in the alleys of knowledge without
   purpose, but I have received His news in these
   alleys of knowledge.

I have a letter from my Beloved: in this letter is an
    unutterable message, and now my fear of death is
    done away.
Kabir says: "O my loving friend! I have got for my gift
    the Deathless One."

When I am parted from my Beloved, my heart is full of
    misery: I have no comfort in the day, I have no
    sleep in the night. To whom shall I tell my sorrow?
The night is dark; the hours slip by. Because my Lord is
    absent, I start up and tremble with fear.
Kabir says: "Listen, my friend! there is no other
    satisfaction, save in the encounter with the
    Beloved."

He is the real Sadhu, who can reveal the form of the
    Formless to the vision of these eyes:
Who teaches the simple way of attaining Him, that is
    other than rites or ceremonies:
Who does not make you close the doors, and hold the
    breath, and renounce the world:
Who makes you perceive the Supreme Spirit wherever
    the mind attaches itself:
Who teaches you to be still in the midst of all your
    activities.
Ever immersed in bliss, having no fear in his mind, he
    keeps the spirit of union in the midst of all
    enjoyments.

The infinite dwelling of the Infinite Being is
    everywhere: in earth, water, sky, and air:

Firm as the thunderbolt, the seat of the seeker is
    established above the void.
He who is within is without: I see Him and none else.

O man, if you do not know your own Lord, why are you
    so proud?
Put your cleverness away: mere words shall never unite
    you to Him.
Do not deceive yourself with the witness of the
    Scriptures:
Love is something other than this, and he who has
    sought it truly has found it.

When at last you are come to the ocean of happiness, do
    not go back thirsty.
Wake, foolish man! for Death stalks you. Here is pure
    water before you; drink it at every breath. Do not
    follow the mirage on foot, but thirst for the nectar;
The saints are drunk with love, their thirst is for love.
Kabir says: "Listen to me, brother! The nest of fear is
    broken.
Not for a moment have you come face to face with the
    world:
You are weaving your bondage of falsehood, your words
    are full of deception:
With the load of desires which you hold on your head,
    how can you be light?"
Kabir says: "Keep within you the truth, detachment, and
    love."

If God be within the mosque, then to whom does this
world belong?
If Ram be within the image which you find upon your
pilgrimage, then who is there to know what happens
without?
Hari is in the East: Allah is in the West. Look within
your heart, for there you will find both Karim and
Ram;
All the men and women of the world are His living
forms.
Kabir is the child of Allah and of Ram: He is my Guru,
He is my Pir.

The jewel is lost in the mud, and all are seeking for it;
Some look for it in the east, and some in the west; some
in the water and some amongst stones.
But the servant Kabir has appraised it at its true value,
and has wrapped it with care in the end of the
mantle of his heart.

O my heart! you have not known all the secrets of this
city of love: in ignorance you came, and in
ignorance you return.
O my friend, what have you done with this life? You
have taken on your head the burden heavy with
stones, and who is to lighten it for you?
Your Friend stands on the other shore, but you never
think in your mind how you may meet with Him:
The boat is broken, and yet you sit ever upon the bank;
and thus you are beaten to no purpose by the waves.

The servant Kabir asks you to consider; who is there that
    shall befriend you at the last?
You are alone, you have no companion: you will suffer
    the consequences of your own deeds.

To whom shall I go to learn about my Beloved?
Kabir says: "As you never may find the forest if you
    ignore the tree, so He may never be found in
    abstractions."

I am neither pious nor ungodly
I live neither by law nor by sense,
I am neither a speaker nor hearer,
I am neither a servant nor master,
I am neither bond nor free,
I am neither detached nor attached.
I am far from none: I am near to none.
I shall go neither to hell nor to heaven.
I do all works; yet I am apart from all works.
Few comprehend my meaning; he who can comprehend
    it, he sits unmoved.
Kabir seeks neither to establish nor to destroy.

SOJOURNER TRUTH

Ray Berry

W HEN the spirit of the divine chooses to manifest itself in a person, it does not take into account the position of that person in society. In the continual unfoldment of spiritual genius, men and women of enormous spiritual stature have risen from the most abject conditions, and they have gone on to inspire the lives of many. Let us take a look at one called Sojourner Truth, who overcame the cruelest and most unpleasant outward circumstances to live a life that was filled with spiritual experience and faith in God — an all consuming faith, that, coupled with her overpowering personality, helped her carve out a remarkable life of service and leadership to all people in difficult and troubling times.

Isabella — her given name — was born into slavery on a Dutch estate in the Hudson Valley of New York around the year 1779. Her father was called Baumfree and her mother Mau Mau Bett. At the time of Isabella's birth they were quartered in a dismal cellar beneath a hotel run by their master. This hovel, consisting of a few planks laid over a mud floor and two windows below ground level, they shared with other slave families. One can hardly imagine the poor food and ill-health they endured under these oppressive conditions.

But even living under such conditions Mau Mau was to instill in Isabella a belief in a God who would listen to her prayers. "My children there is a God who hears and sees you."

"A God, Mau Mau! Where does he live?" asked the children.

"He lives in the sky," she replied, "and when you are beaten, or cruelly treated, or fall into any trouble, you must ask help of him, and he will always hear and help you."

Her ten or twelve brothers and sisters had been sold away from the family while they were very young. Isabella herself was sold at auction at the age of nine, and in order to sweeten the deal of a hundred dollars some sheep were thrown into the bargain. At this tender age her trials in life started. It was with this family that Isabella got her first taste of the rod. She received a particularly vicious beating over a trifle at the hands of her master, and she bore the scars of it for the rest of her days. Later in life, recalling the memory of this beating, she was to say, "And now when I hear them tell of whipping women on the bare flesh, it makes my flesh crawl, and the very hair rise on my head! Oh! My God! What a way is this of treating human beings?"

Yet in times of distress Isabella did not forget the instructions of her mother. She went to God in all her trials, telling Him all and asking Him if He thought it was right, and begging His protection from her persecutors. And later she said, "Though it seems curious, I do not remember ever asking for anything but what I got it. And I always received it as an answer to my prayers."

The conditions under which she lived became so unbearable that she knew she must find a new master. She set about praying that her father would come to her. And he did come. He heard her story and saw her scars. Baumfree got the word out, "Isabella must be traded."

It was not long before Isabella was traded to a good-tempered, hard working family who were not concerned about differences between slaves and their masters. Isabella was overjoyed. This was the answer to her prayers.

She worked hard for the family for a year and a half. She grew tall and strong and self-confident. One day she caught the eye of John Dumont a near-by landowner. He offered three hundred dollars for her. The deal was accepted and Isabella now had a new master.

Dumont had many slaves, but Isabella endeared herself to him by her hard work. At the same time she alienated the other slaves who called her "white man's pet". Yet Isabella gloried in the fact that she was faithful and true to her master. "It made me true to my God," she said. Life was not so easy here for her for many years. She was subject to occasional beatings, and she constantly incurred the displeasure of Mrs. Dumont. Isabella often wondered how she was to overcome her misfortunes and Mrs. Dumont's evil designs. Her mother's lessons on prayer came back to her, and she decided she must have a sanctuary. On the Dumont farm was a small island in a stream overgrown with willow and interwoven with hidden paths made by the grazing sheep. It was an ideal place for a retreat, and the roar of a nearby waterfall would allow vocal prayer to her God.

It was to this refuge that Isabella would retire at least once a day to pray and to relate all her troubles and sufferings. And it was here she got into the habit of exchanging promises with God. "You help me out of this piece of trouble, God," she would say, "and I will pay you back by being a good girl." "Of course, God," she would cajole, "you realize that as much as I would like to keep my part of the bargain, this is impossible under the circumstances; but if you will remedy this present difficulty, you will see whether I won't do all that I have promised . . . But you must be sure to help me!"

Her part of the bargain would be promptly forgotten, but her inclination to the mystical and religious life was developing, as a direct result of her prayers.

Isabella's freedom was fast approaching. The emancipation of slaves was passed into law and her time was soon over. But Dumont went back on his word, even though she had done extra work to complete her part of the bargain. She longed for her freedom.

She decided to plead before the highest judge, "Oh, God, I been a-askin' you, an' askin' you, an askin' you, for all this long time to make my massa an' missis better, an' you don't do it; an what *can* be the reason? Why — maybe you *can't!* Well, I shouldn't wonder if you couldn't. Well, now, I tell you, I'll make a bargain with you. If you'll help me to get away from my massa an' missus, I'll agree to be good; but if you don't help me, I really don't think I can be."

"Now," she continues, "I want to get away; but the trouble's just been, if I try to get away in the night, I can't see; an' if I try to get away in the daytime, they'll see me an' be after me."

Her appeals got results. A little while later she thought she heard the Lord suggest to her, "Get up two or three hours before daylight, and start off."

Happily she replied, "Thank you, Lord, that's a good idea."

She did not wait long to put her plan into action. With some apprehension and the joy of the promise of freedom she walked off, a bundle in one hand, her infant daughter in the other. After walking some distance she sat down to feed her baby. Then she knelt down to pray once more for guidance. "Well, Lord," she called out in her intimate way, "you started me out; now please show me where to go."

She came upon a friendly man who suggested the home of the Van Wagener's some miles off. It took her all day to reach this house, recognizing it from a dream that she had had recently. "That's the place for me," she said. "I'll stop here."

The Van Wageners immediately took her in, offered her employment, and made her feel like a member of the household. They fed her and showed her to her room which contained a huge white bed. Isabella took one look at that bed and crept underneath it to sleep on the floor. In the morning Mrs. Van Wagener saw the untouched bed and said, "Isabella, you haven't slept in the bed."

And Isabella answered in surprise, "Lord, ma'am, you didn't think of such a thing as me sleeping in that there bed, did you? I never heard of such a thing in my life!"

Isabella knew that Dumont would come looking for her, and, indeed, he showed up a few days later expecting to take her back. "Well, Belle," he said, "so you've run away from me."

"No", she replied, "I did *not* run away. I walked away by daylight. You promised me a year of my time if I did all my work."

"You must go back with me" he said.

But Isabella firmly replied, "No, I won't go back with you."

"Well, then," Dumont countered, "I shall take the child. It belongs to me."

"You shall not," Isabella blazed back.

At this moment Van Wagener intervened. He proposed to buy Isabella's freedom, and the matter was settled.

Freedom did not sit easily with Isabella. Life at the Van Wageners was all peace and quiet, and after some months she became bored and restless, anxious to return to her former master and her own people on the plantation.

One day she abruptly announced to the Van Wageners, "My master, Dumont, is coming for me today, and I shall return with him."

"And how did you come by such information?" they asked.

"No one told me," she replied. "I just feel that he will come."

Wonder of wonders, Dumont showed up at the house that very day, and Isabella informed him that she would like to return home with him. "Not on your life," he countered, "I shall not take you back again. You ran away from me."

But Isabella paid no attention to his rebuff. She took her child in her arms and started towards his carriage. Then a most unexpected experience overtook her. With the suddenness and power of a bolt of lightening, God revealed Himself to her. She recalled, "In the twinkling of an eye God was over everything . . . there was no place where God was not."

She was consumed by the gaze of the Being with whom she had been so familiar all her life. She was terrified and wished to hide herself where she could not be seen or found, but she realized that there was no place to hide. There really was no place where God was not.

Greatly relieved when she returned to a somewhat more normal state, she exclaimed, "Oh God, I did not know You were so big!"

By this time Dumont had left in his carriage, and Isabella returned to the house and went to her room. Here she tried to talk to God, but her previous double dealing attitude and broken promises put her off. She was scared and said, "What! Shall I lie again to God? I have told Him nothing but lies; and shall I speak again and tell another lie to God?"

This first impersonal experience of God led to a second more personal experience. She wished for someone, a friend, to stand between herself and the God she thought she had offended. Someone to temper this great power she was experiencing. Then she had a vision, and a friend appeared. "Who are you?" She called out to this person radiant with the beauty of holiness and warm with love. "I *know* you, and I *don't* know you. You seem perfectly familiar. I feel that you not only love me, but that you always *have* loved me— yet I know you not— I cannot call you by name." "Who are you?" she cried, and she became deeply absorbed in prayer.

About to lose consciousness she heard a voice distinctly say, "It is *Jesus.*"

"Yes," she responded, "it *is* Jesus."

How great a blessing He conferred, in that He should stand between her and God! And God was no longer a terror and a dread to her.

Now there could be no doubt. Her years of prayer and trust culminated in this experience. As it ripened she could only surrender herself more and more into the hands of God and trust to Him for guidance in all her actions.

She said about prayer, "Let others say what they will of the efficacy of prayer, I believe in it, and I shall pray. Thank God! Yes, *I shall always pray!"*

Certainly this profound spiritual experience, this direct knowledge of both the impersonal and personal aspects of God was to change Isabella's life in every way. Now she knew what life was all about. Now she could see her trials and sufferings in a new light.

From this time so much love flowed through her heart that she was concerned with only one reason for living: to let the love of God work miracles in the hearts of men — her friends, her enemies, her ex-masters, and white folk in general — so that men and women everywhere, of every race, would be united and free.

Isabella was now to embark on the rest of her journey through life with a new confidence and self assurance that came from complete reliance on and trust in God.

MANY challenging incidents presented themselves to Isabella. When she left Dumont's, she had left behind a five year old son Peter, who had been sold to a slaveholder in Georgia just a year before his emancipation. This was clearly against the law. Isabella surmounted overwhelming odds to win back her son through legal means. When she was re-united with Peter she saw his terrible scars and bruises. "Heavens! what is all this?" she cried.

He answered, "It is where Fowler whipped, kicked, and beat me."

"Oh, Lord Jesus, look! See my poor child!" she exclaimed. And in her anguish she cursed them, "Oh Lord, 'render unto them double' for all this!"

God heard this curse and took His vengeance. Shortly after this, Fowler brutally murdered his wife Eliza Gedney. Eliza's mother, who had scoffed at Isabella's distraction at the sale of Peter, went completely insane, walking about deliriously and crying out constantly, "Eliza, Eliza!"

Isabella recalled her vindictive petition. But now that she had her son back she had no stomach for such retribution. She called out, "Oh my God, that's too much. I did not mean quite so much, God!" But this was God's business. She had better let Him settle this matter as He saw fit.

THE year was 1828. Slavery in New York had ended. Isabella and her children were free. She left the New York countryside to settle in New York City. Here were many more lessons to be learned and a new life to be started. But now she had the most tangible knowledge of God and the faith that accompanies it to take with her as she travelled through life.

Many years passed, and Isabella was dissatisfied and restless with her life in New York City. She said, "Here in New York, the rich rob the poor, and the poor rob one another." Although no longer a slave, she was still doing work for white folk. One day the thought came to her, "These worldly things, are they to be my concern forever? Money? Food? Clothing? Drudgery? No! Never! I am no longer Isabella. The Spirit calls me, and I must go. My new name will be Sojourner Truth. The Lord will provide for and protect me."

She was strong with the faith that her true work was to testify to the hope she held in her heart. The Lord was her director.

A few notable incidents show how Sojourner's life bore wonderful fruit, and how her words and actions were evidence of her strength of character and independence of thought.

Near Hartford, Connecticut she attended a Seventh Day Adventist meeting. The camp was engulfed in an emotional frenzy. When she was asked about her thoughts on the Seventh Day Adventist principles, she replied, "It has not been revealed to me what to think. Perhaps, if I could read I might see it clearly."

"Don't you believe that the Lord is coming?" another asked pointedly.

She replied, "I believe the Lord is as near as He can be, and not be it."

Sojourner wandered through the agitated crowd and in the midst of it she climbed up on a stump and called out, "Hear, hear!" The people gathered around her. Her bearing commanded respect. She spoke in quiet tones, "Children, why do you make such a to-do? Are you not commanded to watch and pray? But you are neither watching or praying. Now go to your tents. Watch and pray without so much noise and tumult. The Lord will not come to such a scene of confusion. He comes still and quiet."

She changed her tone and called out to them, "Here you are, talking about being changed in the twinkling of an eye. If the Lord should come, He'd change you to nothing, for there is nothing in you. You seem to be expecting to go to some parlor away up somewhere, and when the wicked have been burnt, you are coming back to walk in triumph over their ashes — this is to be your New Jerusalem! Now I can't see anything so very nice in that, coming back to such a mess as that will be, a world covered with the ashes of the wicked! Besides, if the Lord comes and burns — as you say He will — I am not going away; I am going to stay here and *stand the fire,* like Shadrach, Meshach, and Abednego! And Jesus will walk with me through the fire, and keep me from harm. No, I shall remain. Do you tell me that God's children *can't stand fire?* It is absurd to think so!"

With confrontations like this Sojourner's reputation preceeded her. It was becoming increasingly easier for her to speak at meetings. Note this letter of recommendation:

Sister, I send you this living messenger, as I believe her to be one that God loves . . . You can see by this sister, that God does by His Spirit alone teach His own children things to come. Please receive her, and she will tell you some new things. Let her tell her story without interrupting her, and give close attention, and you will see she has got the lever of truth, that God helps her to pry where but few can. She cannot read or write, but the law is in her heart.

One fact bears mentioning here. During her travels whenever Sojourner studied the scriptures, she preferred to hear them without comment. If adults read to her, they would invariably slip in their own commentaries. This tried her feelings. Whenever possible she asked children to read the Bible to her, because they would read and reread the same sentence as often as she wished, without comment. In that way she was able to see what her own mind could make out of the record, not what others thought it meant. She wished to compare these truths of the Bible with her own inner experience, another proof of her strength of character and independence of thought.

At Northhampton, Massachusetts, Sojourner attended another camp meeting with remarkable results. A large group of local ruffians was harassing the gathering, interrupting the services and causing a great disturbance.

The organizers tried to persuade the boisterous crowd to desist, but to no avail.

When the decision was made to call the sheriff, the group of toughs became enraged and general mayhem was part of their agenda. They threatened to set fire to the tents and to beat the congregants.

Sojourner realized the seriousness of the situation. Caught up in the contagious atmosphere, she found herself shaking with fear. She hid herself in a far corner of one of the huge tents, saying to herself, "I am the only colored person here, and on me their wicked mischief will probably fall first, and perhaps fatally."

She understood how insecure her position was, and she thought, "Shall I run away and hide from the Devil? Me, a servant of the living God? Have I not faith enough to go out and quell that mob, when I know it is written, 'One shall chase a thousand, and two put ten thousand to flight!' I know there are not a thousand here, and I know I am a servant of the living God. I'll go to the rescue, and the Lord shall go with me and protect me.

"Oh, I felt as if I had *three hearts,* and that they were so large my body could hardly contain them!"

By now the noise and confusion were terrific. Disaster was imminent. Yet Sojourner left her hiding place and walked to the top of a small rise of ground and commenced to sing with all the strenth of her most powerful voice this hymn of Christ's resurrection:

It was early in the morning,
It was early in the morning,
Just at the break of day.
When he rose, when he rose, when he rose,
And went to heaven on a cloud.

As she sang, the boisterous young men, many armed with clubs, rushed towards her, and she was soon surrounded. As the circle closed around her, she stopped singing and inquired in a gentle but firm voice, "Why do you come about me with clubs and sticks. I am not going to harm anyone."

"We aren't going to hurt you, old woman; we came to hear you sing," they cried. "Sing to us. Talk to us. Pray, old woman. Tell us your experiences," they called out one after another.

"You stand and smoke so near me, I cannot sing or talk," she rejoined.

"Stand back, stand back!" shouted the leaders. The crowd gave way amid calls for more singing and talking, and the leaders called out that they would knock down any fool who insulted her in the smallest way.

She saw this unexpected display of respect and said to herself, "Here must be many young men in all this assemblage, bearing with them hearts susceptible of good impressions. I will speak to them."

She spoke and they listened. But it was not just her words that charmed the unruly mob. It was her presence, her inner strength of *three hearts* that won them over.

Those in the back of the crowd called out, "Sing

aloud, old woman, we can't hear." The ringleaders requested that she use a nearby wagon for a pulpit.

But Sojourner objected, "If I do they'll overthrow it."

"No we won't, nobody shall harm you," answered the mob. She mounted the wagon and started to talk to them: "Well, there are two congregations on this ground. It is written that there shall be a separation, and the sheep shall be separated from the goats. The other preachers have the sheep, I have the goats. And I have a few sheep among my goats but they are very ragged." This thrust produced a peal of laughter. She knew she had them in the palm of her hand. She went on talking, singing, and praying for over an hour. When she grew tired she paused, but they clamored for more.

She motioned them to be quiet and called out to them, "Children, I have talked and sung to you as you asked; and now I have a request to make of you. Will you grant it?"

"Yes, yes," they called out.

"Well, if I sing one more hymn for you, will you then go away and leave us this night in peace?"

"Yes, yes, yes," shouted many hearty voices.

"I repeat my request once more," said she, "and I want you *all* to answer."

This time a long loud Yesss! came up from the mob.

"AMEN! IT IS SEALED," answered Sojourner in her powerful voice, and then she began to sing:

I bless the Lord I've got my seal—today and today;
To slay Goliath in the field—today and today;
The good old way is a righteous way,
I mean to take the kingdom in the good old way.

While singing she heard the leaders start to enforce the exodus of the mob. Some refused to go, but before she was finished, she saw the group turn and run as fast as they could in such a solid mass of bodies that they looked like a swarm of bees, so dense was their phalanx, so straight and determined their course. And well before the awed members of the meeting could recover from their surprise, the rioters were gone. A few rebellious spirits wanted to return, but the leaders said, "No — we have promised to leave — all promised, and we must go, all go, and you shall none of you return again."

Oh, Sojourner Truth, you have the heart of a lion.

SOJOURNER now widened her travels from the East to the Mid-West. She lectured against slavery and became involved in the Women's Rights issue. She attended a Women's Rights convention in Akron, Ohio, in 1852. Clergymen of different denominations were the principal speakers, because few women in those days dared to *speak in meeting.*

Many of the women were afraid to let Sojourner Truth say anything. Her reputation for outspokenness had preceded her, and they were worried this meeting would turn into an abolitionist affair.

Slowly, ever so slowly, with great determination Sojourner rose from her seat and proceeded to the podium, amid the jeers and hisses of the unsympathetic crowd. The chairwoman announced, "Sojourner Truth," and pleaded with the audience to remain silent. At her first words there was a profound hush. Here are her words, recorded as closely as possible to her strange dialect, by the chairwoman:

"'Well, chilern, whar dar is so much racket dar must be something out o' kilter. I tink dat 'twixt de niggers of de Souf and de women at de Norf all a talkin' 'bout rights, de white men will be in a fix pretty soon. But what's all dis here talkin' 'bout? Dat man ober dar say dat women needs to be helped into carriages, and lifted ober ditches, and to have de best place every whar. Nobody eber help me into carriages, or ober mud puddles, or gives me any best place, and ar'n't I a woman? Look at me! Look at my arm! I have plowed, and planted, and gathered into barns, and no man could head me — and ar'n't I a woman? I could work as much and eat as much as a man (when I could get it), and bear de lash as well — and ar'n't I a woman? I have borne thirteen chilern and seen 'em mos' all sold off into slavery, and when I cried out with a mother's grief, none but Jesus heard — and ar'n't I a woman? Den dey talks 'bout dis ting in de head — what dis dey call it?' 'Intellect,' whispered some one near. 'Dat's it honey. What's dat got to do with women's rights or niggers' rights? If my cup won't hold but a pint and yourn holds a quart, wouldn't ye be mean not to let me have my little half-measure full?' And she pointed her significant finger and sent a keen glance at the minister who had made the argument. The cheering was long and loud.

"'Den dat little man in black dar, he say women can't have as much rights as man, cause Christ warn't a woman. Whar did your Christ come from?' Rolling thunder could not have stilled that crowd as did those deep, wonderful tones, as she stood there with outstretched arms and eyes of fire. Raising her voice still louder, she repeated, 'Whar did your Christ come from? From God and a woman. Man had nothing to do with him.' Oh! what a rebuke she gave the little man.

"'Turning again to another objector, she took up the defense of mother Eve. I cannot follow her through it all. It was pointed, and witty, and solemn, eliciting at almost every sentence deafening applause; and she ended by asserting that 'Ef de fust woman God ever made was strong enough to turn the world upside down, all 'lone, dese togedder [and she glanced her eye over us], ought to be able to turn it back and get it right side up again, and now dey is asking to do it, de men better let em.' Prolonged cheering. 'Bleeged to ye for hearing' on me, and now ole Sojourner ha'n't got nothing more to say.'

"Amid roars of applause, she turned to her corner, leaving more than one of us with streaming eyes and hearts beating with gratitude."

Yet these same women, who were now applauding Sojourner Truth for her penetrating wisdom and support in the fight for their rights, were not spared her steadfastness to the truth regarding their own weaknesses. She addressed them at another meeting with these cutting remarks:

"Women, you forget that you are the mothers of creation; you forget your sons were cut off like grass by the war, and the land was covered with their blood. You rig yourselves up in panniers and Grecian bend-backs and flummeries; yes, and mothers and gray-haired grandmothers wear high-heeled shoes and humps on their heads, and put them on their babies, and stuff them out so that they keel over when the wind blows. O mothers, I'm ashamed of you! What will such lives as you live do for humanity? When I saw the women on the stage at the Woman's Suffrage Convention, the other day, I thought, 'What kind of reformers are you, with goose-wings on your heads, as if you were going to fly, and dressed in such ridiculous fashion, talking about reform and women's rights?' It appears to me, you had better reform yourselves first. But Sojourner is an old body, and will soon get out of this world into another and wants to say when she gets there, 'Lord, I have done my duty, I have told the whole truth and kept nothing back!'"

This was Sojourner Truth — battling injustice and ignorance and man's inequity to his fellow man. She battled from the fort of God-experience and was surrounded with God's love. She was always positive, clear, and bright. Her trust was in God, and she knew he was *good*.

She never feared death, saying confidently, "When we are done with these old bodies, their aches and pains, we shall be Gods." She compared death to stepping out of one room into another, from darkness into light. "Oh," she cried, "won't that be glorious!"

Sojourner Truth died at her home in Battle Creek, Michigan at three o'clock in the morning, November 26, 1883.

It was early in the morning,
It was early in the morning,
Just at the break of day,
When he rose, when he rose, when he rose
And went to heaven in a cloud.

Sojourner Truth - God's Sojourner - God's Truth.

SAYINGS OF SOJOURNER TRUTH

God is from everlasting to everlasting.

There was no beginning till sin came.

All that had a beginning will have an end.

Truth burns up error.

God is the great house that will hold all His children.

We dwell in him as the fishes in the sea.

Of the fashionable so called religious world she says "It is empty as the barren fig-tree, possessing nothing but leaves."

I think of the great things of God, not the little things.

LAOTSE

Nancy Pope Mayorga

It is a pleasant legend. Lao Tan, affectionately nicknamed Laotse, the "Old Boy", full of years and wisdom and service to his Emperor, was leaving by water buffalo for the far mountains to spend the remainder of his life in contemplation. At the gate to the Pass of Han-Ku, he was stopped by the gatekeeper, Yin Hsi, himself a philosopher, who engaged him in conversation and persuaded him finally to pause long enough to write down the essence of his lifetime of thinking. Affable and serene, Laotse turned back and in three days' time wrote the eighty-one stanzas which comprise the classic mystical scripture of the Chinese, the *Tao Te Ching*. Presumably he entrusted the verses to Yin Hsi and then, discharged of his obligation to mankind, climbed once more upon his buffalo and rode off into the hills. Some say he lived to be 160; others claim 200 years. It is not known where he died.

As is often the case with holy men about whom not many facts are known, legends grew up around the figure of Laotse. The most fanciful one being that his mother, after a supernatural conception, carried him in her womb for sixty-two years so that he was born already white-haired and wise. The date of his birth is set at 604 B.C.

The most credible biography of Laotse appears in the historical records of Szema Chien, written about 100 B.C. According to Chien, the philosopher was born in Honan Province and became historian and librarian of the Emperor's royal library at the Court of Chow. Chien makes note of the fact that "Laotse was a superior man who liked to keep in obscurity. He taught that the transformation of man takes place, as a matter of course, from being pure and still."

It is fairly well substantiated that Laotse had at least one interview with Confucius in 517 when the Old Boy was 87 and the younger man 35, after which meeting Confucius is quoted as saying, "This day I have seen Laotse. This day I have seen a dragon. Birds have wings to fly with, fish have fins to swim with, wild beasts have feet to run with. For feet there are traps, for fins nets, for wings arrows. But who knows how dragons surmount wind and cloud into heaven?" Who knows, if not Laotse, the Old Dragon? And where can one learn, if not in the *Tao Te Ching?*

Did Laotse write the book? It is a controversy that has been occupying scholars for centuries. Laotse himself had great disdain for scholars and their controversies. He would be the first to say that from the point of view of a spiritual aspirant, it does not matter in the least who wrote the *Tao Te Ching.* There it is. Make use of it. As a matter of fact, whether or not he was the one who put down the words, the teaching must be an accretion, as the Upanishads are, of hundreds of years of mystical thought and practice. And, as one commentator, Huston Smith, says, it is a book that can be read in half an hour, or in a lifetime.

The word *Ching* means authoritative scripture. The book is divided into two parts, the first discussing the nature of the *Tao,* the second, the use of *Te* or Tao's power. The character of the book is aphoristic and lends itself to innumerable interpretations. There are at least thirteen versions in English alone, each one with its author's individual annotations, definitions, clues. It seems that a new translation has almost always been made because of someone's dissatisfaction with all other translations.

The trouble arises at the very beginning with the attempt to define the indefinable Tao. Each translator seems to think that the Tao must be explained before the translation begins. The trouble is compounded by the fact that Chinese words, perhaps more than the words of any other language, trail with them subtle emanations of other meanings, implications, connotations, even puns. The result is that in many versions, the translator's introduction comes out longer than the *Tao Te Ching* itself. So it becomes a matter of individual interpretations of wide latitude, and we who do not know Chinese, must search among the translators for the man who is most like us. Or better yet, study them all.

But the fact is that every reader, even the Chinese, comes to the *Tao Te Ching* from where he stands on the spiritual ladder, brings to it just as much understanding as he is capable of, finds in it just as much help as he is presently able to assimilate. Moreover, without doubt, it grows in him and he grows in it. Every time he reads it, he finds greater meaning. One can well imagine a translator becoming dissatisfied with his own translation and trying anew.

LAOTSE knew the incurable propensity of men to define. His very first sentence reads, "If the Tao could be comprised in words, it would not be the indefinable Tao." No one pays any attention to that warning. The most usual English word for Tao is "The Way". There is a reluctance even to write it down, so inadequate is it. For the Tao is the path but also the goal; it is the Perennial Philosophy, it is the ground of all existence, the essence of being, it is the greatest of the great, the smallest of the small, immanent as well as transcendent, eternally existent, and so forth. By using such equally inadequate words, we have failed with all the others, and like them attempted to express the inexpressible — the boldest of all contradictions. On the other hand, if we are to use words at all, perhaps the more names the better. When the color wheel has all the colors on it, it spins white.

The Tao is unmoving. But it is inseparable from Te, its creative power, like fire and its power to burn, like water and its wetness. Te brings forth the "ten thousand creatures" which comprise the whole universe.

Well, if Laotse does not define the Tao, at least he spends much time and many verses in examining it and singing its praises.

There is a force at work in the Universe that guides all things. To imitate this force is called 'falling in line with the Way of Heaven.' It is the way of this force to yield. It is the way of this force to endure. Holding fast to the 'Way', all things are accomplished by this force. The force does not strive, yet all things obey it. Mystery of mysteries, this force is the Mother of all things; mystery of mysteries, he who knows it knows the Eternal.

If one looks for Tao, there is nothing solid to see; if one listens for it, there is nothing loud enough to hear. Yet if one uses it, it is inexhaustible.

The 'Way' cannot be escaped. All creatures obey the laws of heaven though they know it not. The law of 'reap what you sow' is a Universal law; though it does not contend, enforce or insist, it is ever in effect. Sow violence, and violence is gained; sow anger, and anger is bred within; sow confusion, and confusion is your home. But he who sows peace, receives peace, lives in peace, and is able thus to sow much more of peace.

Tao is eternal but has no name.

WITH this lure, Laotse goes on to teach about the Te and its use. According to him, ignorance and troubles arise from the fact that men have separated themselves from their divine source. Spiritual practice consists in learning to live in harmony with the Tao, to give up ego and self-will, and lay ourselves open to the workings of Te within us.

The sage holds to the inner-light, and is not moved by the passing show. Quiet and serene he watches the merchants with their merchandise pass by, watches the seller and the buyers parading to the market and returning to their homes. Quiet and serene, he is fixed upon the

Eternal. When the moment comes, he will do what is right without pausing to consider its rightness; when the moment comes he will act for the welfare of all.

What is the first step? "To know men," he says, "is to be wise; to know oneself is to be illumined."

THERE are, of course, certain preparations for knowing one's self. The wise man gives up extravagances, excesses, pride; he does not fight, does not boast, and puts himself in the background; he becomes humble like water which seeks the low places, becomes like the window which is useful because of its clarity, the pitcher because of its emptiness, becomes once more what the Chinese called the "uncarved block" of wood, a symbol of man's pristine simplicity.

The next step is to be still. Laotse uses the familiar metaphor of muddy water which, when allowed to stand, becomes clear. "Tao can only be mirrored in a still pool." He says:

Block the passages, shut the doors. Let all
sharpness be blunted, all tangles untied, all
glare tempered, all dust smoothed. This is
called the mysterious levelling.

The result of the practice of this mysterious levelling will eventually be the melting of the little self into the great Tao. There, on that level, "all is peace, quietness, security." Living in the presence of the Tao is the ultimate contentment. "Truly," says Laotse, "he who has once known the contentment that comes simply through being contented, will never again be otherwise than contented."

Laotse is once described by his great commentator, Chuangtse, as being found sitting like a log of wood as though he had no consciousness of any outside thing and were wandering somewhere all by himself. When the disciple commented in surprise on his state, Laotse is supposed to have replied, "True. I was wandering in the Beginning of Things." And in a section of the *Tao Te Ching*, he himself speaks of the ecstasy called "Far Away Wandering," which he says means returning to "What There was at the Beginning."

LIKE all mystics, Laotse was eminently pragmatic, and, possessing the Tao, he used it with the greatest common sense. "Meditate on the Tao within yourself," he says, "and the power of your personality will be true power." He had no liking for organized administration, but put his faith in intuition and conscience — in other words, in the Tao. He was absolutely nonviolent.

Force is not of the Tao, and what is not of
the Tao quickly perishes.

Success may have been an unavoidable
step. But the real success must not be one of
force.

To be incapable of harm, remain low; to be
incapable of being harmed, remain low. None
are jealous of, none contend with, that which is
below them. None seek to overthrow that which

takes the lowest place. That is why the low endures; that is why the low is able to outlast the high. All pass over the low, without a glance, and so the low remains undisturbed by the world, remains at peace.

He believed that government should be in the hands of the sages, for then all action will be balanced, pure and effective. The sage knows "how to be on top without crushing the people with his weight. He speaks as though he were lower than the people, puts himself in the background. Thus they do not find him irksome. Because he does not strive, none can contend with him." He had homespun comparisons: "Rule a kingdom gently, as you would fry a small fish."

What kind of a man is he who has possessed himself of the Tao? He acts without personal motive. He is compassionate and forgiving, repaying evil with good, injury with kindness. In his description of the ideal man, we see Laotse himself — simple, spontaneous, serene, at the same time outspoken and powerful because of the Tao within him.

That which is steady and constant is to be trusted. That which is unwavering and Eternal is to be taken as a guide. He who is not shaken by the winds of passion, nor upset by the desires on this side or by the refusal of that on the other, he it is that has taken as guide the 'Way'. All things come from Heaven, therefore the sage refuses nothing; therefore he is overjoyed at nothing. The pleasant and the unpleasant, the day and the night, the winter and the summer, all are accepted in the same calm spirit. Into his hands come all things, and the sage offers thanks to Heaven for all.

In the face of misfortune, the Taoist is undisturbed; in the face of death he is calm. As Chuangtse said quietly about the loss of his wife, "She has gone to rest awhile in the Inner Room. Shall I disturb her with my wailing and lamentation?" For Laotse, death was to be an endless enjoyment of Tao. And for us he has a reassuring word, "All eventually will come to Tao, as streams and torrents flow into the sea."

This comprehensive view of life and death and freedom, then, is the *Tao Te Ching*. This is what the Old Boy wrote down in just three days' time at the gate to the pass of his final liberation, and then rode off to his meeting with the Tao. There must have been a radiance about his going. He knew, and he said it plainly:

Tao is forever, and he that possesses it, though his body ceases, is not destroyed.

ST. JOHN OF THE CROSS

Nancy Pope Mayorga

O<small>NE OF THE</small> greatest *bhaktas* (lovers of God) the Christian faith has ever known was that luminous Spanish mystic of the sixteenth century, St. John of the Cross. He was first and always a lover, and God his Beloved. But these are pale words. He was a living ember blown upon by the breath of God, an ember glowing ever brighter on account of that breath. All he ever spoke of, all he ever admitted was the love of God, and the events of his life, grim and painful as they sometimes were, seemed only to quicken this constant act of love.

St. John is rare, if not unique, among Christian saints, for although the Church claims him, and his daily work was in and for the Church, he can not be encompassed by a church, nor even by Christianity in its broadest sense. He was purely and simply, widely and deeply, a man of God. But if this makes him sound unapproachable, it should be mentioned that he was greatly loved when he lived. He was a very small man, less than five feet tall, thin-faced, with dark, compelling eyes. His manner was unobtrusive. Whatever came to him, honors or humiliations, he accepted, with more than serenity, with joy. The love of God kept him joyful under all conditions. His greatest poems, passionate poems of love for God, on which he later based his whole teaching, were actually written while he was a prisoner in a very small cell, subject to indignities and cruelty.

His early life was unremittingly hard. His mother was widowed shortly after he was born, and he was educated at an institute for children of the poor, where he was also fed and clothed. At seventeen he enrolled in a Jesuit college and received a first-class education in the humanities. In 1563, at twenty-one, he took vows as a Carmelite.

At this time the strictness of the Carmelite Order had relaxed considerably, the monks and nuns dressing and living in comfort and luxury. Brother John was unhappy about this and was considering transferring to a more austere order. But then he met Teresa of Avila, who had felt the same dissatisfaction as a Carmelite nun. It was her hope to reform the Order, to restore the Carmelite Primitive Rule for friars and nuns for a life more restricted and more given to solitude and contemplation. She persuaded John that this was where his call was, to work within the Order to reform it. So John agreed to join with Brother Antonio de Heredia, a man of fifty-seven, who had willingly given up a comfortable and important position as a prior to work with Teresa for establishing a monastery according to the strict Primitive Rule.

We have Teresa's humorous and affectionate description of Brother John at this time. She was surprised to find him so small, and she called her two monks "a friar and a half." But she was impressed by John, by the depth of his dark eyes, by his composure, also by his common sense and his courage. And she was to say much later, "I never came across any imperfection in him."

For her new monastery Teresa had been made a gift of a tumble-down house in an isolated village called

Duruelo. She was dismayed at her first sight of the place, nothing more than a pigsty, she said, but her "friar and a half" took it over with joy, and Brother John felt "free at last from the fetters of material things." The places in the garret where the two men slept were so close under the roof they could only sit or lie, and at first in such bad repair that often while they meditated, the snow sifted in on their habits. They considered it a time of great rejoicing. At a later visit Teresa reported that she found the prior, Brother Antonio, "in front of the monastery, this little stable of Bethlehem, busy sweeping like a simple lay brother, his face alight with happiness. I was amazed at the spirit which God had infused into the place. The two merchants who traveled with me did nothing but weep."

IT seemed that there was a need in the Carmelite Order for just such a reform, because once it was started, it grew rapidly. The friars and nuns of the reform wore the plainest of clothes and rope sandals instead of fine Moroccan leather shoes. They became known as the Discalced, or unshod, Carmelites. At first they were ignored by the Calced members, but inevitably, as they drew new enthusiasts to their lists, jealousy arose. There began a struggle over jurisdiction. Though he never wished it so, the influence of Brother John grew until he stood, with Teresa, almost as a symbol of what came to be thought of as a rebellion. Certain factions of the established order decided to stop the expansion. They kidnapped John, took him to Toledo, and put him in a cell six feet by ten feet with the only light from a slit high up in the wall. He was there for nine months during which time he was treated with harshness and even punishments such as might be given to a criminal. Yet it was during this time that he composed most of his great poems. It is said that at night his cell glowed, but that when the prison guards would come to investigate the source of the light, it would disappear. His escape from that prison was extraordinary, if not miraculous. He said the Virgin released him. The guards seemed to be deaf and blind, locks and walls no obstacle to him.

By the time Teresa died in 1582, the reform had become well established. Brother John had presided over several new foundations and was now consultant on the new administrative council. But again problems and jealousies arose, this time within the organization. The original Discalced Carmelites were being eliminated one by one, and, after five years as a consultor, Brother John was suddenly ordered out of the country to a post in Mexico. He never reached it. Before he could leave, he fell mortally ill at a convent in Ubeda, southern Spain, where the prior disapproved of him and made things as uncomfortable for him as he could. However, his sanctity became known by the people of that district, and his funeral was the occasion of a great outburst of love and appreciation. He was only forty-nine when he died.

It had never been Brother John's intention to be a teacher. As a matter of fact, in his writing he deferred to what he considered the superior wisdom of Teresa. His poems of love for God, however, he allowed to pour out of him without restraint. He could not help it. The most exquisite poetry, perfect in form, flowed from his heart with joyous spontaneity. When he visited Teresa's convents, he found his verses on the lips of all the nuns. They were constantly asking him for interpretations of certain lines. Finally, Teresa's companion, the saintly

Ana de Jesus, persuaded him that he should write commentaries on his poems, and so he began the work of his lifetime, four great books — *The Ascent of Mount Carmel, The Dark Night of the Soul, The Spiritual Canticle of the Soul*, and *The Living Flame of Love*.

St. John is not easy to read. His poems are a delight, but his prose is wordy, diffusive, and repetitive. As a teacher, he is a religious psychologist, analyzing in astonishingly minute detail the religious process. But he is not like Teresa who talked endlessly about herself, her sufferings, and her ecstasies. Unselfconsciously, almost accidentally, he reveals the sublimity of his own experiences. At any unexpected moment, his difficult prose will burst forth, lofty, poetic, ardent, joyful, and soul-stirring. It is a glimpse of the fire that is burning within.

The essence of his own experience is in his three greatest poems — *The Ascent of Mount Carmel, The Living Flame of Love*, and the *Spiritual Canticle*. These he used like sutras, or threads to which his commentaries were to be strung. If he is diffuse, he is not disorderly. His commentaries make up four, carefully planned, progressive books.

THE first: *The Ascent of Mount Carmel*, based on the poem of that name, describes the task of a spiritual aspirant taking his first steps in the upward path to union with God.

> In a dark night,
> With anxious love inflamed,
> O happy lot!
> Forth unobserved I went,
> My house being now at rest.

The going forth is the decision to find God. The house at rest is the first step on the journey, and detachment is the key to setting the house at rest. In his commentary, St. John makes it very plain what he means by detachment. "It is not the things of this world that occupy or injure the soul, for they do not enter within, but rather the wish for and desire of them . . . Oh would that spiritual persons knew how they are losing the good things of the spirit because they will not raise up their desires above trifles!" *[The Ascent]*

The first dark night is the purgation of these sense desires, and St. John takes up the job with vigor and thoroughness. He himself has struggled from the bottom of the path to the heights and knows every pitfall and stumbling block. The disciple who is willing to surrender himself to this basic book, to this determined teacher, will be made over, will be finally and wholly convinced that the only purpose in life, the only thing that matters at all, is to unite mind, heart and soul with God. This is St. John's constant message, this is his purpose in writing, to impress upon us the absolute necessity, as well as the ways and means, for stripping ourselves of all hindrances to the knowledge of and ultimate union with God. It is simple really. The whole of religion is love, and the whole of spiritual exercise is to free the soul from worldly entanglements which prevent it from loving God completely.

THE second: *The Dark Night of the Soul*, the second of the four books, is also based on the poem, *The Ascent*. Once the apprentice soul sets out on this path of purification, God begins to draw it very quickly to Himself. After the strenuous gaining of a measure of self-control, after learning to "abide with attention in loving waiting upon God" *[The Ascent],* then the aspirant's duty is to allow God to work. All his activity now should be bent toward submitting his will to God's will. This St. John calls "the passive night," and he is very careful to give all the signs that show when an aspirant is ready for passivity, lest the disciple fall into laziness or complacency. When all attachments and ties are broken, when all worldly pleasures have become tasteless, then is the time to resign oneself utterly to God. What is required for this is faith. "The soul, when it least uses its own proper ability, travels most surely, because it walks most by faith. Who shall hinder God from doing His will in a soul that is resigned, detached, self-annihilated?" *[The Dark Night]*

THE third: *The Living Flame of Love.* Then after much practice, there comes a blessed state in which the soul communes easily with God and exercises itself in love. The description of this state is the substance of St. John's third book. "The soul already transformed and glowing interiorly with the fire of love, is not only united with the divine fire, but becomes a loving flame. Hence then we may say of the soul which is transformed in love, that its ordinary state is that of the fuel in the midst of the fire; that the acts of such a soul are the flames which rise up out of the fire of love." "When the soul is on fire with love, it will feel as if a seraph with a burning brand had struck it . . . and when the burning brand has thus touched it, the soul feels that the wound it has received is delicious beyond imagination." *[The Living Flame]*

At this point then there is nothing to do but wait for

God's grace. But there need be no anxiety about this waiting, for St. John assures us, "It is impossible, according to the divine goodness and mercy, that God will not perform His own work. Yes, more impossible than that the sun should not shine in a clear and cloudless sky." And he adds, "If we are seeking the Beloved, He is seeking us much more." *[Living Flame]*

Now the soul has to acknowledge that all is the grace of God and there is nothing else. The sooner we surrender, the better for us. The Beloved is waiting.

THE fourth: *The Spiritual Canticle.* In this beautiful book comes the moment for which we have long been preparing, toward which we have been struggling, the moment which alone gives life its meaning. "When the soul has lived for some time in this perfect and sweet love, God calls it and leads it into His flourishing garden for the celebration of the spiritual marriage. Then the two natures are so united, what is divine is so communicated to what is human, that, without undergoing any essential change, each seems to be God." This is the "flame that consumes and gives no pain. The love of God is now perfect in the soul, has changed it into God, wherein its movements and actions are now divine. The soul in this estate of the Spiritual Betrothal walks habitually in union with the love of God." *[Spiritual Canticle]*

> My soul is occupied,
> And all my substance in His service;
> Now I guard no flock,
> Nor have I any other employment;
> My sole occupation is love.

THE LIVING FLAME OF LOVE

O Living Flame of Love,
That woundest tenderly
My soul in its inmost depth!
As Thou art no longer grievous,
Perfect Thy work if it be Thy will,
Break the web of this sweet encounter.

O sweet burn!
A delicious wound!
O tender hand! O gentle touch!
Savouring of everlasting life,
And paying the whole debt,
By slaying Thou hast changed death into life.

O lamps of fire,
In the splendors of which
The deep caverns of sense,
Dim and dark,
With unwonted brightness
Give light and warmth together to their Beloved!

How gently and how lovingly
Thou wakest in my bosom,
Where alone Thou secretly dwellest;
And in Thy sweet breathing
Full of grace and glory,
How tenderly thou fillest me with thy love.

THE ASCENT OF MOUNT CARMEL

In a dark night,
With anxious love inflamed,
O happy lot!
Forth unobserved I went,
My house being now at rest.

In darkness and in safety,
By the secret ladder, disguised,
O happy lot!
In darkness and concealment,
My house being now at rest.

In that happy night
In secret, seen of none,
Seeing nought myself,
Without other light or guide
Save that which in my heart was burning.

That light guided me
More surely than the noonday sun
To the place where He was waiting for me,
Whom I knew so well,
And where none appeared.

O guiding night;
O night more lovely than the dawn;
O night that hast united
The lover with His beloved,
And changed her into her love.

On my flowery bosom,
Kept whole for Him alone,
There He reposed and slept;
And I caressed Him, and the waving
Of the cedars fanned Him.

As I scattered His hair in the breeze
That blew from the turret,
He struck me on the neck
With His gentle hand,
And all sensation left me.

I continued in oblivion lost,
My head was resting on my love;
Lost to all things and myself,
And amid the lilies forgotten,
Threw all my cares away.

THE SOUL OF THE INDIAN
The Great Mystery
Charles Alexander Eastman (Ohiyesa)

THE ORIGINAL ATTITUDE of the American Indian toward the Eternal, the "Great Mystery" that surrounds and embraces us, was as simple as it was exalted. To him it was the supreme conception, bringing with it the fullest measure of joy and satisfaction possible in this life.

The worship of the "Great Mystery" was silent, solitary, free from all self-seeking. It was silent because all speech is of necessity feeble and imperfect; therefore the souls of my ancestors ascended to God in wordless adoration. It was solitary because they believed that He is nearer to us in solitude, and there were no priests authorized to come between a man and his Maker. None might exhort or confess or in any way meddle with the religious experience of another. Among us all men were created sons of God and stood erect, as conscious of their divinity. Our faith might not be formulated in creeds nor forced upon any who were unwilling to receive it; hence there was no preaching, proselytizing, or persecution, neither were there any scoffers or atheists.

There were no temples or shrines among us save those of nature. Being a natural man, the Indian was intensely poetical. He would deem it sacrilege to build a house for Him who may be met face to face in the mysterious, shadowy aisles of the primeval forest, or on the sunlit bosom of virgin prairies, upon dizzy spires and pinnacles of naked rock, and yonder in the jeweled vault of the night sky! He who enrobes Himself in filmy veils of cloud, there on the rim of the visible world where our Great-Grandfather Sun kindles his evening camp-fire, He who rides upon the rigorous wind of the north, or breathes forth His spirit upon aromatic southern airs, whose war canoe is launched upon majestic rivers and inland seas—He needs no lesser cathedral!

THAT solitary communion with the Unseen which was the highest expression of our religious life is partly described in the word *Hambeday*, literally "mysterious feeling," which may be interpreted as "consciousness of the divine."

The first *Hambeday*, or religious retreat, marked an epoch in the life of the youth. Having first prepared himself by means of the purifying vapor-bath, and cast off as far as possible all human or fleshly influences, the young man sought out the noblest height, the most commanding summit in all the surrounding region. Knowing that God sets no value upon material things, he took with him no offerings or sacrifices other than symbolic objects, such as paints and tobacco. Wishing to appear before Him in all humility, he wore no clothing save his moccasins and breech-clout. At the solemn hour of sunrise or sunset he took up his position, overlooking the glories of earth and facing the "Great Mystery," and there he remained, naked, erect, silent, and motionless, exposed to the elements and forces of His arming, for a night and a day to two days and nights, but rarely longer. Sometimes he would chant a hymn without words, or offer the ceremonial "filled pipe." In this holy trance or ecstasy the Indian mystic found his highest happiness and the motive power of his existence.

When he returned to the camp, he must remain at a distance until he had again entered the vapor-bath and prepared himself for intercourse with his fellows. Of the vision or sign vouchsafed to him he did not speak, unless it had included some commission which must be publicly fulfilled. Sometimes an old man, standing upon the brink of eternity, might reveal to a chosen few the oracle of his long-past youth.

THE native American has been generally despised by his white conquerors for his poverty and simplicity. They forget, perhaps, that his religion forbade the accumulation of wealth and the enjoyment of luxury. To him, as to other single-minded men in every age and race, from Diogenes to the brothers of Saint Francis, from the Montanists to the Shakers, the love of possessions has appeared a snare, and the burdens of a complex society a source of needless peril and temptation. Furthermore, it was the rule of his life to share the fruits of his skill and success with his less fortunate brothers. Thus he kept his spirit free from the clog of pride, cupidity, or envy, and carried out, as he believed, the divine decree — a matter profoundly important to him.

It was not, then, wholly from ignorance or improvidence that he failed to establish permanent towns and to develop a material civilization. To the untutored sage, the concentration of population was the prolific mother of all evils, moral no less than physical. He argued that food is good, while surfeit kills; that love is good, but lust destroys; and not less dreaded than the pestilence following upon crowded and unsanitary dwellings was the loss of spiritual power inseparable from too close contact with one's fellow-men. All who have lived much out of doors know that there is a magnetic and nervous force that accumulates in solitude and that is quickly dissipated by life in a crowd. Even his enemies have recognized the fact that for a certain innate power and self-poise, wholly independent of circumstances, the American Indian is unsurpassed among men.

The red man divided mind into two parts, the spiritual mind and the physical mind. The first is pure spirit, concerned only with the essence of things, and it was this he sought to strengthen by spiritual prayer, during which the body is subdued by fasting and hardship. In this type of prayer there was no beseeching of favor or help. All matters of personal or selfish concern, as success in hunting or warfare, relief from sickness, or the sparing of a beloved life, were definitely relegated to the plane of the lower or material mind, and all ceremonies, charms, or incantations designed to secure a benefit or to avert a danger, were recognized as emanating from the physical self.

The rites of this physical worship, again, were wholly symbolic, and the Indian no more worshipped the Sun than the Christian adores the Cross.

The elements and majestic forces in nature, Lightning, Wind, Water, Fire, and Frost, were regarded with awe as spiritual powers, but always secondary and intermediate in character. He believed that the spirit pervades all creation and that every creature possesses a soul in some degree though not necessarily a soul conscious of itself. The tree, the waterfall, the grizzly bear, each is an embodied Force, and as such an object of reverence.

The Indian loved to come into sympathy and

spiritual communion with his brothers of the animal kingdom, whose inarticulate souls had for him something of the sinless purity that we attribute to the innocent and irresponsible child. He had faith in their instincts, as in a mysterious wisdom given from above; and while he humbly accepted the supposedly voluntary sacrifice of their bodies to preserve his own, he paid homage to their spirits in prescribed prayers and offerings.

In every religion there is an element of the supernatural, varying with the influence of pure reason over its devotees. The Indian was a logical and clear thinker upon matters within the scope of his understanding, but he had not yet charted the vast field of nature or expressed her wonders in terms of science. With his limited knowledge of cause and effect, he saw miracles on every hand, the miracle of life in seed and egg, the miracle of death in lightning flash and in the swelling deep! Nothing of the marvelous could astonish him; as that a beast should speak, or the sun stand still. The virgin birth would appear scarcely more miraculous than is the birth of every child that comes into the world, or the miracle of the loaves and fishes excite more wonder than the harvest that springs from a single ear of corn.

The logical man must either deny all miracles or none, and our American Indian myths and hero stories are perhaps, in themselves, quite as credible as those of the Hebrews of old. If we are of the modern type of mind, that sees in natural law a majesty and grandeur far more impressive than any solitary infraction of it could possibly be, let us not forget that, after all, science has not explained everything. We have still to face the ultimate miracle, the origin and principle of life! Here is the supreme mystery that is the essence of worship, without which there can be no religion, and in the presence of this mystery our attitude cannot be very unlike that of the natural philosopher, who beholds with awe the Divine in all creation.

The Indian did not, so long as his native philosophy held sway over his mind, either envy or desire to imitate the splendid achievements of the white man. In his own thought he rose superior to them! He scorned them, even as a lofty spirit absorbed in its stern task rejects the soft beds, the luxurious food, the pleasure-worshiping dalliance of a rich neighbor. It was clear to him that virtue and happiness are independent of these things, if not incompatible with them.

There was undoubtedly much in primitive Christianity to appeal to this man, and Jesus' hard sayings to the rich and about the rich would have been entirely comprehensible to him.

It is my personal belief, after thirty-five years' experience of it, that there is no such thing as "Christian civilization." I believe that Christianity and modern civilization are opposed and irreconcilable, and that the spirit of Christianity and of our ancient religion is essentially the same.

In the life of the Indian there was only one inevitable duty, the duty of prayer, the daily recognition of the Unseen and Eternal. His daily devotions were more necessary to him than daily food. He wakes at daybreak, puts on his moccasins and steps down to the water's edge. Here he throws handfuls of clear, cold water into his face, or plunges in bodily. After the bath, he stands erect before the advancing dawn, facing the sun as it dances upon the horizon, and offers his unspoken orison. In our own tongue His name was not spoken aloud, even with utmost reverence.

His mate may precede or follow him in his devotions, but never accompanies him. Each soul must meet the morning sun, the new, sweet earth, and the Great Silence alone!

It has been said that the position of woman is the test of civilization, and that of our women was secure. There was nothing of the artificial about her person, and very little disingenuousness in her character. Her early and consistent training, the definiteness of her vocation, and, above all, her profoundly religious attitude gave her a strength and poise that could not be overcome by any ordinary misfortune.

Long before I ever heard of Christ, or saw a white man, I had learned from an untutored woman the essence of morality. With the help of dear Nature herself, she taught me things simple but of mighty import. I knew God. I perceived what goodness is. I saw and loved what is really beautiful. Civilization has not taught me anything better!

As a child, I understood how to give; I have forgotten that grace since I became civilized. I lived the natural life, whereas I now live the artificial. Any pretty pebble was valuable to me then; every growing tree an object of reverence. Now I worship with the white man before a painted landscape whose value is estimated in dollars! Thus the Indian is reconstructed, as the natural rocks are ground to powder, and made into artificial blocks which may be built into the walls of modern society.

The first American mingled with his pride a singular humility. Spiritual arrogance was foreign to his nature and teaching. He never claimed that the power of articulate speech was proof of superiority over the dumb creation; on the other hand, it is to him a perilous gift. He believes profoundly in silence, the sign of a perfect equilibrium. Silence is the absolute poise or balance of body, mind, and spirit. The man who preserves his selfhood ever calm and unshaken by the storms of existence — not a leaf, as it were, astir on the tree; not a ripple upon the surface of shining pool — his, in the mind of the unlettered sage, is the ideal attitude and conduct of life.

If you ask him: "What is silence?" he will answer: "It is the Great Mystery!" "The holy silence is His voice!" If you ask: "What are the fruits of silence?" he will say: "They are self-control, true courage or endurance, patience, dignity, and reverence. Silence is the corner-stone of character."

"Guard your tongue in youth," said the old chief Wabashaw, "and in age you may mature a thought that will be of service to your people!"

The moment that man conceived of a perfect body, supple, symmetrical, graceful, and enduring — in that moment he had laid the foundation of a moral life! No man can hope to maintain such a temple of the spirit beyond the period of adolescence, unless he is able to curb his indulgence in the pleasures of the senses. Upon this truth the Indian built a rigid system of physical training, a social and moral code that was the law of his life.

WHENEVER, in the course of the daily hunt, the red

hunter comes upon a scene that is strikingly beautiful or sublime — a black thundercloud with the rainbow's glowing arch above the mountain; a white waterfall in the heart of a green gorge; a vast prairie tinged with the blood-red of sunset — he pauses for an instant in the attitude of worship. He sees no need for setting apart one day in seven as a holy day, since to him all days are God's.

Every act of his life is, in a very real sense, a religious act. He recognizes the spirit in all creation, and believes that he draws from it spiritual power.

NATIVE AMERICAN WISDOM

Trouble no man about his religion — respect him in his view of the Great Spirit, and demand of him that he respect yours. Do not force your religion on anyone.

Wabasha *Santee Sioux*

The Great Spirit sketches out the path of life roughly for all the creatures on earth, shows them where to go, where to arrive at, but leaves them to find their own way to get there. He wants them to act independently according to their nature.

Lame Deer *Lakota*

We do not worship creation. We worship the Great Spirit in the creation He has made.

Pete Catches Sr. *Lakota*

For the Great Spirit is everywhere; he hears whatever is in our minds and hearts, and it is not necessary to speak to Him in a loud voice.

Black Elk *Oglala Sioux*

We each have a duty to cast out our doubt, to turn aside our ignorance, and . . . to realize that . . . the creative principle, the Great Mystery, is within ourselves.

Dhyani Ywahoo *Cherokee*

This center which is here, but which we know is really everywhere, is *Wakan-Tanka*.

Black Elk

There is no word for "God"; we call it a Great Mystery, because of its formlessness.

Dhyani Ywahoo

Children are taught to go directly to the source of the Great Mystery. In order that knowledge does not get separated from experience or wisdom from divinity, wait and listen. Do not ask why. A child that cannot sit still is a half-developed child.

Luther Standing Bear   *Lakota Sioux*

You don't ask questions when you grow up. You watch and listen and wait, and the answer will come to you. It's yours then, not like learning in school.

Larry Bird   *Keres*

I was raised not to ask *why* but to listen, become aware. I take for granted that people have some knowledge of themselves. That is religion.

Soge Track   *Taos Pueblo*

My father went on talking to me in a low voice. That is how our people always talk to their children, so low and quiet, the child thinks he is dreaming. But he never forgets.

Maria Chona   *Papago*

163

Grown men may learn from very little children, for the hearts of little children are pure, and, therefore, the Great Spirit may show to them many things which older people miss.

Black Elk

Without spiritual practice confusion reigns.

Dhyani Ywahoo

No one will tell you how to pray, how to live. You must prepare yourselves; you have to find yourselves.

Matthew King   *Lakota*

Do not wrong or hate your neighbor for it is not him that you wrong, you wrong yourself.

Thomas Wildcat Alford   *Shawnee*

We Indians know the One true God, and . . . we pray to Him continually.

Black Elk

Whatever our tribe, our language, our race, our culture, there is one truth, one reality, that unites us as people.

Dhyani Ywahoo

The two are really only one: it is only the ignorant person who sees many where there is really only one.

Black Elk

Sin is trespass against the laws of the Great Spirit; it brings its own punishment, for sin *is* its own punishment.

Wabasha

To still the mind is very important, so that you may truly know yourself.

Dhyani Ywahoo

I am blind and do not see the things of this world; but when the light comes from above, it enlightens my heart and I can see, for the Eye of my heart sees everything; and through this vision I can help my people. The heart is a sanctuary at the center of which there is a little space, wherein the Great Spirit dwells, and this is the Eye. This is the Eye of the Great Spirit by which He sees all things, and through which we see Him. If the heart is not pure, the Great Spirit cannot be seen.

Black Elk

To see our work as prayer and an opportunity to bring forth a flash of truth is a great gift. To know that even the busy world is a holy world is quite a change of heart.

Dhyani Ywahoo

First responsibility: to know yourself, understand your own mind.

Dhyani Ywahoo

It does not require many words to speak the truth.

Chief Joseph   *Nez Perce*

The first peace, which is the most important, is that which comes within the souls of men when they realize their relationship, their oneness, with the universe and all its powers, and when they realize that at the center of the universe dwells *Wakan-Tanka*, and that this center is really everywhere, it is within each of us. This is the real Peace, and the others are but reflections of this. The second peace is that which is made between two individuals, and the third is that which is made between two nations. But above all you should understand that there can never be peace between nations until there is first known that true peace which, as I have often said, is within the souls of men.

Black Elk

By prayer and fasting and fixed purpose, you can rule your own spirit.

Wabasha

Essentially there is one truth underlying our attempts to describe what is indescribable.

Dhyani Ywahoo

Remember your nothingness in the presence of the Great Spirit.

Black Elk

Every man should have his own Holy Place where he keeps lonely vigil, harkens for the Voices, and offers prayer and praise.

Wabasha

True wisdom is only to be found far away from people, out in the great solitude, and it is not found in play but only through suffering. Solitude and suffering open the human mind, and therefore a shaman seeks his wisdom there.

Igjugarjuk   *Caribou Eskimo*

We should be as water which is lower than all things, yet stronger even than the rocks.

Black Elk

By your thinking and desire you will be brought here again and again until you awaken to the sacred light within yourself and every being.

Dhyani Ywahoo

The body is a robe stitched together by desire, thought, and action.

Cherokee Elder

Now is the result of all our yesterdays and the basis of all our tomorrows, so why don't you just pay attention to what's happening now?

Great-Grandfather Eli Ywahoo

So live your life that the fear of death can never enter your heart.

Wabasha

For after all the great religions have been preached and expounded, or have been revealed by brilliant scholars, or have been written in books and embellished in fine language with fine covers, *man— all men— is confronted with the Great Mystery.*

Luther Standing Bear

No one is going to influence my soul unless I'm the one who's going to. I'm the only one who's responsible for that soul. If I don't do the right thing here, I'm at fault. No one is going to bring you up to your grave but yourself.

Alex Saluskin   *Luiseño*

We all know that we came here naked and without possessions, and that we will leave without anything.

Dhyani Ywahoo

Do not grieve. Misfortunes will happen to the wisest and best of men. Death will come, always out of season. It is the command of the Great Spirit, and all nations and people must obey. What is past and what cannot be prevented should not be grieved for . . . Misfortunes do not flourish particularly in our lives — they grow everywhere.

Big Elk   *Omaha*

It is good to have a reminder of death before us, for it helps us to understand the impermanence of life on this earth, and this understanding may aid us in preparing for our own death. He who is well prepared is he who knows that he is nothing compared with *Wakan-Tanka,* who is everything; then he knows that world which is real.

Black Elk

There is no death. Only a change of worlds.

Chief Seattle   *Suqwamish*

Let my soul be draped in various flowers; let it be intoxicated by them; for soon must I weeping go before the face of our Mother.

Aztec

RAMPRASAD

Nancy Pope Mayorga

ONE OF THE deep-rooted Hindu ideas most alien to Western minds is the idea of worshipping God as Mother, worship known as *Shakti,* whose logic, nevertheless, is inescapable. For it is based on the following dualistic principal: *Brahman* is impersonal, inactive; Divine Mother is creative, sustaining, and destructive. God has to be beyond change and activity. Yet, here is the world and it cannot be ignored; hence Mother, God's power, the producer and sustainer of this phenomenal universe. It is a profound idea, which was pondered over, used, and refined through the long, slow Indian centuries and reached a radiant flowering in the last century in Sri Ramakrishna at Dakshineswar.

For this idea of Shakti, Ramakrishna was a remarkable bridge, not only between the ancient and the modern, not only between legend and logic, but more important for us, between Eastern and Western psychology. From his days as a young boy, crying to the Mother and rubbing his face despairingly in the dust, feeding a cat in the temple with holy food because he saw the Mother in it, to his later days as the rational, illumined teacher, psychologist supreme, he spanned in one lifetime those great rolling centuries, and gave us in simple and universal language the essence of their matured wisdom. This is what he said:

> When I think of the Supreme Being as inactive — neither operating nor preserving nor

destroying — I call Him Brahman or *Purusha* or the superpersonal God. When I think of Him as active — creating, preserving and destroying — I call Him *Shakti* [Divine Mother] or *maya* or *prakriti*, the personal God. But the distinction between them does not mean a difference. The superpersonal and the personal are the same thing, like milk and its whiteness, the diamond and its luster, the snake and its wriggling motion. It is impossible to conceive of the one without the other. The Divine Mother and Brahman are one.

The principal seat of Shakti worship is the northeastern part of India — Bengal, Assam, and Behar. And one of the most famous, prolific, and inspired worshippers of the Divine Mother was the Bengali singer of hymns, Ramprasad (1718-1775). Readers of M's *Gospel of Sri Ramakrishna* know what a great inspiration the life of Ramprasad was to Ramakrishna in his early spiritual struggles. At every kirtan, at every gathering of devotees, some song of Ramprasad's was sung. Again and again, Ramakrishna, calling on the Mother with tears, reminded her, "You revealed Yourself to Ramprasad. Why not to me?"

BORN at Kumarhati, Ramprasad was given a good education. His father was a physician who expected that his son would follow the same career. The boy showed great promise in his early school years; but after studying medicine for awhile, found himself disinclined to be a doctor. Then his father suggested he study languages, Sanskrit, Persian, and Hindi, to prepare himself for a business career; but it soon became apparent that the boy's mind yearned only for the religious life. It was thought that marriage might cure this disease; and so he was married and soon had a family of four children, a responsibility which fell heavily upon his conscience and for which, temperamentally, he was very poorly equipped.

Like many saints, he was a failure at practical life; but it can be said of him what can not be said of all saints, that he had an understanding wife. Sarvani stood by him, and struggled to make ends meet, till finally he managed to get a job in Calcutta as a bookkeeper and accountant for the manager of an estate. But he was incorrigible, and instead of keeping accounts he wrote hymns to the Divine Mother on the pages of the ledger. This was reported by his immediate superior to the manager, who came in annoyance to see for himself. Ramprasad had written a plea to the Divine Mother that he didn't want that job as bookkeeper, but "appoint me your treasurer, Mother, and trust me. I will be your servant without pay. I want only the dust of your feet." To his employer there was something so moving about these lines that tears came to his eyes. In Ramprasad he recognized a great soul, and agreed with him that there was something more to life than keeping books. He said, "Go home. Seek your Divine Mother, and my family will pay you an allowance the rest of your life."

The man's name was Vakulachandra Ghosal and deserves to be remembered; for in giving Ramprasad his freedom to sing, he made a gift to the world of many beautiful songs sung today by rich and poor alike, by villagers of Bengal, by coolies, by holy men, by school boys. And those dying on the banks of the Ganges often ask to hear a song by Ramprasad.

His patron did something else for him — he introduced him to the Krishnagar Court, where he rose in
favor with the rajah and won the title of "Entertainer of
Poets." Here, among men of his own intellectual level,
he seemed to have found himself. There was even a
good-humored running feud between him and a rival
poet, Aju Goswami, who was a materialist, a wit, and
clever in poking fun at Ramprasad up on his transcendental level. To Ramprasad the world was a "mere
framework of illusion," but his less ascetic friend
insisted it was a "very mansion of mirth; here I can eat,
here drink, and make merry." "Free me from the net of
maya," prayed the saint; but Aju begged mischievously,
"Bind me in your wide chains." "Dive deep, oh mind,"
Ramprasad sang, and Aju came right back with his
doggerel, "Oh mind, dive not! Just go floating . . ." They
both seemed to have enjoyed this exchange.

WITH his family's material wants taken care of,
Ramprasad plunged into severe spiritual practices.
During this period of his life, he wrote his most beautiful
and pathetic poems of pleading, with their endless
complaints that the Divine Mother had not shown herself
to him. "In what way have I offended?" he asks. "Unen-
durable has become my lot, and all day I sit and weep."
And, "When the child weeps, uttering the dear name of
the mother, then the mother takes it on her lap. Throughout the whole world I see this come to pass. I alone am
excepted."

Finally out of his faithfulness and his agony, he
received the vision. The Divine Mother appeared to him
in a garden near his home. It is said that the physical
appearance of Ramprasad became transformed; and a

174

divine glow which everyone could see, came from his body. Miracles began to happen of which he spoke in his poems. Once he was tying up a hedge and his little daughter was on the other side passing the cord to him as he passed it through to her. After a while, the child grew tired of the work and ran off to play, but Ramprasad never knew, for someone else kept up the work from the other side until the job was finished. When the little girl came back, she was astonished to find the work done and confessed that she had not been there for a long time. Ramprasad was dumbfounded and could only conclude that the Divine Mother Herself had been helping him.

On another occasion, on his way to the Ganges to bathe, Ramprasad met a very beautiful young woman who asked him to sing for her. He requested her to wait a few minutes, but when he got back to his house she had gone, leaving a note for him in the family chapel. She said she was Kali [Divine Mother] and she commanded him to go to Benares to sing for her. Twice he started and twice fell ill on the road, but the second time he saw Kali in a vision telling him to never mind, that the journey was not necessary. In joy over this vision, he composed a song about the futility of pilgrimages. "The lotus feet of Kali are places of pilgrimage enough for me. Deep in my heart's center meditating upon them, I float in an ocean of bliss . . . What care I for going to Benares? See, around my neck as a garland I have bound the name of Kali."

It was Ramprasad's peculiar habit and pleasure to wade into the Ganges up to his neck, then stand and let his songs to the Divine Mother pour spontaneously out over the water. Boats on the river would stop, and people would gather on the shore to listen to him.

What did they hear? They heard a language they understood, earthy and colloquial, full of puns. For example, he said, punning in his own name. "Prasad has offered his prasad." They heard illustrations drawn from their own familiar rural life, racy, salty, and sometimes vulgar. To us today he gives a fascinating, authentic look at the thought and customs of that time and place. He spoke of his mind as a "bad farmer." Speaking of rebirth, he compared himself to a "blindfolded ox that grinds the oil," bound to the log of the world, turning round incessantly. He described the six passions as "crocodiles haunting the bathing *ghat*" or as robbers leaping over the low mud wall of his courtyard. Very often he thought of death when his friends would leave him, "bones and ashes on the burning ground." And in an oft-quoted reproof to his soul about its fear of dying, he said scornfully, "Thou, a snake, fearing frogs!"

Sometimes it must have been a stirring sound over the surface of the Ganges, for many of his verses ring with vitality and enthusiasm:

Jagadamba's watchmen go out into the dread, black
    night!
Jagadamba's watchmen!
"Victory! Victory to Kali!" they cry,
And clapping their hands and striking upon their cheeks,
They shout, "Bam! Bam!"

But when he touches the ground of the Universal Mother, it is then his poetry springs up to divine heights. When he talks directly and sweetly to Mother, he reaches our hearts. "Let us have a word or two about the problem of suffering. Let us talk about suffering, Mother, let me express my mind." "Present art Thou within my lotus-heart. Spurn me not at the last, Mother, me who have found refuge at Thy feet." And, "In the world's play, what was to be has been. Now at eventide, taking your child to your bosom, go home."

Like many a great saint, Ramprasad seemed to have been aware of his approaching death. His last songs are almost all about the subject of death. They are vigorous and assured. There is no fear in them. "Death the thief is close behind thee. Awake, my mind, and slumber not." "Herald of Death, get hence! I can be the death of Death, if I remember the Almighty Mother's power."

His last day was the last day of the annual celebration of Kali puja. Ramprasad, so the story goes, followed the clay image of Kali as it was taken to be immersed in the Ganges. Standing up to his neck in the water, he sang his final song, "My mind is firm, and my gift well made. Mother, my Mother, my all is finished." And soaring with the song, his pure and rejoicing soul left his body.

HYMNS OF RAMPRASAD

Come, let us go for a walk, O mind, to Kali, the wish-
    fulfilling Tree,
And there beneath it gather the four fruits of life.
Of your two wives, Dispassion and Worldliness,
Bring along Dispassion only, on your way to the Tree,
And ask her son Discrimination about the Truth.

When will you learn to lie, O mind, in the abode of
    Blessedness,
With Cleanliness and Defilement on either side of you?
Only when you have found the way
To keep these wives contentedly under a single roof,
Will you behold the matchless form of Mother Shyama.

Ego and Ignorance, your parents, instantly banish from
    your sight,
And should Delusion seek to drag you to its hole,
Manfully cling to the pillar of Patience.
Tie to the post of Unconcern the goats of Vice and
    Virtue,
Killing them with the sword of Knowledge if they rebel.

With the children of Worldliness, your first wife, plead
    from a goodly distance,
And, if they will not listen, drown them in Wisdom's sea.
Says Ramprasad: If you do as I say,
You can submit a good account, O mind, to the King of
    Death,
And I shall be well pleased with you and call you my
    darling.

In the world's busy market-place, O Shyama, Thou art
    flying kites;
High up they soar on the wind of hope, held fast by
    maya's string.
Their frames are human skeletons, their sails of the three
    gunas made;
But all their curious workmanship is merely for
    ornament.
Upon the kite-strings Thou has rubbed the manja paste
    of worldliness,
So as to make each straining strand all the more sharp
    and strong.
Out of a hundred thousand kites, at best but one or two
    break free,
And Thou dost laugh and clap Thy hands, O Mother,
    watching them!
On favoring winds, says Ramprasad, the kites set loose
    will speedily
Be borne away to the Infinite, across the sea of the world.

Taking the name of Kali, dive deep down, O mind,
Into the heart's fathomless depths,
Where many a precious gem lies hid.
But never believe the bed of the ocean bare of gems
If in the first few dives you fail;
With firm resolve and self-control
Dive deep and make your way to Mother Kali's realm.

Down in the ocean depths of heavenly wisdom lie
The wondrous pearls of Peace, O mind;
And you yourself can gather them,
If you have but pure love and follow the scriptures' rule.
Within those ocean depths, as well,
Six alligators lurk—lust, anger, and the rest—
Swimming about in search of prey.
Smear yourself with the turmeric of discrimination;
The very smell of it will shield you from their jaws.

Upon the ocean bed lie strewn
Unnumbered pearls and precious gems;
Plunge in, says Ramprasad, and gather up handfuls there!

I drink from no ordinary wine, but Wine of Everlasting
    Bliss,
As I repeat my Mother Kali's name;
It so intoxicates my mind that people take me to be drunk!
First my guru gives molasses for the making of the Wine;
My longing is the ferment to transform it.
Knowledge, the maker of the Wine, prepares it for me
    then;
And when it is done, my mind imbibes it from the bottle
    of the mantra,
Taking the Mother's name to make it pure.
Drink of this Wine, says Ramprasad, and the four fruits of
    life are yours.

Mother, this is the grief that sorely grieves my heart,
That even with You for Mother, and though I am wide
    awake,
There should be robbery in my house.
Many and many a time I vow to call on You,
Yet when the time for prayer comes round, I have
    forgotten.
Now I see it is all Your trick.

As You have never given, so You receive naught;
Am I to blame for this, O Mother? Had You but given,
Surely then You had received;
Out of Your own gifts I should have given to You.
Glory and shame, bitter and sweet, are Yours alone;
This world is nothing but Your play.
Then why, O Blissful One do You cause a rift in it?

Says Ramprasad: You have bestowed on me this mind,
And with a knowing wink of Your eye
Bidden it, at the same time, to go and enjoy the world,
And so I wander here forlorn through Your creation,
Blasted, as it were, by someone's evil glance,
Taking the bitter for the sweet,
Taking the unreal for the Real.

O mind, you do not know how to farm!
Fallow lies the field of your life.
If you had only worked it well,
How rich a harvest you might reap!
Hedge it about with Kali's name
If you would keep your harvest safe;
This is the stoutest hedge of all,
For Death himself cannot come near it.

Sooner or later will dawn the day
When you must forfeit your precious field;
Gather, O mind, what fruit you may.
Sow for your seed the holy name
Of God that your guru has given to you,
Faithfully watering it with love;
And if you should find the task too hard,
Call upon Ramprasad for help.

How are you trying, O my mind, to know the nature of
    God?
You are groping like a madman locked in a dark room.
He is grasped through ecstatic love; how can you fathom
    Him without it?
Only through affirmation, never negation, can you know
    Him;
Neither through Veda nor through Tantra nor the six
    darsanas.

It is in love's elixir only that He delights, O mind;
He dwells in the body's innermost depths, in Everlasting
    Joy.
And, for that love, the mighty yogis practise yoga from
    age to age;
When love awakes, the Lord, like a magnet, draws to
    Him the soul.

He it is, says Ramprasad, that I approach as Mother;
But must I give away the secret, here in the
    market-place?
From the hints I have given, O mind, guess what that
    Being is!

PEACE PILGRIM

Ray Berry

A TRULY ALL-AMERICAN Sannyasini. That is the best way to describe this remarkable woman called Peace Pilgrim. In the traditional sense a *sannyasini* is a wandering nun, consumed with an eagerness to merge herself with the divine force, travelling the length and breadth of India, begging her food, sleeping where chance may bring her, sharing her spiritual thoughts with others, and just accepting what the Lord may dole out to her.

This was the pattern of Peace Pilgrim's life for more than twenty-eight years. She travelled literally the length and breadth of North America, all fifty states, the ten provinces of Canada, and parts of Mexico. Well, one might not think this so remarkable if it weren't for the fact that she did this continuous journeying on foot, *never* asking for anything: food, shelter, or transportation. She walked without a penny in her pocket. She had only the clothes she wore, and those consisted of pants, shirt, tennis shoes, and a short sleeveless tunic lettered boldly on the front "*Peace Pilgrim.*" How many pairs of tennis shoes she must have worn out during those years! Years that were counted from the time she was forty-four until a few days before her seventy-third birthday. Just imagine her living like this, travelling, walking "like a leaf blown in the wind" until she was almost seventy-three years old. Her message to all she met was simple, "This is the way of peace: overcome evil with good, and falsehood with truth, and hatred with love." She talked about peace between nations, between groups, among people and the most important *Inner Peace*, which she talked about most often because that is where real peace begins.

There is only one thing that could inspire and support a journey of this extent and provide the strength to see it through for all those years, and that is absolute, uncompromising faith in herself and in God. Faith which comes and is sustained by the realization and direct experience of the ultimate truths of life.

PEACE Pilgrim was born July 15, 1908 into a hard-working, resourceful family on a small farm in the eastern United States. In her youth she was happy to play in the woods and streams of the countryside. She had no formal religious training as a child. She said it would be less that she would have to undo from her mind later on. In her late teens she began her search for God. "What is God? What is God?" she inquired of many people, but never received an answer. Then she took another approach, she asked herself. She pondered deeply and was ultimately answered from within. She said, "I touched God intellectually as truth, emotionally as love, as goodness, kindness, a creative force, a motivating power, an over-all intelligence and an ever-present, all pervading spirit. That brought God close. I could not be where God is not. You are within God. God is within you."

As she looked about the world, she became increasingly uncomfortable about having so much while others had so little. From this gnawing dissatisfaction she sought a meaningful way of life. After much prayer and contemplation she felt a complete willingness to dedicate her life to serving others. She began to live to give instead of to get, and she entered a new and wonderful world, and a great peace came over her.

Then began her years of intense spiritual practice. And this stage continued for fifteen long hard fought but joyously rewarding years.

She explained her own inner process:

During the spiritual growing up period the inner conflict can be more or less stormy. Old habits and tendencies don't die an easy death. The self-centered nature is a very formidable enemy and it struggles fiercely to retain its identity. It defends itself in a cunning manner and should not be regarded lightly. It knows the weakest spots of your armor and attempts a confrontation when one is least aware. During these battles, one must maintain a humble stature and be intimate with *none* but the promptings of the higher self.

The process toward inner peace is not necessarily taken in any particular order. The first step for one may be the last step for another. So just take whatever steps seem easiest for you, and as you take a few steps, it will become easier for you to take a few more.

The first preparation is to take a right attitude toward life. Stop being an escapist! Face life squarely and get down beneath the surface where the truths and realities of life are to be found. There is an art to living. No problem ever comes to you that does not have a purpose in your life, that cannot contribute to your inner growth. When you perceive this, you will recognize that problems are opportunities in disguise. It is through solving problems in accordance with the highest light we have, that spiritual growth is attained.

It takes the living quite a while to catch up with the believing, but now there is a living to give instead of to get. As you concentrate on the giving, you discover that just as you cannot receive without giving, so neither can you give without receiving. There is a feeling of endless energy, it just never runs out, it seems to be as endless as air. You seem to be plugged in to the source of universal energy.

You are now in control of your life. Your higher nature, which is controlled by God, controls the body, the mind, and the emotions.

Henry Thoreau said. "If a man does not keep pace with his companions, perhaps it is because he hears a different drummer." Now you are marching to that different drummer: the higher nature instead of the lower nature.

Another preparation she emphasized is the simplification of life. "Try to bring inner and outer well-being into harmony in your life, to keep your desires down to need level. In this materialistic age we have such a false criterion by which to measure success. We measure it in terms of dollars, in terms of material things. But happiness and inner peace do not lie in that direction. Unnecessary possessions are only unnecessary burdens. If you know and do not do, you are a very unhappy person indeed."

The following story was told by a professor of religion and philosophy. He and his wife were hosting Peace Pilgrim in their home for a few days. "I went to pick up Peace Pilgrim at the station. Seeing her standing at the curb as I drove up, I got out to greet her and then went to get her bags to put them in the trunk. Well, there were no bags, *nothing*. Whatever she carried was in the pocket of her tunic: a comb, toothbrush, her mail, some paper and a pen. This woman is serious business. My wife said that she felt she was in the presence of a tiger. We had another visit with Peace some fifteen years later, and she actually looked younger this second time."

Peace Pilgrim continually emphasized, "Anything beyond need tends to become burdensome. If you have it, you have to take care of it! There is a great freedom in simplicity of living where you can find harmony between inner and outer well-being. We have gotten ourselves so far out of harmony, because we are so way off on the material side. This is due to our inner well-being lagging so far behind our outer well-being. The valid practice for the future is on the inner side, on the spiritual side, so that we will be able to bring these two into balance.

"No one is truly free who is still attached to material things, or places, or people. Material things must be put into their proper place. They are there for use. But when they have outlived their usefulness be ready to relinquish them and perhaps pass them on to someone who needs them. Anything that you cannot let go of when you are finished with it possesses you, and in this materialistic age a great many of us are possessed by our possessions. We are not free.

"There is a well-worn road which is pleasing to the senses and gratifies the ego and worldly desires, but leads nowhere. And there is the less traveled path, which requires discrimination and renunciation, but results in untold spiritual blessings."

Sri Ramakrishna said, "You have to turn the key to this world in the opposite direction, if you want to realize God."

During this period of her spiritual practice and deliberate living there were hills and valleys, lots of hills and valleys. Then, in the midst of the struggle, there came a wonderful mountaintop experience — the first glimpse of what the life of inner peace is like.

In her own words: "I was out walking in the early morning. All of a sudden I felt very uplifted, more uplifted than I had ever been. I remember *I knew* timelessness and spacelessness and lightness. I did not seem to be walking on the earth. There were no people or even animals around, but every flower, every bush, every tree seemed to wear a halo. There was a light emanation around everything and flecks of gold fell like slanted rain through the air. This experience is sometimes called the illumination period.

"The most important part of it was *not* the phenomena. The important part of it was the realization of the oneness of all creation. Not only all human beings — I knew before that all human beings are one. But now I knew also a oneness with the rest of creation. The creatures that walk the earth, and the growing things. The air, the water, the earth itself. And, most wonderful of all, a oneness with That which permeates all and binds all together and gives life to all. *Oneness.* A oneness with That which many would call God."

The inspiration for the pilgrimage came at this time.

TWENTY-EIGHT years. Tens of thousands of uncounted miles. How many people Peace Pilgrim met and inspired through her quiet joyous ways!

A man once said to her, "I'm surprised at the kind of person you are. After reading your very serious message on the way of peace I expected you to be a very solemn person, but instead I find you bubbling over with joy." She said, "Who could know God and not be joyous?"

To the end she stressed this message: "When you find peace within yourself, you become the kind of person who can live at peace with others. Inner peace is not found by staying on the surface of life, or by attempting to escape from life through any means. Inner peace is found by facing life squarely, solving its problems, and delving as far beneath its surface as possible to discover its verities and realities. Inner peace comes through strict adherence to already quite well-known laws of human conduct, such as the law that the means shape the end: that only a good means can ever attain a good end. Inner peace comes through relinquishment of self-will, attachments, and negative thoughts and feelings. Inner peace comes through working for the good of all. We are all cells in the body of humanity — all of us, all over the world. Each one has a contribution to make and will know from within what this contribution is, but no one can find inner peace except by working, not in a self-centered way, but for the whole human family.

"The key word for our time is practice. We have all the light we need, we just need to put it into practice."

CONVERSATIONS WITH PEACE PILGRIM

Q. What is the goal and purpose of mankind?

A. Our goal and purpose is to bring our lives into harmony with God's will.

Q. Is the goal of self-knowledge to know God?

A. If you really know yourself you will know you are a child of God and you will become aware of God.

Q. What is mysticism?

A. One who takes the mystic approach receives direct perceptions from within. This is the source from which all truth came in the first place.

Q. Where did you learn meditation?

A. I did not learn meditation. I just walked, receptive and silent, amid the beauty of nature — and put the wonderful insights that came to me into practice.

Q. Do you suggest meditation or breathing exercises to the seeker?

A. I suggest a time apart or a time alone with God, walking in receptive silence amid the beauties of God's nature. From the beauty of nature you get your inspiration, from the silent receptiveness you get your meditation, from the walking you get not only exercise but breathing— all in one lovely experience.

Q. Can spiritual growth be accomplished quickly or does it take awhile?

A. Spiritual growth is a process the same as physical growth or mental growth. Five year old children do not expect to graduate into college at the end of the term; the student of truth should not expect to attain inner peace overnight. It took me fifteen years. The spiritual growing up is a very interesting and enjoyable process. There should be no wish to either hasten it or slow it down. Just experience it and take the steps toward inner peace and let it unfold.

I talk to groups studying the most advanced spiritual teachings and sometimes these people wonder why nothing is happening in their lives. Their motive is the attainment of inner peace for themselves — which of course is a selfish motive. You will not find it with this motive. The motive, if you are to find inner peace, must be an outgoing motive. Service, of course, *service*. Giving, not getting. Your motive must be good if your work is to have good effect. The secret of life is being of service.

Q. When I try to help someone, I never know whether my action will be truly beneficial or not. I try to have good motives but I never really know.

A. Yes, you have to do the best you can, and motive is extremely important, extremely important. For instance, if you are doing some good thing because you feel it will benefit you, you will receive no benefit. You must be doing the good thing out of love, you see, with a good motive in order for it to benefit you. It is very interesting.

Q. How does an ordinary housewife and mother find what you seem to possess?

A. One who is in the family pattern, as most people are, finds inner peace in the same way that I found it. Find and fit into your special place in the divine plan, which is unique for every human soul. You might try sitting in receptive silence, as I did. Being in the family pattern is not a block to spiritual growth, and in some ways it is an advantage. We grow through problem-solving, and being in the family pattern provides plenty of problems to grow on.

Only when we realize that we do not possess people — that they must live in accordance with their own inner motivations, do we stop trying to run their lives for them, and then we discover that we are able to live in harmony with them.

Pure love is a willingness to give without a thought of receiving anything in return.

Q. How can one break bad habits of thought and action?

A. Bad habits of thought and action lessen as spiritual growth progresses. You can work on replacing negative thoughts with positive thoughts.

Q. What is the spiritual life?

A. That which cannot be perceived by the five senses. Spiritual things will endure, physical things will not. The spiritual life is the real life; all else is illusion and deception. Only those who are attached to God alone are truly free. Only those who live up to the highest light live in harmony. All who act upon their highest motivations become a power for good. It is not important that others be noticeably affected; results should never be sought or desired. Know that every right thing you do, every good word you say, every positive thought you think, has good effect.

Q. Where do I look to find spiritual truth?

A. In the final analysis you find spiritual truth through your own higher nature. There is no glimpse without walking the path. You can't get it from anyone else nor can you give it to anyone. Just take whatever steps seem easiest for you, and as you take a few steps, it will be easier for you to take a few more.

Q. Do you feel that if the person is highly motivated, there is some kind of guidance beyond himself?

A. Well, we all have tremendous guidance, but especially those who are willing to allow their lives to be governed by the higher nature. You see, that higher nature is there and to a certain extent you receive some guidance, but if you allow it to govern your life (and you have free will as to whether you will allow it to govern your life or not); then, of course, you will receive constant guidance. Our lives are ordered and arranged for us in many wonderful ways if we allow it to happen.

Q. What overcomes fear?

A. When you know that you are only wearing the body, which can be destroyed— that you are the reality which activates the body and cannot be destroyed— how can you be afraid?

When we have found inner peace we feel unity with the Divine within all human beings and unity with God, so all fear is gone from our lives. As long as we feel separate we are afraid to be and act alone — as soon as we feel oneness that feeling is gone.

Q. Do you accept disciples?

A. Of course I do not. Only God takes disciples. It is not healthy to follow another human being. Every person must find his or her maturity. The process takes time, the growth period is different for each individual.

Why do you look at me? Look at your own self. Why do you listen to me? Listen to your own self. Why do you believe in what I say? Do not believe in me or any other teacher, rather trust in your own inner voice. *This* is your guide, this is your teacher. Your teacher is within not without. Know yourself, not me!

Q. What is it like to communicate with God?

A. Communication with God is a deep inner knowing that God is within you and around you. God 'speaks' through the still, small voice within. When you have constant communion with God, a constant receiving from within, there is never any doubt; you know your way. You become an instrument through which a job is done, therefore you have no feeling of self-achievement.

The main things, if you are to find inner peace, are to bring your life into harmony with the laws which govern this universe (these are the same for all of us), and to find and fit into your special work in this world—your job in the divine plan.

Many people are suffering from spiritual starvation even though what they need is within them and all around them.

One in harmony with God's law of love has more strength than an army, for one need not subdue an adversary; an adversary can be transformed.

For guidance and for truth it is much better to look for the source through you own inner teacher, than to look to people or books.

The path of the seeker is full of pitfalls and temptations, but the seeker must find it alone— with God.

In all people I meet I see that divine spark, and that's what I concentrate on.

Receptive prayer results in an inner receiving, which motivates to right action.

I can say this to you. Live in the present. Do the things you know need to be done. Do all the good you can each day. The future will unfold.

Only those who are attached to God alone are truly free.

BROTHER LAWRENCE

Nancy Pope Mayorga

BROTHER LAWRENCE LIVES for us in one slim little volume of fifty pages called *The Practice of the Presence of God*. Opening this book is like opening the window to a fresh spring morning. His simple prose reflects the purity and directness of his approach to God. "You need not cry very loud," he says in words of unadorned beauty. "He is nearer to us than we are aware of." Brother Lawrence wastes no words, yet the amount of information and inspiration in the fifty short pages of this book is almost past belief. It is the finest and most powerful distillation of a lifetime of spiritual practice.

The first eighteen pages of the book consist of four interviews he granted (in 1666) to M. Beaufort, Grand Vicar to M. Chalons, the Cardinal, at the monastery where Brother Lawrence worked as cook. The Vicar, having heard reports of this man, came to check for the Cardinal on, perhaps, subversion or insubordination or heresy. He found not a rebel — that was the last thing Brother Lawrence would be — but certainly not a conformist. He was impressed enough to go home and try to write down every word he had heard from this kitchen laborer, impressed enough to ask respectfully if he might come again to visit him. To this request the Vicar received a calm and authoritative answer that, if Monsieur's interest was genuinely spiritual, he, Brother Lawrence, would be glad to talk to him. Otherwise, he was too busy in his kitchen.

The Vicar came at least four times, and from him

we have the only description of this humble and glorious lay brother, whose "very countenance was edifying, such a sweet and calm devotion appearing in it as could not but affect the beholders. He spoke quite freely, and what he said was very simple, to the point and full of sense." Two years after Brother Lawrence died, the Vicar wrote what he called *The Character of Brother Lawrence,* in which he said: "He had a frank and open manner, which, when you met him won your confidence at once, and made you feel that you had found a friend to whom you could unbosom yourself wholly. Behind his rather rough exterior, one found a singular sagacity, a spaciousness of mind quite beyond the range of the ordinary lay brother, a penetration that surpassed all expectation."

The last thirty-two pages of Brother Lawrence's little book are made up of letters written by him in his old age to people earnestly desiring to know the method by which he had arrived at the "habitual sense of God's presence." Now, after three hundred years, these letters are for us; this friend is ours. And what a never-ending comfort it is to hear him tell frankly of his spiritual struggles, to have him encourage us again and again in ours.

He was alerted to God, converted to the godly life at the age of eighteen by seeing in winter a tree stripped of its leaves, and reflecting upon the fact that it would be, by God's grace, leafy and flowery in the spring. From this experience he received a "high view of the providence and power of God" which was never effaced from his soul, and from it he received the impetus to start his search.

He began by studying books for the way to God, but he was not an intellectual, or the books were not inspiring, and he found that he was simply being confused. So he put aside books, and, gave, as he says, "the all for the all." "I renounced for the love of Him everything that was not He, and I began to live as if there was none but He and I in the world." How simple! Yet he is careful not to mislead the hopeful aspirant, and he confesses, "I must tell you that for the first ten years I suffered much . . . I fell often and rose again presently. It seemed to me that all creatures, reason, and God Himself were against me." Nevertheless, he did not make vain attempts to pierce the future, nor did he dwell on his present anguish. He said firmly, "Let what may come of it, however many be the days remaining to me, I will do all things for the love of God." Thus, in putting aside self, he in truth found God. "When I thought to end my days in these troubles, I found myself changed all at once; and my soul felt a profound inward peace, as if she were in her center and place of rest. Ever since that time, I walk before God simply, in faith, with humility and love."

NICHOLAS HERMAN of Lorraine was his name. He started life, he tells us, as a footman, but he was a "great awkward fellow who broke things." He decided then to join the Carmelite monastery at Paris in the hope that God would punish him and make him suffer for his faults. But, he says with strange ruefulness, God disappointed him in this matter and gave him nothing but happiness and satisfaction in his life. This in spite of the fact that he was lame, that he worked for sixty years in the kitchen at a job he did not particularly relish, much of the time under great pressure and bustle, and that he was sometimes given assignments for which he felt he was inadequate. He was sent, for example, into Burgundy to buy wine for his society, an errand which made him apprehensive because of his lameness and his lack of knowledge of business. But he managed to go about the boat by rolling himself over the casks; and as for the business, he simply told God that it was His affair, and without his knowing how, it all turned out very well. We get a vivid picture of him in the monastery kitchen when he tells us, "The time of business does not with me differ from the time of prayer, and in the noise and clatter of my kitchen, while several persons are at the same time calling for different things, I possess God in as great tranquility as if I were upon my knees at the blessed sacrament."

His calm and continuing satisfaction resulted from the fact that he had discovered the true secret of work, always "pleasing myself by doing things to please God," rejoicing, as he says in a famous line, "to pick up a straw from the ground for the love of God."

But although Brother Lawrence is a lover of God, a true *bhakta*, it is as a karma yogin that he is best known, as a karma yogin that he teaches. "Make one hearty renunciation," he says, and as we study him, it begins to be clear what he means by renunciation — namely, work for God — "that we ought not to be weary of doing little things for God, who regards not the greatness of the work but the love with which it is performed." He says firmly that our progress does not depend in changing our position or work, but in doing our ordinary work purely for the love of God. He himself made a practice of offering all his actions to God. He thought of God at the beginning of his work. When he finished, if it had gone well, he gave thanks to God. If otherwise, he asked pardon, and without being discouraged, continued to exercise the presence of God within him. He says, "By rising after my falls, and by frequently renewed acts of faith and love, I am come to a state wherein it would be as difficult for me not to think of God as it was at first to accustom myself to it."

No one speaks with more authority than the man of experience. No teaching carries such conviction as that from a man of illumination. With all his humility, the authority and conviction of Brother Lawrence is clear. He is an illumined soul. He says, "I see Him in such a manner as might make me say sometimes, I believe no more, but I see." As if by divine appointment, he fearlessly accepts responsibility: "Knock, persevere in knocking, and I will answer for it that He will open to you."

As a teacher, Brother Lawrence is neither a philosopher nor a theologian. He is a practical mystic. What interests him are the everyday problems of spiritual practice. "Think often on God, by day, by night, in your business, and even in your diversions. Lift up your heart to Him, sometimes even at your meals, and when you are in company . . . It is not necessary for being with God to be always at church. We may make an oratory of our heart."

He is conscientious about his correspondents. "You tell me nothing new," he writes to one struggling aspirant. "You are not the only one that is troubled with wandering thoughts." And he goes on to advise that if the mind wanders, do not worry; bring it back in tranquility. "One way to recollect the mind easily in time of prayer is not to let it wander too far at other times."

Like a good teacher, Brother Lawrence is constantly urging and encouraging. "Let us set about it seriously." "I say again, we must work at it. Time presses, there is no room for delay; our souls are at stake." "Set heartily about this work. I will assist you with my prayers." "Resolve to persevere to death!" Such pleading cannot be resisted. We not only feel that he is convinced about God, but that he cares deeply about us.

AT the end of his life, in his eightieth year, God answered Brother Lawrence's long-cherished prayer and sent him some suffering to bear. He received it with joy because, as he said in a letter written shortly before he died, "When we know that it is our loving Father who distresses us, our sufferings will lose their bitterness and become even a matter of consolation." At the end of the letter he says, "I hope from his mercy the favor to see Him in a few days."

Two days later, when he had received the last sacraments, a brother asked him if he was easy and what his mind was busied with. This was his reply: "I am doing what I shall do through all Eternity — blessing God, praising God, adoring God, giving Him the love of my whole heart. It is our one business, my brethren."

MAXIMS OF BROTHER LAWRENCE

I engaged in a religious life only for the love of God, and I have endeavored to act only for Him; whatever becomes of me, whether I be lost or saved, I will always continue to act purely for the love of God. I shall have this good at least, that till death I shall have done all that is in me to love Him.

We ought to act with God in the greatest simplicity, speaking to Him frankly and plainly, and imploring His assistance in our affairs, just as they happen. I have often experienced that God never fails to grant it.

We should establish ourselves in a sense of God's presence by continually conversing with Him. It is a shameful thing to quit His conversation to think of trifles and fooleries.

There is not in the world a kind of life more sweet and delightful than that of a continual conversation with God. Those only can comprehend it who practice and experience it; yet I do not advise you to do it from that motive. It is not pleasure which we ought to seek in this exercise; but let us do it from a principle of love, and because God would have us.

I do not advise you to use multiplicity of words in prayer, many words and long discourses being often the occasions of wandering. Hold yourself in prayer before God like a dumb or paralytic beggar at a rich man's gate.

That there needed neither art nor science for going to God, but only a heart resolutely determined to apply itself to nothing but Him, or for His sake, and to love Him only.

Believe me, count as lost each day you have not used in loving God.

That the most excellent method he had found of going to God was that of doing our common business, without any view of pleasing men, and purely for the love of God.

In the beginning I had often passed my time appointed for prayer in rejecting wandering thoughts and falling back into them. I could never regulate my devotion by certain methods as some do. At first I had meditated for some time, but afterward that went off, in a manner I could give no account of.

Useless thoughts spoil all; the mischief begins there; but we ought to reject them as soon as we perceived their impertinence to the matter in hand, and return to our communion with God.

I am more united with God in my outward employments than when I leave them for devotion and retirement.

It is a great delusion to think that the times of prayer ought to differ from other times; we are as strictly obliged to adhere to God by action in the time of action as by prayer in the season of prayer.

I tell you that all consists in one hearty renunciation of everything which we are sensible does not lead to God.

Sometimes I consider myself there as a stone before a carver, whereof he is to make a statue; presenting myself thus before God, I desire Him to form His perfect image in my soul, and make me entirely like Himself.

I am in the hands of God, and He has His own good purpose regarding me; therefore I trouble not myself for aught that man can do to me.

The trust we put in God honors Him much and draws down great graces.

You would go faster than grace, but one does not become holy all at once.

The greater perfection a soul aspires after, the more dependent it is upon divine grace.

God seems to have granted the greatest favors to the greatest sinners, as more signal monuments of His mercy.

Ah, did I know that my heart loved not God, this very instant I would pluck it out.

I again say, let us enter into ourselves. The time presses, there is no room for delay; our souls are at stake.

YOSHIDA KENKO
The Harvest of Solitude
Clive Johnson

T HE QUEST FOR solitude, whether it be for the space of an hour or a lifetime, has been a part of nearly everyone's experience. And although few are drawn to it as a permanent way of life, there has been a sufficient number to attract the interest of the historian as well as the serious student of religion. Nearly all solitaries have fled the world in order to seek a higher and fuller life— away from the tumult of the crowd. The chains of the world weigh heavily on them. "What do we want most to dwell near to?" wrote Henry David Thoreau in *Walden.* "Not to many men surely, the depot, the post-office, the bar-room, the meeting-house . . . but to the perennial source of our life . . ."

One of these solitaries, who would undoubtedly have remained obscure if it were not for a slim volume of his writings, was Yoshida Kenko, a Japanese court official and nobleman who renounced a life of luxury and ease for one of frugality and simplicity. And although he was born nearly seven hundred years ago, his thoughts and expressions create a sense of timelessness which serves to bridge the distance of the centuries.

The story of Kenko the monk is so typically Japanese in its subtle intertwining of irony, quiet wisdom, and re-flectiveness that one is tempted to regard it as a tale of fiction. But the character of this fourteenth-century Buddhist monk possesses that noble and enduring quality which at once reassures us that though such men are indeed rare, they are true. And, as history has shown, their worthiness is often communicated to us through their writings. In the case of Kenko these are few. But those we do have display a depth of insight and beauty of expression which cannot fail in some measure to touch all those who sincerely search, as he did, for inner peace and joy.

Yoshida Kenko was born in the year 1283 in a small village near Kyoto, Japan. He died in the spring of 1350 at the age of sixty-eight. He spent more than half his life — until the age of forty-two — among the world of men as a nobleman and court official. Grief over the emperor's death severed Kenko's link with the world of pomp and wealth and drew him for the remainder of his days to the life of a simple hermit and monk.

He loved solitude. After he had made up his mind to leave the world, he determined not to choose the communal life of a monastery, but a small house in the wilds of Arashiyama some distance from the busy rush of Kyoto. Near his hut, still runs a narrow river, which hurls itself down upon the quiet valley below, winding through deep gorges carpeted with bristling pines. Even now the place is described as intimate and natural and must have been more so during Kenko's time. Those who have chosen to spend their lives alone invariably select places like Arashiyama. It is the companionship of trees, streams, birds, flowers — and not men — that they seek. These become their companions and sustainers. As one of them, a Zen monk, wrote long ago:

> The wind gives to me
> Enough of fallen leaves
> To make a fire.

Not all of Kenko's days were spent alone. Occasionally he would visit some old friend in Kyoto, but his persistent yearning for the contemplative life would invariably lead him back to his little hut. "To live devoted to the Lord Buddha in the mountain solitudes is never wearisome," he wrote on one occasion, "and it drives away the clouds from the thoughts, leaving them clear and serene."

A DECIDED advantage of the solitary life is its removal from any externally imposed routine. One more or less lives and works as one pleases. In this regard, Kenko proved no exception — particularly where his writing was concerned. Inspiration ruled his creative efforts. When an idea or memory came to him, he simply wrote it down on a scrap of paper, stuck it to the wall of his hut, and then promptly forgot about any further writing until another flash set him going again. Many years after his death a friend collected these scraps of paper and had them published, at which time they became known as the *Tsure-zure Gusa*. They were soon treasured by cultured Japanese for their mixture of delicate beauty and sound wisdom and have persisted in popularity to this day.

Individuals like Kenko, who have chosen to flee the embrace of society to live by themselves, usually arouse in others a mixed reaction of curiosity and antipathy. For although people have always been vaguely fascinated by hermits, anchorites, and the like, they have also generally resented the fact that such men should find the company of others so unnecessary. Even if such a reaction is immature, it is an understandable one. For by choosing to withdraw from society, the solitary is, in effect, saying:

"I'm sorry, but what you offer is not enough. I want something more." Of course there is the very strong chance that the "something more" will not be enough either. He might easily go mad or become an incurable egocentric. The approbation of society provides most men with sufficient self-confidence and encouragement to lead reasonably happy, useful lives. In addition, such approval gives us a valuable measure of our own character; thus, we are less likely to become anti-social or grow destructive personalities. But the solitary, driven to this extreme way of life by an overpowering desire to insulate himself from the rush of men, is thoroughly prepared to forsake these supports.

Still, he must be prepared for many battles within. The peace of isolation can be quickly broken by the intrusion of irrelevant notions or disturbing distractions and obsessions — all of them upsetting to the mind. By renouncing diversion, the solitary also renounces the protective wall he has for years constructed around the inner recesses of his mind. Like angry devils suddenly released from captivity, thoughts long-buried fly out to haunt and torment him, and he is forced at last to confront the inconsistent and incomprehensible things of life instead of simply ignoring them. But all these struggles are willingly faced by the solitary if he is convinced that behind the world he has forsaken lie only temporal happiness and passing joys; and that in the apparently barren life he has adopted there is the seed of a lasting and eternal joy which will one day germinate. One of these men, an anonymous Christian recluse, makes good his point when he writes:

> In the midst of a civilization visibly

crumbling away before us, the vision of men and women going apart into solitude — for the quest still goes on — silently, yet stridently bears witness to the reality of the unseen, to the lordship of mind over matter, to the supremacy in man of the spirit. It trumpets abroad the tremendous question: What exchange shall a man give for his soul?

Although we cannot with any certainty attach a religious motive to Thoreau's famous two-year period of solitude, we can see the characteristics which mark him a true solitary. "I find it wholesome to be alone the greater part of the time," he wrote in *Walden*. "To be in company, even with the best, is soon wearisome and dissipating. I love to be alone. I never found the companion that was so companionable as solitude. We are for the most part more lonely when we go abroad among men than when we stay in our chambers."

Now, we might well ask the question: What enables the solitary to escape the punishments of loneliness? Kenko suggests the reason:

If a man should desire the Great Adventure, he cannot have it both ways, nor can he succeed also in the beloved affairs of the world. Difficult as it may be to bid fare-well to duty, he should ruthlessly set it aside. But he argues far otherwise. "Such and such a thing must be attended to, or people will certainly laugh at me. When I consider the years I spent in arranging such matters it would be sheer weakness to fly off to some new notion in such hot haste.

Well, that is his point of view, but if he accepts it the world strengthens its bonds, and preoccupations crowd in upon him in endless procession, and the moment of relinquishment will never arrive.

What does this tell us? That if we wish a higher life we must eventually abandon the vain pleasures of the world and the attachments they breed—in short, conquer desire. It is unfulfilled desires which torment the lonely person. The solitary has learned to go beyond them. Desirelessness is the foundation of spiritual life. If we are controlled by something finite, something which has the capacity to cause us pain and distract our minds from higher aspirations, how is it possible to grow in spirit? Naturally, temptations assault everyone. But when man surrenders to an obsessive self-concern—as certainly the lonely are apt to do — he is marked for sorrow. It is desire which nourishes the small self, and it is this self which every aspirant is eventually required to transcend.

Of course, Kenko must have been aware that not everyone is suited for monastic life. It takes a particular type of individual to exchange the pleasures and diversities of the world for a life of sameness and simplicity. But at the same time, he was aware there are a number of people who in the face of problems and woes, attempt to escape them through retreat to the forest or cave. "For my part," he wrote, "if a man drops into the monastic way simply because life has treated him unkindly, I cannot think well of it. I like better those who are glad to choose solitude and to pass their time in such retirement that none seek them any more."

Despite the quiet flow of his life, there is no record

that Kenko ever found a single day of it dull or boring. He wrote on one piece of paper:

What sort of creatures are they who find life tedious? I cannot understand the drift of such thoughts. Well indeed is the life of him who lives in solitude! If we live according to the world's measure our hearts move to the rhythm of wealth and reputation. If we must have friendly social relations, how can we insist upon truths which would offend those we meet? We must jest, argue, quarrel, be merry and always amid uncertain conditions. Thoughts flit hither and thither, advantage and disadvantage appear and disappear. A drunkard's dream, inebriate and inebriating, a noisy activity stupefying and lapsing into dullness as age creeps on. And in this all ends. True pleasure lies in extricating oneself from this sort of business, in forsaking human relations, and laying worldly affairs aside. Even if the absolute truth of the universe be too high for understanding, much peace can thus be attained.

Kenko's writings reveal another characteristic to mark him as a healthy-minded solitary — his love of beauty. Simply because he looked upon the world as transitory does not mean that he denied its loveliness. On the contrary, he embraced it, but lightly and with dispassion. Note in the following selection how poetically he describes the passing seasons, yet, at the same time, maintaining a respectable distance between himself and the subject. Observe how few references he makes to his feelings or to what the scenes create in him. Only in the final sentence does he intrude:

> How profound is the interest of the revolving pageant of the seasons! Spring, summer, autumn, and winter encircle us in turn. The universal feeling is that autumn makes the deepest appeal to sentiment. That is true but, O how enchanting is the spring when the singing birds return on a warm spring breeze! How sweet the sunshine! It is a stirring of spring within us to see the grass thickening beneath the fences on a mild misty day and to watch the early budding of the flowers. Rain and wind follow and disturb our thoughts with pity, until the lengthening leaves break out in green flame upon all the trees. There is a strange fascination in the withered leaves of winter, and in watching their fall at the edge of the brook on a cold morning when the frost rims them with white glitter and the morning mist rises like breath from the stream. I find all this very lovely.

WISDOM is eternal and universal. It is bound by no religion or philosophy, neither does it recognize time or place. We are drawn to the thoughts of this unusual Japanese monk because the truths expressed in his writings harmonize to some degree with the Truth that is in us all and struggles for expression. "The egg is the world, and the bird breaks the shell; afterwards, it flies toward God . . ." wrote Hermann Hesse in his novel *Demian*. Whether we prefer to regard the world as transitory and unreal or as a joyful manifestation of His power, we will, sooner or later, have to break its shell and fly to God. This, the wise tell us, is man's ultimate purpose in life. To realize it means constant struggle against not only the impulses of our lower nature, but victory as well over the more subtle, refined temptations of the intellect and ego. We can extend Hesse's simile further. We are bound by *five* shells or "sheaths" — the physical body, the breath (or "vital" force), mind (i.e., the mind that receives sense impressions), intellect, and ego. When, one by one, these are pierced through by spiritual effort and God's grace, then He, the supreme Self, is found; the Atman is revealed, the ever-blissful soul of man.

As a way of life, solitude offers small evidence for providing man with a final solution to the problem of existence. In fact, the majority of the world's saints and thinkers have generally lived in close association with other men. And it has some great dangers. By removing himself from society, the solitary escapes any objective or corrective evaluation of his own behavior. In time, the abnormal may appear normal to him, the destructive, harmless. To lead balanced, productive lives, most of us need the reinforcement and love of others. Naturally, there are always exceptions, such as Kenko and Thoreau, and from such exceptions the world has profited. For by their experiment with life they have been able to pass on to those who would listen some essentials of happiness: freedom from attachment, simplicity in living, love of nature, and removal from distraction. And somehow we stand in awe of these men who have flung aside honor and wealth to travel an unmarked and lonely road.

SELECTIONS FROM KENKO THE MONK

For my part, I say fix your mind on the most important object before you. Choosing that and discarding all the rest, work at it with a will. In one day or even one hour many things will present themselves for decision. Choose the best of them for yourself and lose not a moment in attacking it. If you are attacking everything, you conquer nothing.

A moment's indolence may condition the indolence of a lifetime. Fear it!

Resolving on a certain course, why trouble your head if you do not shine in other matters, and why bemoan the slanders that may assail you? Nothing worth doing can be accomplished without devotion to that and neglect of all else.

We should relish this world while keeping the next in mind, following the Way of the Buddhas. This is to comprehend true beauty.

There are many parasitic things in the world which destroy the objects upon which they batten. Such are vermin about the body, mice in the house, traitors to the country, wealth to an avaricious man, earthly desires to the spiritual man, religious dogma and ceremonies to the monk.

When I reflect upon the thought of mankind and its purpose, I compare it to a man who models a snow image of the Buddha and proposes to decorate it with precious substances and jewels in spring and to build a temple to house it. But can the snow tarry until spring? Truly a man's life is like an image of snow thawing and wasting daily.

The shoals of the Asuka river shift every year. So also change the conditions of men's lives. Time passes. Events fall behind us and fade. Pleasure and sorrow succeed each other. The garden of prosperity becomes a wilderness. The house remains, but the masters flit through it and change. I long to hold conference with the noble people of old, but, alas! themselves, their houses, and even their tombs have passed away.

He little knows the world who says that a man can live in whatever manner he wishes, and that at home and in the usual social relations he can lead the religious life adequately. I cannot think this is so. We monks, unlike ordinary people, desire to live so that we may transmit the Unchanging Law of Changes, and how is this to be done if we are to serve the Emperor or to be troubled with family concerns? It is for me to cling to the Unchanging and having resolved to follow the Buddha we must also follow the quiet life. Yet if we live in the mountains we must defend ourselves from cold and hunger. So, while I declare that the return to epicure-anism and fine clothes kindles the flame of worldly desire and renders the religious life impossible, I cannot agree with the extreme view that the monk's life must be wholly desireless. Surely he also must have his desires, though very unlike those of the impassioned worldling. It must be permitted to him to desire his humble bed, his poor clothing, his one bowl of food, his vegetable soup, and these frugal desires are soon satisfied. As to his inward life, if he is free from false shame and pays reverent attention to his rule, he will soon learn to distinguish the right from the wrong in this matter. But being mortal and longing for enlightenment, we monks must certainly surrender the world, for if we lead the ordinary life we shall soon be overcome by passionate desires, and so far from attaining the wisdom of the Buddhas we shall sink into the ignorance of animals.

"It is not well to stay for age in travelling the Way. Do not the graves of early youth cry loud against delay?"

Ah, it is when unheralded sickness grips a man and the world forsakes him that he begins to taste the pangs of unavailing regret for the irretrievable. Regret! The mildest form it can assume is remorse for the misspent moments of the past: the doubt instead of decided action, the foolish hurry in the place of wise delay. But when the end is at hand how useless is regret!

There is the story of a long-dead sage. When people pressed upon him for his counsel in important affairs of their own and of other peoples' he habitually replied: "But I myself am plunged even now into anxiety respecting an important transaction. At this very instant it may turn into frightful urgency," and so saying he would turn a deaf ear and immerse himself in meditation.

Sexual desire is an impulse which leads men into ridiculous situations. Here the nature of man is certainly folly. Strange to think what agonies men have suffered from a passion for some woman, and how a woman may lie tossing all night careless of all else and enduring inconceivable miseries from this passion. Such is the power of love. But the truth is that it is rooted in deep things much beyond our knowledge and its source is far away indeed. There are desires attached to all the six senses, yet all but this one may be conquered. And from this neither the old nor young, the wise or foolish are exempt.

I do not deny that this is a transitory world, and that our dwellings are only temporary shelters, but since we have to live here I like to see them furnished with taste.

In the overabundance of certain things I find vulgarity. Thus I object to an overcrowding of furniture in the sitting-room, to a whole bunch of writing-brushes beside the ink-slab, too many images of the Buddha in the chapel, too great a profusion of stones, trees and grass in a garden, too many children in a house, too many words to a friend, too verbose dedications of sacred offerings.

Why be so toilsomely luxurious in a world not permanently our own? And who can promise that these things may not perish in fire and end only as smoke defiling the sky?

Man's life is transitory. But if it were otherwise what a frightful monotony! If life were eternal all interest and anticipation would vanish. It is the uncertainty which lends it fascination. Observe all life, and you will find that man's span probably exceeds the others, and yet it resembles the ephemera which lives but a day. Death lies in wait in the evening. Does Death time his arrival to suit your pleasure? Death in his swift attack is more ruthless than the pursuing rush of flame or wave. where then shall we place the true worth of life?

Having fully realized the fleeting nature of human existence, I find every day not too long to be spent in the posture and practice of unceasing inward prayer.

Life draws near its close, but the way of peace is still distant, though sunset is in the sky. Surely it is then high time to sever all the relations of life, to abandon those loyalties and to trouble no longer about etiquettes. No doubt we shall be censured as cruel, people will call us mad, deluded, what not! But need we care for such critics — they who understand nothing of the truth? For my own part it troubles me not at all when they slander me, and I am deaf to their praise.

Don't be too proud to ask for guidance when you don't exactly know where you are going.

I have been reading a book in which the reflections of a wise man are recorded. Here are a few excerpts very much to my taste.

"Leave undone whatever you hesitate to do."

"He whose heart is engrossed in things spiritual should not hoard so much as a jar of rice-husks with salt. But let him remember that a well-written copy of a Scripture and a beautiful image of the Buddha are equally dangerous possessions."

"A hermit should always manage his housekeeping carefully lest he should come to want."

"A man of high birth should have the humility of a man of low position. A wise man should not display his book learning. A wealthy man's tastes should be as simple as a poor man's. A skillful man must in no case be arrogant."

"The first principle of true service to the Buddha is to divorce the mind from all earthly considerations and never to recur to them."

I have forgotten the rest.

THOMAS A KEMPIS

Nancy Pope Mayorga

THOMAS HAMMERKEN, born in 1380 at Kempen, Germany, lived his long life, from age twelve to age ninety-one, in a monastery. It was there, isolated from the business of the world, that Thomas grew in wisdom and spirit — exploding once and for all the notion that man must perform actions in the world in order to live a full and successful life. Thomas' success lay in the world of the spirit, carrying out the commands which God dictated to him through the heart. And from these travels in the country of his heart, he produced a phenomenally successful book, a book which has gone through more than six thousand editions, has been translated into at least fifty languages, and is second only to the Bible in popularity. It is called *The Imitation of Christ*. He wrote it as a handbook of spiritual instruction meant primarily for the monks of his order, but so fundamental and incontrovertible is its message that people of every age, in every walk of life, in every country, have been and still are profoundly moved by its teachings.

Thomas' father, John, was a poor man and a silversmith— hence the name Hammerken which means "little hammer." His mother, Gertrude, devout and intelligent, helped the family finances by running a nursery school for the children of the town. There was one other son, John, who was thirteen years older than Thomas. Their parents gave the boys a careful religious training, and John very early left home to enter a religious school.

The school to which he went and to which Thomas

would follow him later, was at Deventer, Holland. It had been established by an inspired lay preacher, Gerhard Groot, and was the first belonging to a number of communities known as the Brothers of the Common Life. Thomas was later to write a biography of Groot and an account of the life of these lay brothers.

Groot was converted from a luxurious, secular and selfish life to one of meditation and prayer, and from this contemplative state he emerged to be a brilliant preacher. According to Thomas, people left their businesses and their meals to hear him preach and the churches could not hold the crowds. Groot had been to visit the beautiful and serene mystic, Ruysbroek, and was greatly attracted to the life of the community which Ruysbroek had gathered around him. There he got the idea for his Brothers of the Common Life, an establishment for devout men to live together without monastic vows. The first house was founded at Deventer, and about a hundred others followed later. These brothers lived lives of poverty, chastity, and obedience. They did not beg, but worked at jobs and placed all earnings in a common fund. Their ambition was to live as the early Christians did, simply, in the love of God and neighbor, with humility and devotion. Thomas probably never heard Gerhard Groot preach. He was only four years old when Groot, at forty-four, died of the plague.

Groot's idea was carried forward by Florentius Radewyn, and it was to Radewyn that Thomas' brother John sent him when, at the age of twelve, Thomas left home and trudged off to Holland. Radewyn was greatly drawn to the young boy. He treated him as a son, kept him in his own home for a while, then found him board and lodging, helped him with his school fees and gave him books. Thomas was seven years at the Deventer school. There, according to the fashion of the time, he dropped his family name and became just Thomas from Kempen (à Kempis). There he developed the two accomplishments which seemed to have given him the most satisfaction— singing and the art of manuscript copying. His other great satisfaction was the presence of Radewyn, whom he not only admired, but revered. "The mere presence of so holy a man," he wrote, "inspired me with such awe that I dared not speak.

"On one occasion it happened that I was standing near him in the choir and he turned to the book we had and sang with us. And standing close behind me, he supported himself by placing both his hands on my shoulders. and I stood quite still, scarcely daring to move so astonished was I at the honor he had done me."

It was Radewyn who advised him that the monastic life would suit him best. By his own admission, Thomas was the kind of man who was happiest "in a little nook with a little book." So at twenty, he joined the Augustinian Order and entered the monastery of Mount St. Agnes at Zwolle where his brother John was already prior.

LIFE was busy within the walls. Thomas took his turn at hauling water and fuel, working at kitchen and other household tasks. There was choir singing, and of course, the lifelong business of copying manuscripts. Of this latter work, he noted that to the monk, writing was far more than just a trade. He is quoted as saying, "If he shall not lose his reward who gives a cup of water to a thirsty neighbor, what will not be the reward of those who, by putting good books into the hands of those neighbors, open to them the fountains of eternal life? Blessed are the hands of such transcribers." Manuscript copying was ever his favorite work and he is known to have made one copy of the whole Bible, which took him fifteen years.

At thirty-four he entered the priesthood, and after that he began to preach. His sermons were fervent and thoughtful. The fame of his eloquence spread, and he preached to crowded audiences. In 1425 he was promoted to superior, which meant spiritual adviser and instructor. Later his brothers elected him prefect of the monastery, but it turned out that he was too simple-minded in business, too absent-minded, and altogether temperamentally unsuited to the administrative job. He went back very happily to his old position.

Besides his sermons, he found time to write many tracts on the monastic life: *The Discipline of Cloisters, The Life of the Good Monk, Sermons to Novices, The Solitary Life*, and so forth. From these, and from contemporary accounts of him, we get a fairly rounded picture of the man. He was diligent, kind, most reserved, but not anti-social. He enjoyed religious talks with his brothers and was eloquent and inspired in the subjects of God and the soul; but whenever the subject turned to mundane matters, he grew uncomfortable. "My brothers," he would say, "I must go. Someone is waiting to converse with me in my cell." About his physical appearance it is written that he had a sweet expression and lustrous, at times, intense brown eyes. His complexion to the day of his death was fresh-colored, vivid. He must have stooped a little from so much bending over his desk, for it is mentioned that he straightened up when singing, even rose upon his toes with his face turned upward. He worked to the last days of his life and never needed spectacles for even the most delicate tracing.

His reading was wide. Besides the scriptures he read the writings of St. Bernard, St. Gregory, St. Ambrose, St. Thomas, but also Aristotle, Ovid, Seneca, and Dante. However, his experience was entirely bookish, his life entirely within. The turbulent world outside the monastery, wars and revolts, the split in the church and two popes anathematizing each other, one in Rome, one in France, futile church councils trying to restore peace, left him undismayed. He believed that all problems could be solved by retiring into Christ. If life is lived with the sole purpose of drawing near to God, then, no doubt, the fever of living dies down. It is this glimpse of a fruitful peace within the endless, futile turmoil of worldly life that gives *The Imitation* its perennial appeal.

SHORTLY after he was ordained as a priest, Thomas began work on his great book. It was to occupy him for ten years. He wrote it meticulously in the finest medieval Latin and in a rhythmical style that suggests he intended it to be chanted. The book is a miracle of simplicity and straight-thinking. There is very little theology. "Of what use is your subtle talk about the Blessed Trinity if you are not humble?" he asks. He goes right to the heart of Christianity, of all religion. And the heart of the matter is, as Henri Bergson put it, that this universe is nothing but a machine for the making of gods. This is not a book for the pretender, the dilettante, nor the faint-hearted. "Heaven help us if we find easy reading in *The Imitation of Christ!*" exclaims Monsignor Knox, one of its translators. But any sincere aspirant,

229

wondering how self-purification is to be accomplished, can take a course in sainthood here.

HE starts out in Book I in a most businesslike manner. Here is a man who knows what he is dealing with, and he is dealing with psychology. After a short chapter of propaganda for the godly life, he begins searching out every corner of the human psyche for weaknesses and falsities. The chapter headings show what he is about: On taking a low view of oneself; About immoderate passions; How to get rid of self-conceit; About useless gossiping; Why it is good for us not to have everything our own way; On putting up with other people's faults; How temptations are to be kept at bay.

Where human behavior is concerned, he is shrewd. "How can a man expect to have peace when he is always minding other people's business?" Prune away your own bad habits now, he urges, for nothing will be more consolation to you than a clean conscience. "Forgive an injury with your whole heart." More than forgive, be indifferent to it. How is this to be done? Live in the inner world. "Turn to God and you will be lifted out of yourself and rest in Him contentedly."

He does not pretend that all this is going to be easy. He says, "The conquest of self demands the hardest struggle of all; but this has got to be our real business in life, the conquest of self." Because, "Once a man is integrated, once his inner life has become simplified, all of a piece, he begins to attain a richer and deeper knowledge — quite effortlessly, because his knowledge comes from above." How beautiful are these words of his: "Speak, O Lord for thy servant heareth. Silence, all ye teachers!

And silence, ye prophets! Speak Thou alone, O Lord, unto my soul!"

This would be the effortlessness of the athlete integrally trained for the moment of contest. One who has earnestly tried to follow Thomas à Kempis through such a strenuous preparation must come from this pitiless paring away and rooting out and exercise of will with a feeling of cleanness, power, exhilaration, "rejoicing as a strong man to run a race." Many tired and jaded people of the world might consider this state of health enough reward. But to Thomas this was just a prelude. He had something more in mind.

BOOK II, which is much deeper, follows naturally and logically. It deals with the compensations, consolations, and joys of living an interior life. Here he discusses peace, purity, singleness of purpose, and God's grace. "You must make room deep in your heart to entertain Him as He deserves; it is for the inward eye, all the splendor and beauty of Him; deep in your heart where He likes to be. Where He finds a man whose thoughts go deep, He is a frequent visitor; such pleasant converse, such welcome words of comfort, such deep repose, such intimate friendship are well-nigh past belief." And "the more a man dies to himself, the more he begins to live in God. So then, when we have made an end of reading and studying, this is the conclusion we should reach at last."

IN BOOK III the character of *The Imitation* changes. The format changes, too. It becomes a dialogue between God, whom Thomas calls The Beloved, and the human soul, whom he calls The Disciple or The Learner. In it

God instructs, exhorts, encourages, promises. The disciple reveals his doubts and discouragements, has his questions answered, is even allowed to put God to the test. The intimate friendship between Thomas and God is touching. He complains to God with utter familiarity, "Lord, what a state things have got into these days!" And God answers him as reassuring father and friend, "Stand your ground, son, and trust in Me."

It is no wonder that in the course of this long dialogue, the disciple falls in love with God and breaks forth again and again into hymns of praise and adoration.

"If anyone has this love, he will know what I mean. A loud cry in the ears of God is that burning love for Him in the soul which says, 'My God, my love, You are all mine and I am all Yours.'"

"Let me sing the song of love and follow You, my Beloved, to high heaven. Let my soul grow faint in praising You, rejoicing in Your love. Let me love You more than myself, love myself only for Your sake; let me love in You all who truly love You."

But the great value of Book III for spiritual aspirants is that we can identify with the learner. The disciple's doubts are our doubts. He asks the questions that are in our hearts. And the answers come surely from God to every question, from every angle. *The Imitation* becomes a handhold in the swamp of our life, a handhold to help us up and out of the mire.

BOOK IV is a short discussion of the Holy Communion. Thomas raises the subject above ritualism and puts it where it belongs on the lofty and universal basis of mysticism. "This most high and adorable

Sacrament is the health of body and soul, the remedy for every spiritual disease." The Beloved advises us: "If you have no wish to drown in the deep gulf of doubt, don't busy yourself with useless attempts to analyze this deep Sacrament. There are many people who in their desire to fathom mysteries too deep for them, have lost all feeling of devotion. He is a happy man who can simply turn away from the uncharted ways of theological discussion and walk ahead by the sure and open road of God's commandments. What God wants of you is faith and a life of unalloyed goodness, not loftiness of understanding . . . Do you, then, if you would be my disciple, offer yourself to Me in this Sacrament, together with all the powers of your heart."

TOWARD the end of the great dialogue, God says, as a kind of summing up, "It is a pure heart that I look for; that is the place in which I rest." And Thomas, from his long lifetime of friendship with the Lord, has these final, warm words of advice:

"Go forward, then, with simple, unfaltering faith. Leave your worries behind and trust in Almighty God. God never misleads you."

FROM THE IMITATION OF CHRIST

Surely great words do not make a man holy and just; but a virtous life makes him dear to God.

It is vanity to desire to live long, and not to care to live well.

This is the highest lesson: a true knowledge and humble estimation of ourselves; to think nothing of one's self and highly of others.

It often wearies me to read and hear many things; in You I find all that I desire.

A man of pure, simple, and steadfast mind, although occupied in many works, does not become distracted; for he does all things for the glory of God and tries to be free from all self-seeking.

He who strives to overcome himself has a greater combat. And this ought to be our chief endeavor: to conquer ourselves, to grow daily stronger than we were, and to make progress in virtue.

Every perfection in this life is accompanied by some imperfection; and all our knowledge is not without some obscurity.

A humble knowledge of self is a surer way to God than a deep search after learning.

When the day of Judgement comes, we shall not be asked what we have read, but what we have done; not how well we have spoken, but how well we have lived.

How quietly does the glory of the world pass away!

He is truly great who has great love.

He is truly learned who does the will of God and renounces his own will.

Do what lies in your power, and God will assist your good will.

Spiritual talks greatly further our growth, especially when persons of one mind and spirit associate together in God.

So long as we live in this world, we cannot be without suffering and temptation. As Job says: "The life of man upon earth is a warfare."

We want others to be perfect; and yet we do not correct our own defects. We do not weigh our neighbor in the same scale as ourselves.

If you cannot continually collect yourself, do it at least twice a day, in the morning and at night.

In your little room you will find what you often lose abroad.

In silence and stillness a devout soul advances in virtues and learns the mysteries of the Scriptures.

Happy is he who casts aside whatever may defile or burden his conscience.

Resist manfully; one habit overcomes another.

Why do you wish to defer your good purpose? Arise, begin this very moment, and say: "Now is the time to be doing; now is the time to fight; now is the time to better myself."

You ought so to regulate yourself in all your actions and thoughts, as if you were to die today.

Oh that we might spend a single day well in this world!

Men soon change, and quickly fail; but Christ remains forever, and stands by us firmly to the end.

There must be simplicity in our intention; and purity in our desires.

A pure heart penetrates Heaven and hell.

To walk with God and not to be held by any outward affection, is the state of a spiritual man.

Those that are established in God can in no way be proud.

Blessed are the eyes which are closed to outward things, and open to inward things.

Use temporal things, and desire eternal.

Without labor there is no rest, nor without fighting can the victory be won.

From a pure heart proceeds the fruit of a good life.

You must be lord and master of your own actions, not a servant or a hireling.

If I love the Spirit, I shall delight to think on things spiritual.

Divine love conquers everything and increases all the powers of the soul.

There is neither in Heaven nor on earth anything sweeter than love, nothing stronger, nothing loftier, nothing happier, nothing more precious; for love is born of God.

MIRA BAI
Nancy Pope Mayorga

EVERY SPIRITUAL ASPIRANT comes to know the saints as his best friends. In his pain, their words bring him loving comfort. In his joy, they carry him upward on the wings of their ecstatic songs. He grows avid for saints. And when he has exhausted the words of all the saints of the West, he is drawn inevitably to that inexhaustible mine of saints, India.

What is a saint? According to the dictionary, a holy, godly, or sanctified person. But this definition leaves out the very essence, which is dedication. A saint is first and foremost a dedicated person, dedicated to God. One such greatly dedicated person in India was Mira Bai.

Mira Bai, Queen of Chitor—it's a lovely name that sings itself. And Mira Bai's whole life was a continuing song of love. Her sorrow was sweet, and it overflowed in song. "Cherish pain," she said, "it is dear to Him." Her joy was irrepressible. "Rejoice, rejoice! He is my own!" She was the flute at Krishna's lips.

Among the scanty and conflicting records of her life, one charming story appears consistently. As a little girl of five, Mira Bai was sitting in the window of her home when a wedding procession passed by, bright with flowers, joyful with music. She watched it out of sight, then came running to her mother, her dark eyes shining.

"Mother," she asked eagerly, "who is my sweetheart?"

Her mother answered carelessly, as busy mothers do, yet characteristically as a Hindu mother:

"Giridhar Nagar (Krishna) is your sweetheart."

The little girl must have stood quite still as that familiar name fell sweetly into her young heart which was waiting for it. From that day, the Name was on her lips, in her heart, motivating her life — "Krishna, my love, my bridegroom."

At the age of eight, as was the custom, Mira Bai was married to the son of the ruler of Mewar; and at eighteen she went to the capitol city, Chitor, to live and rule the kingdom with her husband, the young Raja Bhojraj. For ten years her life was serene. Her husband sympathized with her love of Krishna, and built her a temple in the city. Here, with silver bells on her ankles and tiny cymbals on her fingers, she worshipped Krishna with song and dance, and by her intense devotion brought life to the image in the shrine. But then Bhojraj died. The serene years came to an end.

Mira Bai's brother-in-law, Vikramaditya, who became Rana of Chitor, was quite a different person from his brother. He had his villainous role to play in the drama of Mira's life. But in his defense, let's say that it is socially inappropriate, even in India, to have a widowed sister-in-law forever singing and dancing in ecstasy in public. It is awkward to have holy men of all beliefs, of all castes, in all stages of poverty and disarray, always hanging around the royal castle. For Mira Bai's fame was spreading, and her love of God cut through all custom and caste, embraced all beliefs. She drew devotees to herself. They wept with her, rejoiced with her, and danced with her. And many a long hour was spent in heart-stirring religious talk and song.

Let people try to restrain me,
O friend, I will not be stopped.
I will remain in the Saints' company
And gain the bliss of the Lord's love.
I will not bother with the world;
If all my wealth goes, let it go;
Even if my head be severed
I will not complain.
My mind is absorbed in *simran;*
I meet all censure with cheer.
Mira's Lord, Thou everlasting One,
Grant me the shelter
Of my Master's feet.

It was exasperating, too, to the Rana, that all the emissaries he sent to try to dissuade her ended up by being her converts. In a moment of rage, it is said, he sent her a cup of poison. Mira Bai smiled, spoke the name of Krishna, and the poison was nectar on her lips. He sent her a cobra in a basket, hoping for the worst, and Krishna changed the cobra into a picture of himself. Then the Rana asked Mira Bai why, in heaven's name, she didn't become sati and commit the respectable suicide of a virtuous Hindu widow. Upon receiving this message, Mira calmly stripped the bracelets from her arms, put on the gerua cloth of renunciation, and left the castle with these words:

I will not be restrained now, O Rana,
Despite all you do to block my path.
I have torn off the veil of worldly shame;
The company of Saints alone is dear to me.

Merta, my parents' home, I have left for good.
My vision wakened, now shines bright.
My Master has revealed unto me
The mirror within my own body;
Now I'll sing and dance in ecstasy.
Keep to yourself your gems and jewelry,
I have discarded them all, O Rana.
My true Lord I have come to behold;
None knows of this wealth within the body.
I fancy not your forts and palaces,
Nor want silken robes wrought with gold.
Mira, unadorned and unbedecked,
Roams intoxicated in the Lord's love.

It was more than just a going out from her home. It was an adventure of the soul. Her Western brother, John of the Cross, told of his same experience:

In a dark night,
With anxious love inflamed,
O happy lot!
Forth unobserved I went . . .
Without other light or guide
Save that which in my heart was burning.

And Mira Bai's songs, from this early period of her wandering, are very like the songs of St. John—searching, sighing, seeking with the heart, crying,

Where have you gone, dear Lord,
After planting Your love in my heart?
You have forsaken me, O deceitful One,
After setting the wick of love aflame.

After launching love's boat, You have
Left it adrift in the sea of separation.
Beloved Lord, when will You meet me?
Mira can live no more without You.

She became a dried leaf in the breeze of God. But
the breeze of God was not just whimsical. It carried her
to all the great shrines of Krishna.

At some time, at some place, she met the pure and
exalted saint, Raidas, a cobbler, the Jacob Boehme of
India, and became his disciple. It is said that she was
initiated by him into the worship of the impersonal One
and Infinite. Be that as it may, her sweet songs to
Krishna went on in an unbroken flow, and it is through
them, in this period of her wanderings, that we can
follow the thread of her life.

The Lord's Name is all that I own,
Nothing else belongs to me.

I have given up my father,
Given up mother and brother,
Given up all that were once
Close to my heart.
Through the company of Saints
I am rid of the fear of public opinion.
To meet the Saints I rush with joy;
A look at the worldly gives me pain.

With the stream of my tears
I have watered love's everlasting vine.
In my life I met two saviors—
The Saint and the Lord's Name.

The Saint ever adorns my forehead,
The Name is embedded in my heart.
I took the essence of the ultimate truth,
and unto me the mystery unfolded:
'I am He' and 'He is me'.

Inevitably she came to Brindavan, the place of Krishna's play with the gopis. The radiant joy in Mira's face was such that the people of Brindavan acclaimed her as an incarnation of one of those love-intoxicated milkmaids. At the time of Mira's arrival in Brindavan, there was living at the temple of Krishna a famous devotee, Jiv Goswami, of the school of Chaitanya. Mira Bai, always eager to meet and talk with saints, stood at the temple gate and asked for an audience with him. He sent word that since he was a monk and a sannyasin, he did not look upon the face of a woman. Then Mira Bai, as intelligent and spirited as she was pure, answered:

"I thought Krishna was the only male in Brindavan, and that everyone else was female. Now I understand that there is a second Krishna here."

Jiv Goswami was struck by her message. He recognized a great soul. Quickly he came out to the temple gate, humbly took the dust of her feet, and received her embrace.

After a short stay in Brindavan, Mira moved on to Dwaraka, the "City of Many Gates," founded by Sri Krishna, himself, on the shore of the Arabian sea. There she settled and spent the rest of her life, some twenty years, until the end came in 1614 at the age of sixty-seven.

WHY is it that the saints of all ages and all countries

wander? And again, why do they finally settle down? Mira Bai gives the answer very clearly in this song.

> I laugh to hear
> When a fish is thirsty in water.
> Man, without realizing his true self
> Roams now from here to there.
> Renouncing all, he wanders in quest of God;
> Defeated, he drifts in the world's ocean vast.
> But Mira, through the Inner Path,
> Has met her dear Eternal Lord.

The facts of her outer life may be scanty, unsubstantiated, and seemingly irrelevant. The facts of her inner life are teeming and undisputable. Within herself, she lived an intense, one-pointed, and absolutely relevant life. It is laid bare for all to see and study, in over 300 beautiful and deeply personal songs.

Why did she wander? Because she was driven by her love and her longing. Hear her—

> For Thy sake, my Beloved, I forsake all
>   comforts.
> Why dost Thou now remain away from me?
> Pining, I rush in all directions and know no
> rest. Nights I pass without sleep, days without
> food. Truly, for Thy sake I became a wander-
> ing mendicant in the wilderness.

After her initiation by the saint Raidas, there is shown a slightly different spirit, more determination. The guru has encouraged and steadied her.

My mind is fixed on the Lord, no obstacle in
    the pursuit of him can obstruct me.
In the shelter of the Lord I have no fear.
My eyes are set on no other sight but Thee.

She still wandered, chanting the name of the Lord,
and associating with the holy. These two activities made
up her life, and the sum and substance of her life's
teaching. Chant the Name. Keep company with the holy.

Repeat the Lord's Name, O man,
It washes off a million sins.
The records of your actions
Of numerous previous births,
In no time are torn to tatters
On repetition of the Name.
When nectar in a cup of gold
Is offered to you free,
Why should you be loath to drink it?
Says Mira, let the Eternal Lord
Now permeate your body and heart.

But when she reached Dwaraka, she settled down.
Why? The change in the spirit of her songs is very
significant.

The One I longed for has come home.
The raging fire of separation is quenched;
Now I rejoice with Him, I sing in bliss.
The peacocks at the cloud's roar
Dance with unbound joy;
I rejoice in ecstasy
At the sight of my Beloved.

I am absorbed in His love;
My misery of wandering
In the world has ended.
The lily bursts into bloom
At the sight of the full moon;
Seeing Him my heart blossoms in joy.
Peace permeates the body of mine,
His arrival has filled my home with bliss.
That very Lord has become my own,
Who is ever the redeemer of His devotees.
Mira's heart, scorched by the blaze of
    separation,
Has become cool and refreshed;
The pain of duality has vanished.

What happened? It is not hard to guess, and, as a matter of fact, here again comes one of those few events whose description appears consistently in all accounts of her life, too consistently to deny.

One night, as every night, Mira Bai was worshipping her Lord in the quiet, fragrant temple at Dwaraka. The prayer had melted into the mantra, the mantra into the Name, and Mira Bai's song now consisted of one word, "Krishna!" In her longing, she suddenly held out her arms to the image in the shrine, and, it is said, the Image stretched forth His arms to receive her. "O Thou, the treasure of my heart! Oh Thou, the breath of my breath!" Mira fell unconscious, tears of joy streaming from her eyes. No more lamenting now. No more wandering. Only peace. And joy. She was one at last with the blissful One Who is All.

MEISTER ECKHART
Philip L. Griggs

A NUMBER OF MYSTERIES and surprises surround the figure of Meister Eckhart, thirteenth-century monk and mystic. One of these is the fact that although so many of his teachings have come down to us, we know very little about his life. He seems to have lived between the years 1260 and 1328. But just what the forces were which went into the making of his singular character, and how he became what some regard as the greatest teacher in Christianity since its Founder, we do not know.

When he was about fifteen years old we see him entering a Dominican monastery to study for the priest-hood, and we see that in 1300 he was a popular preaching monk and author of tracts. His neatly reasoned and lofty sermons were noted more for their power and directness than for their scholastic niceties, and filled the Churches with common working people whose interest in theology appears to be comparable to the modern worker's interest in politics. He gave these in the German language instead of Latin, and is often called the first man to use this vernacular for metaphysics.

Although we have no direct knowledge of his religious experiences at any time, it is significant that when teachers in the Vedantic tradition come to study the message of Eckhart they recognize in him a Christian who must have experienced *nirvikalpa samadhi,* the superconscious experience of the formless, non-dual Godhead. There is certainly nothing in his life to contradict this, and much to suggest it.

He was sent on many preaching missions, given honorary degrees, and was soon made Provincial (local head) of the Order in Saxony and later also for Bohemia. He must have been at this time a tremendous worker. But now the Church which made and honored him began to disclaim him. His teachings struck some unfamiliar notes, and detractors sought to connect him with certain "wild" mystical sects which were under inquisition; a list of his "errors" was drawn up by Church authorities. In 1327 Eckhart made a brilliant public defense in the Cologne church, in which he denied any heresy or unbecoming conduct and offered to retract any errors proved. He failed to convince the Papal appointees, however, or perhaps he only fanned the flames of their suspicions, for a Papal bull was issued in 1329 condemning Eckhart as one deceived by the devil and deceiving others. But the good Meister never had to read his own final condemnation; death had intervened. We are told nothing of the circumstances of his death.

The influence of his teachings is to be seen in mystics who followed him — Tauler, Suso, Ruysbroeck, and others — but his own writings and recorded sermons lay nearly forgotten for five hundred years, until they were uncovered in the last century.

THE real problem one faces in gleaning from a field as rich as the works of Meister Eckhart is how to discard. It is all wheat, so to speak; there are virtually no tares. But in making this selection I have had in mind three principal points of reference, and, inevitably, I have chosen what I liked best.

The first was to show that Meister Eckhart is no medieval antique but very much a man of our own time.

In fact, it may even be fairly said that he was much ahead of his time. Perhaps only now are we able properly to understand and appreciate Eckhart's particular facet of the Perennial Philosophy.

Secondly, this master has long been considered and reported as a jnani, one who emphasizes the path of reason. This may indeed have been his emphasis, but it should be quite evident from what follows that he was a well-rounded spiritual personality, equally at home in the paths of action and devotion also and well qualified thereby for his monastic position as spiritual director of hundreds of monks and nuns.

Finally, I have hoped to show how far Meister Eckhart transcended the limitations of his Christian tradition. Eckhart climbed about as far out on the limb of the Christian Church and its doctrine as a man could, but he was too simple and pious to cut clean through that limb by his own choice. He outgrew the dogma which nurtured him, but so gracefully that he was hardly conscious of having done so. Of course his near excommunication is only one dismal landmark in the Christian Church's general tendency to discourage mysticism, but it was a fateful and perhaps fatal decision for the Church. It is interesting to speculate what might have happened if, instead of being condemned and set aside, Eckhart's ideas and experiences had been allowed to flourish throughout the Christian world.

At any rate, one familiar with the Vedantic tradition will find in this discourse many familiar phrases and perspectives which he may never have expected to see in the West. See how Meister Eckhart urges the practice of *neti-neti,* "not this, not that." Hear him as he describes what Hindus clearly know as samadhi, and assures us that unitive knowledge of Godhead can be had here and now. How reminiscent of Swami Vivekananda are his stirring notes of nondualism and the complete renunciation of ego! Note his understanding of the mother-principle in the Deity. His doctrine of the Word which is eternally being spoken in us is the heart of his cosmology and reminds us of the Indian emphasis on the Divine Name. Again, Eckhart knows that religion is far beyond mere dharma — his word is virtue — and assures us that it should be fun, not long-faced. Many such parallels the reader will see: his description of the unconventional behavior of saints, his matter-of-fact attitude toward heaven and hell, and how the perfect knower, "even if there were" many Persons in the Godhead, "would see them all as One."

Here then is proof that in the highest religious experience time, culture, and geography play no part, that all men who know God — who have become God — speak the same language, the language of the spirit.

All the teachings here have been drawn from recorded and translated material attributed to Eckhart. Only the style of speech has been somewhat modernized, and the teachings have been arranged in the form of a dialogue. The conversations are conceived as having taken place some time between the years 1311 and 1320, between the Meister and one or another of his many monks.

Q. How can I find God?
A. No man ever found God; He gave Himself away.

Q. Ah! Then let me put it another way. What prevents us from knowing God?

A. Three things. The first is time; the second is body; and the third, multiplicity. Remember, if you seek anything of yours, you will never find God, for you are not seeking God merely. You are seeking for something with God, making a candle of God, as it were, with which to find something, and then, having found it, throwing the candle away. Creatures have no real being, for their being consists in the presence of God. If God turned away for an instant they would all perish, and having all creatures without God is no more than having one fly without God. God must give me Himself, which He can do only when I have renounced myself wholly; only then shall I know God.

Q. Is this knowledge like our present knowledge?
A. No. Do not foolishly imagine that your reason can grow to the knowledge of God; no natural light can bring it about that God shall shine divinely in you; it must be utterly extinguished and go out of itself altogether, then God can shine with His light, bringing back with Him everything left behind, and a thousand-fold more, besides the new form containing it all. To know God God-fashion, your knowledge must change into downright un-knowing, to a forgetting of yourself and every creature.

Q. But, sir, if God is beyond knowledge, and therefore unknowable, and we can know nothing of the unuttered Godhead, what then shall we do?
A. You must lose your your-ness and dissolve in His His-ness. You see, God is said to be unknown because no creature knows Him as He knows Himself. Nothing we can say of God is really true. When I say "man," I

have in my mind human nature. When I say "gray," I have in mind the grayness of gray. When I say "God," I have in my mind not any of His qualities. God is such that we apprehend Him better by negation than affirmation. The more we can impute to Him not-likeness, the nearer we get to understanding Him. Thus God and I are not like, but one in knowing.

Q. One in knowing? Then just what is the relationship between God and the soul?

A. My child, God and the soul are so near together that there is really no distinction between them. Nothing but God finds its way into God, and once the soul is in God, she is God, borne into God on His eternal Word. Soul is in the middle, between God and creature. If she prefers the lower powers of her five senses to her higher ones whence comes her knowledge of spiritual things, then she grows ignoble and base. The worldly pleasures of the soul God has no stomach for, and when she realizes this, she discards the joys in which God has no share. Therefore, for God and the soul to be one, the soul has to lose her own life and nature. They are one as regards what is left. But for them to be one, one must lose its identity and the Other must keep its identity; then they are the same.

Q. Is there a distinction between "soul" and "spirit"?

A. In her higher powers the soul is spirit, and in her lower, soul; and between soul and spirit is the bond of one common being. You must know how the philosophers say the soul is double-faced— her upper face gazes at God all the time and her lower face looks somewhat down, informing the senses; and the upper face, which is the summit of the soul, is in eternity and has nothing to do with time; it knows nothing of time or of body. There is that something in the soul which is uncreated and uncreatable. It is flowing from the Spirit and is altogether spiritual, and in this power God comes out in the full flower of His joy and glory, as He is in Himself. Such intense delight, such supreme exaltation as no mind can conceive nor tongue express. If a man catches one fleeting glance of the joy and bliss therein, it would make it up to him for having to suffer everything he could ever suffer.

Q. You say the Spirit knows not of the body. But what then is the relationship between soul and body?

A. The soul has no natural concern with the things of this world any more than the ear has with color or the eye has with song. Our natural philosophers teach that the body is rather in the soul than the soul in the body. Even as the cask contains the wine and not the wine the cask, so does the soul keep the body in her, rather than the body the soul.

Q. A very old question, sir: is God one, or is He many?

A. Look you, the narrowest of the powers of my soul is more than heaven-wide, to say nothing of the intellect, wherein there is measureless space, wherein I am as near a place a thousand miles away as the spot I am standing on this moment. Theologians teach that the angel hosts are countless. But to one who sees distinctions as something different from multiplicity, to him, I say, a hundred is as one. If there were a hundred Persons in the Godhead, he would still perceive them as one God.

Q. If God became man in the person of Jesus Christ, how does that help me?

A. God not only became man; He assumed human nature. I make bold to say that every good thing possessed by the saints, and by Mary, and Christ in His human nature, is also mine in this same nature.

Q. But if I already possess in this nature all that Christ does in his humanity, why do we set Christ so high and honor him as our Lord and God?

A. Because he was a messenger from God to us, bringing us our own happiness. The happiness Christ brought us was our own. But I will give you a harder saying; to subsist immediately in this pure nature a man must be so wholly dead to person that he wills as well to one across the seas whom he has never seen, as to his own present and familiar friend. So long as you still wish better to yourself than to one whom you have never seen, you are beside the mark, nor have you even for an instant seen into this simple ground. Again, the eternal Word did not take upon itself this man or that; it took upon itself one indivisible free nature, human nature, bare and formless, for the indivisible form of manhood is wholly without form. Here it is just as true to say that man became God as that God became man. You are, with Christ, the Son of the eternal Father, because you have the same nature which was there made God.

Q. You have spoken often to us of this Word, the

Logos, which is being born eternally in the ground of
our soul; but how are we to hear this Word, Meister
Eckhart?

A. Actually, God never spoke but one word, and
that is still unspoken. But He begets in the soul His
child, His Word, and the soul conceiving it passes it on
to its powers in varied guise — now as desire, now as
good intent, now as charity; it is His, not yours at all. He
prays in us, not we ourselves. So lay no claim to
anything. Let go yourself and let God act for you and
in you as He pleases. This work is His, this birth is His,
and all you are, to boot. God installs Himself in your
nature and powers, when self-bereft of all belongings,
you take to the desert, as it is written: "A voice crying in
the wilderness." Let this eternal voice cry on in you at its
sweet will, and do you be a desert in respect to self and
creatures.

Q. How is it that God can flow out, becoming all
the creatures He has begotten, and still He remains
within Himself?

A. I can only give you an analogy: It is like what I
am now saying; it springs up within me, then I pause in
the idea, and thirdly I speak it out, and all of you receive
it; but really it is in me all the time.

Q. Sir, why is it said that God is light, considering that He is incomprehensible?

A. Ah! Just because He is incomprehensible,
therefore He is light! Don't you see that God's incom-
prehensibility comes from His being unending? But His
unendingness is due to His being simple; simplicity is
the same as purity, and purity is light. So it is well said

that God is light, and when the divine light is flooding the soul, soul becomes merged into God like a light into light. Anything approaching this light the light consumes and turns to its own divine nature.

Q. One book says that God is beyond virtue; this is difficult to understand.

A. It means that the vision of God transcends virtues. Virtue is in the middle, between vice and perfection, and the fruit of virtue— the end and object of virtue — will never be obtained until the soul is caught up above the virtues. Be sure that as long as a man holds fast as slave to virtue, he will never taste the fruit of virtue, which is to see the God of Gods. Be sure of it, mere virtue has never seen this sight.

Q. Surely this does not mean that we are to abandon virtue?

A. No, we are to practice virtue, not to possess it. Not by fasting and good works can we gauge our progress in the spiritual life, but a sure sign of growth is a waxing love for the eternal and a waning interest in temporal things. The man who owns a hundred thousand dollars and gives them all in the name of God to found a monastery is doing a good work. Yet I say it would be better for him to despise and empty himself for love of God.

Q. In your sermon last Sunday you said that we cannot say what God is; why can we not say that He is being?

A. I hold that it is as wrong for me to say that God is being as to say the sun is black or white. God is neither this nor that. But when I say God is not being, is superior to being, I do not thereby deny Him being: I dignify and exalt it in Him. But, being is God's idiosyncrasy. Our whole life ought to be being, for so far as it is, it is in God. The most trivial thing perceived in God, a flower for example, as seen in God, would be a thing more perfect than the universe.

Q. Sir, what happens when we attain to perfect union with God?

A. When the soul, being kissed by God, is in absolute perfection and bliss, then at last she knows the embrace of unity, then at the touch of God she is made uncreaturely; then with God's motion, the soul is as noble as God is Himself. As the drop becomes the ocean, not the ocean the drop, so the soul imbibing God turns into God, not God into the soul. There the soul loses its name, its power and its activity, but not its existence. The soul abides in God as God abides in Himself.

Q. What happens at the moment of this union? What is it like?

A. Ah, my child, if only you could be suddenly altogether unaware of things; yes, could you but pass into oblivion of your own existence as St. Paul did when he said: "Whether in the body I know not, or out of it I know not, God knoweth." Here the spirit had so entirely absorbed the faculties that it had forgotten the body; memory no longer functioned, nor understanding, nor the senses; vital warmth and energy were arrested so that the body did not fail throughout the three days during which he neither ate nor drank.

Q. Is this union with the personal God, or with Godhead?

A. Look you, Christ says: "I have been man for you, and if you do not become God for me, you wrong me." God became man that we might become God. God in His Godnature lay hidden in human nature so that we saw nothing but man. And so this soul shall hide itself in God's nature until we can see nothing but God; not putting on a Person as Christ did, but wholly immersed in the divine nature. God is the nature of each nature; He is all nature's nature, undivided.

Q. Can this state of union be attained in this very life, Meister Eckhart?

A. I have sometimes said that man sees God in this life in the same perfection, and is happy in the same perfect way as in the life to come. Many people are astonished to hear this. Yet this life is attainable while a man still eats and drinks. When a man has reached this point we may well say, this man is God and man. All Christ has by nature he has won by grace. His body is filled with the noble nature as the soul, which it receives from God with divine light; thus we may indeed say, Behold, a man divine!

It may well be that you who search after God will come across such perfected men as we have been speaking of. They are away from home, my child, and no one rightly knows them except those in whom the same light shines. Believe me, if I knew one such, and I had a house full of gold and precious stones, I would give the whole of it for a single fowl for him to eat. If all the things God ever made were mine, I would at once give them all for the enjoyment of that man, for they are all his. God in the fullness of His power is his, too, and if there stood before me all the hungry who are in imperfection, I would not withhold from that man's need a single morsel of the fowl, even if it would feed that multitude. You must remember that in the case of an imperfect man, anything he eats or drinks will drag him down and make him prone to sin. But not the perfect man: what he eats and drinks he raises up in Christ to the Father. Keep a sharp lookout, I warn you, for these men are difficult to tell. For instance, if they should need it, while others are fasting they will be eating; while others keep watch, they will be sleeping; while other folk are praying, they will hold their peace. In short, the things they say and do seem unaccountable, for what God makes obvious to those who are on the way, is foreign to those who have arrived. These have no wants whatever; they are rich in possessing a city of their own. These people do the most valuable work of all, which is within. Blessed is the land wherein one of them lives; in one instant they will do more lasting good than all the outward actions ever done. See that you withhold nothing of theirs. May we all recognize these people, and loving God in them, may we possess, with them, the city they have won.

Q. By what signs may we recognize such a perfect man?

A. There are five: he never complains; he never makes excuses — when accused he leaves the facts to vindicate him; there is nothing he wants in earth or heaven but what God wills; he is not moved by time; and he is never rejoiced: he is joy itself. Perhaps there are six more signs, too. Such people are dead to flesh and blood and all natural appetites. Secondly, the pleasures of the body are like sour breath to them. They are forever listening to God's voice within them. They are not perturbed by the uncertainties of things, neither vexed nor depressed. Again, they turn everything to good account, so nothing can corrupt them. As St. Paul says, "All things work together for good to them that love the Lord." And they have no desire to compete with anyone; they live in the world as if there were no one but themselves and God.

Q. Are these then what is known as free souls, or free men?

A. Right you are. Holy Scripture cries aloud for freedom from self. Self-free is self-controlled and self-controlled is self-possessed and self-possession is God-possession and possession of everything God ever made. This is known as self-mastery. He who for one instant wholly resigns self, unshaken and motionless in himself— that man is free.

Q. Do you mean to say that a man can, in this body, reach a state where he is incapable of sin?

A. Now on this point, the seers debate; the best authorities say, "Yes," alluding to souls so perfectly disciplined, outwardly and inwardly, that they have no propensity to sin.

Q. Can a man fall, so to speak, from the state of divine union, back into sin?

A. I believe — no I am sure — that the man who is established in this can in no way at any time be separated from God. I hold that he can in no way lapse into mortal sin. He would rather suffer the most shameful death, as the saints have done before him, than commit the least of mortal sins. I hold that he cannot willingly commit, nor yet consent to, even a lesser sin, whether in himself or in another. So strongly is he drawn to this way, so much is he habituated to it, that he could never turn to any other; to this way all his senses and powers are directed.

Q. Some say, "To do God's will is the highest state." Do you think there is a higher?

A. There is, and I have just been speaking of it. Because you see, in the abstract Godhead there is no activity. The soul is not perfectly beatified until it casts itself into the desolate Deity where neither act nor form exists, and there, merged in the void, loses itself: as self it perishes, but is alive in God.

Q. Sir, there is much debate: does this power to realize God lie in God or in the soul?

A. I say the power lies in the soul; or better, the energy is in God, and the capacity is in the soul. If I were wholly what I am I should be God; there would be for me neither time nor place nor change. There is nothing so easy to me, so possible, as to be God, to remain what I really am.

Q. How can we please God? In what is He made most happy?

A. In self-perception. All God wants of us is for us to go out of ourselves with respect to our creatureliness, and let God be God in us.

Q. What is needful to attain love of God?

A. Four things: first, a real dispassion toward creatures; second, the right sort of active life; third, the right sort of contemplative life; fourth, an aspiring heart.

Q. Why don't we taste God's love?

A. Because our tongue is furred with the slime of created things, and does not possess the salt of divine affection. If we had Godly love we should savour God and all the works of God, and should receive all things from Him, and be doing the same work as He does.

Q. You speak of doing His work; why is it the saints seem so anxious to serve only the Lord at every moment? What is the great incentive?

A. You see, it is because they have tasted God, and it would be strange indeed if, once tasting and enjoying God, the soul could stomach anything else! As one saint says, once the soul tries God, she finds the things that are not God repugnant and distasteful.

Q. What is God's love for us like?

A. Will you understand if I tell you it is an arrow, sped without anger, and received without pain? You do not need to seek Him here or there. He is no further off than at the door of your heart; there He stands lingering, awaiting whoever is ready to open and let Him in. You do not need to call to Him far off. He waits much more impatiently than you for you to open to Him. He longs for you a thousand times more urgently than you for Him.

Q. What does Christ mean by being "poor in spirit"?

A. He means those who will nothing, know nothing, have nothing. Being poor in spirit means being poor of all *particular* knowledge. As long as it can be said of a man that it is his will to do the will of God, he has not this poverty; he should be empty of will and desire. A man should be as free of his own knowledge as he was when he did not exist, free even of the knowledge of God's work in him. Finally a man should be so poor that he has no place in him for God to work. To preserve place is to preserve distinction. Now I say more: I pray God to rid me even of God! How can I say such a thing? Because conditionless being is above God and above distinction; it was in this that I became myself, herein I willed myself and knew myself to make this man I call "I," and in this sense I am my own cause. For this am I born, and as to my birth which is eternal, I can never die. In my eternal mode of birth I have always been, am now, and shall remain eternally. What I am in time shall die, for it is of the day and passes with the day. In my birth all things were born, and I was the cause of mine own self and all things, and had I willed it, I would never have been, nor any thing, and if I had not been, then God would not have been either.

You do not have to understand this. I see you have not followed me. Never mind; until you are like this truth you will not see my argument, for it is the naked truth straight from the heart of God.

Q. But how can we possibly be "perfect as the Father in heaven is perfect"?

A. You are thinking of an accumulation of virtuous

qualities. But, my child, perfection means fulfillment. Imperfection means time. When time drops from you, your time is fulfilled. Time ends when there is no before and after, when you see at a glance all that has ever happened and will ever happen. In this immediate vision you will possess all things. This is perfection of time, and there you are perfect, and are truly the only son of God, and Christ.

Q. What do you understand by "the kingdom of God," of which Christ speaks so often?

A. God's kingdom means the soul being full of God, and nothing of itself. God's kingdom is Himself, and His perfect nature. There, there is neither time nor space, before nor after, but everything present is one new, fresh-springing *now* where millenniums last longer than the twinkling of an eye. There every spirit rejoices in the joy of every other, relishing it each in his degree; every inhabitant of the kingdom of heaven is, knows, and loves in God, in his own self, and in every other spirit. Again, as you know, Christ has said, "The kingdom of heaven is within you."

Q. Why did our Lord say, "I, if I be lifted up, shall draw all men unto Me"?

A. I believe He meant that when He dawns upon our heart and understanding, He gathers us up into Himself. In this sense all creatures are one man, and that man is God. In this sense man is all things. For He has the nature of all beings, and souls joined to Christ are in this sense one man with Him. And like Christ, loving yourself you love all men as yourself. So long as you love anyone less than your own self, you do not truly love yourself! Love all men in one man who is both God and man.

Q. Why do you think Christ said to his disciples: "It is expedient for you that I go away"?

A. That is not hard to understand. His disciples loved Him as a man and a mortal, so that in spite of His being the most perfect good God ever sent, yet He was a hindrance to His followers by His bodily presence. You have forgotten the latter half of the saying: "For unless I go away, you will not receive the Holy Spirit." Unless the soul is raised to a higher power, from physical to spiritual things, the Holy Spirit cannot enter it to do Its work.

Q. Meister Eckhart, by what name should we call on God?

A. God is called by many names in scripture, is He not? David said, "The Lord is His name." You should remember that words have enormous power. They have got it from the emanation of the eternal Word. All beings are trying to speak God in their actions; they all speak Him as well as they can; but they cannot really pronounce Him. Nevertheless, all are trying to utter God, who still remains unspoken. For God transcends name, transcends nature. We can find no name to give to God, but we are permitted to use the names His saints have called Him by, those whose hearts were flooded with His divine light. We ought to say: "Lord, in those very names which Thou didst instill into the hearts of saints, suffusing them with Thy light, we praise Thee and adore Thee." And again, we should know that in giving God no name at all we also praise and honor Him.

Q. When I think of all the saints I always think of my own impurities. What is the way to be rid of them, to become pure?

A. Pray to Him to purify you, to empty you. If you are empty, God of His very nature is obliged to fill you. The way to be pure is by steadfast longing for the one good—God. How to acquire this longing? By self-denial and aversion to creatures; self-knowledge is the way, for created things are all naught, they come to naught with lamentation and bitterness. So do not concern yourself with worldly trivialities; we are not made for trivial things, and *the glory of the world is only a travesty of truth, a heresy of happiness.*

Q. The prophets of old spoke much about the fear of God. Do you think there is any place for fear in the spiritual life?

A. Only the fear of losing God, of forgetting Him. Man should not be afraid of God. Fear is only the veriest beginning of wisdom. God loves man immeasurably, and man should love God the same. Is it not a wonder that man can be without Him without whom he cannot be? And if a man truly trusts God, he will leave himself in His hands—no fear.

Q. Who can say he really trusts God?

A. True, few there be. Only he can say he trusts God who keeps overnight not so much as a pennyworth of possessions.

Q. Are you speaking literally, sir? Is this what renunciation really means?

A. In truth, my boy, renunciation of self is true

renunciation. The other day a man came to me and told me he had given a quantity of land and goods, to save his soul. Alas, I thought, how paltry, how inadequate, the things you have resigned. It is blindness and folly so long as you care a jot for what you have renounced. Renounce yourself!

Q. Which would you call the greatest virtue?
A. The masters praise humility more than most other virtues, but I rank detachment before any meekness, and for several reasons. Meekness can be had without detachment, but complete detachment is impossible without humility. Also, humility means to abase oneself before all creatures, and in doing this one pays heed to creatures, one goes out to them. But detachment abides in itself. Perfect detachment is without regard, without either lowliness or loftiness to creatures; it has a mind to be master of itself, loving none and hating none; the only thing it wants to be is same.

Q. I think the practice of detachment is most difficult, because the unruly senses do not obey the dictates of the mind. How can the passions be made to obey?
A. When the mind is fixed on God, and stays there, the senses become obedient to the mind. As you would hang a needle to a magnet and then another needle on to that, until there are four needles, say, hanging from the magnet, so long as the first needle stays clinging to that; and when the leader drops, the rest will go as well. Just so, while the mind keeps fixed on God, the senses are subservient to it, but if the mind should wander off from God the passions will escape and be unruly.

Q. Sir, what is the "dryness" of which so many spiritual seekers complain?

A. When the mind is exerting itself in real earnest, God interests Himself in the mind and its work, and then the soul sees and experiences God. But since the uninterrupted vision and passion of God is intolerable to the soul in this body, therefore God withdraws from the soul from time to time, as it is said, "A little while ye see Me, and again a little while and ye see Me not." Our Lord hides Himself sometimes, for if the soul were conscious of God immediately, uninterruptedly, she would not be able to take care of the body. Some people complain much of having no interior life, no devotion, no sweetness, nor any such consolation. I say these folk are unrighteous as yet, and though they suffer, it is not the best, for they seek not God alone.

Q. We may know all this, intellectually, yet when distractions arise, in prayer and remembrance, it seems at times almost too much for us!

A. If we fail to see God, my children, that is due as much to our feeble desire, as to the distraction from creatures. Aim high, be high! To see God requires high aspiration. Ardent desire and abject humility together work wonders. I vow God is omnipotent, but He is impotent to thwart the humble soul which has towering aspiration. I say, and I would stake my life upon it, that by will a man may pierce a wall of steel; and we read about St. Peter that on catching sight of Jesus, he walked upon the water in his eagerness to meet Him.

Q. Some say, Meister Eckhart, that salvation comes by knowledge; others say, by works. Which is it?

A. It is by neither. For the soul is unable to encompass God by any means. Did I tell you, no man ever found God—He gave Himself away?

Q. You did, sir; but this implies dependence on grace, and what if God does not choose to be gracious?

A. Ah, but the higher is ever more ready to pour out its power into the lower, than the lower is ready to receive it. You see this is nature. So God is vastly quicker to pour out His grace than man is to take it in. Do you know, God likes forgiving big sins more than small ones? The bigger they are the gladder He is and the quicker to forgive them. It is the same with grace, and virtues, the greater they are the greater His pleasure in giving them; giving of largess is His nature.

None of you should think it difficult to arrive at this detachment from all things, however hard it may seem at first. Having once got into it, you will find no life more easy, more delightful. God is so very careful to be always with a man, to guide him to Himself in case he takes the wrong way. No man ever wanted anything so much as God wants to make the soul aware of Him. God is ever ready, but we are so unready. God is near to us, but we are far from Him.

Q. Will you tell us which you think is to be preferred, the life of action, or the contemplative life?

A. Precious few succeed in living the contemplative life at all here upon earth. Many begin, but fail to consummate it. It is because they have not rightly lived the life of Martha. As the eagle spurns its young that cannot gaze at the sun, even so it fares with the spiritual child. He who would build high must lay firm and strong foundations. The true foundation is the very way and pattern of our Lord Jesus Christ, who Himself declared, "I am the way, the truth, and the life." Perfect rest is, of course, absolute freedom from motion, and is our goal. St. Bernard says, "The most subtle temptation that can beset us is to occupy ourselves too much in outward works." Our least interior act is higher and nobler than our greatest outward one, and yet our loftiest interior act halts in God's unveiled presence in the soul.

Q. So then we must all be active for some time to come. But how can we know right action from wrong?

A. If any man acts in such a way that his deeds are able to degrade him, be sure he is not acting according to God's law. That is one test. Works done outside the kingdom of God are dead works, but works done in the kingdom are living works. If you want to live and have your work live, you must be first dead to all things, and reduced to nobody. So enter into your own Ground and work; acts done by you there are all living. But there is another aspect to this question. Actually, a man should orient his will and all his works to God, and having only Him in view go forward unafraid, not thinking, "Am I right or am I wrong?"

One who worked out all the chances before starting his first fight would never fight at all. And, if going to some place we must think how to set the first foot down, we shall never get there. A man should not dragoon himself: "This you must do at any cost." That would be wrong for thus he lends importance to himself. Follow your principles and keep straight on; you will come to the right place. That is the way.

Q. Then we need not always know what is best for us?

A. No, my child; whatever it is that lights devotion in your heart and knits you closest to God, that is the best thing for you in every case.

Q. Does the time come, then, when we feel it is the Lord alone who works in us, and not we ourselves?

A. Yes, this God does when He has given us Himself first. Any man who would attain to this must stay in the presence of God the whole time and refuse to let God be put out of his mind by fortune or misfortune or by any creature whatsoever.

Q. Although I try to practice the presence of God in every place, still I find it so much easier in the church and other quiet places, than in busy ones.

A. True. One may go to the fields and say one's prayers and be conscious of God, or go to church and be conscious of God; if we are more conscious of Him by being in a quiet place, however, that comes of our own imperfection after all. For God is in all things and all places and just as ready to give Himself so far as He can; and that man knows God aright who always finds Him the same.

Q. Sir, it is a very ticklish question, whether God is also the material cause of the universe. What do you say?

A. God is not only the Father, but He is the Mother of all things, to boot. He is the Father, for He is the efficient cause of all things as Creator. He is the Mother of all things as well, for when creatures have got their being from Him, He still stays with them to keep them in being. When a house is in being, its builder can depart because it is not the builder alone that makes the house; the materials of it he draws from nature. But God provides a creature with the whole of what it is, with form as well as matter, so He is bound to stay with it or it will promptly drop out of existence.

Q. And what of hell, Meister Eckhart?

A. Theologians speak of hell; I will tell you what hell is. It is merely a state. What you have here is what you have there. This is hell, if you do not see God and His friends. And it is much the same with heaven, for you should know that many a man who goes to heaven no more enjoys the light of God's countenance than sunshine in forest gloom.

Q. Can what we do in this life give joy to the saints who are living in eternity?

A. Yes, surely. Marvelous, incredible to tell, every saint rejoices in each virtuous deed, each good desire or intention; their joy no tongue is able to express nor any heart conceive. So how much greater must God's joy be!

Q. Some weeks ago your sermon was on the will and whether it is free or not; but I confess I was

unable to understand it. Will you elucidate this point?

A. I can put it more simply. Teachers declare that the will is free in the sense that none can bind it excepting only God. God does not bind the will, He sets it free – free to choose nothing but God Himself, and this is real freedom. Some people say, if I have God and the love of God then I am at liberty to follow my own will. They are mistaken. So long as you are capable of anything against the will of God and His law, you have no love of God, though you try to make the world think that you do. No one loves virtue without being virtue.

Q. How do sorrow and depression arise, and how can I overcome them?

A. All sorrow comes from love of something of which I am deprived. If I mind the loss of external things it is a sure sign that I am fond of them, and really love sorrow and discomfort. Is it any wonder that I am unhappy when I like discomfort and unhappiness? I turn toward creatures, whence there comes naturally all discomfort, and turn my back on that which is the natural source of happiness; no wonder I am woebegone and wretched! The fact is, it is quite impossible for God or anyone to bring true solace to a man who looks for it in creatures. But he who loves only God in all beings and all beings in God only, that man finds real and true and equal comfort everywhere. We ought to love things not a whit more than just as much as we love God in them.

People often say to me: "Pray for me." And I think to myself, "Why ever do you go out? Why not stop at home and mine your own treasure? For indeed the whole truth is native in you."

277

Q. The saints suffered all manner of horrible things. When I read of them I cannot help feeling that their suffering was somehow different, as you have implied.

A. Very true. Our Lord's friends do not suffer at all. The least suspicion of God-consciousness and sufferings are all forgot. This may happen while the soul is still in this body; while yet in the body a soul may reach oblivion of all its travail, not to remember it again.

Q. Sir, I have read nearly all the books in our library on prayer, but they seem to give me only hints. What *is* prayer?

A. Prayer is the practice of pure Being and glorying therein. Never pray for any mortal thing, my children. If you must pray for anything at all, pray for God's will and nothing else, for in that you have found everything. God is one, and anything extra that is sought for, or found, is not God but a mere fraction.

Q. What, then, is the prayer of the heart that has found this true detachment?

A. Detachment and emptiness cannot pray at all. The heart detached has no desire for anything, nor has it anything to be saved from. Its only prayer consists in being of one form with God. At the height of its detachment the soul is ignorant with knowing, loveless with loving, dark with enlightenment.

Q. You do not lay any great value on penances, then, in the spiritual life?

A. As I have said, it is not by fasting and good works that we can gauge our progress in the virtuous life. Penitential practices were instituted for a special object. Fasting, watching, praying, kneeling, scourging, hair-shirts, hard beds, or whatever it may be, were all invented because body and flesh stand ever opposed to spirit. The spirit is not at home here, where the body is. So to help the spirit in its distress and put a bridle upon the flesh, these practices are resorted to. But to conquer and curb the flesh *it is a thousand times better to put on the bridle of love*. Love is like the fisherman's hook. Once the fish takes it, it is done for — the fisherman is certain of his catch. God lies in wait for us with this hook above all. He who has found the way of love will seek no other. He who hangs on this hook is so fast caught that foot and hand, mouth, eyes and heart, and all that is man's is bound to be God's.

Whoever is caught in this net, whoever walks in this way, whatever he does is done through love. Such a person's most trivial action is more profitable to himself and to others than the cumulative works of other men. He rests more usefully than others labor. Therefore, await this hook, so you may be happily caught — and the more surely caught so much the more surely freed.

That we may be thus caught and freed, help us, O Thou who art Love Itself.

WILLIAM LAW
Nancy Pope Mayorga

A STRANGELY NEGLECTED FIGURE of the 18th century is William Law (1686-1761), Anglican divine, writer, and mystic. Strange that he should be neglected, because he is not only a master of English prose, but a deep and original thinker— insofar as the discovery of truth can be called original— and a great saint. Those who know him at all usually know him for his little book, *A Serious Call to a Devout and Holy Life*, which sets forth in lively language a plan of life so thoroughly Vedantic that one looks for quotations from Hindu scripture— but looks in vain. He found those practical and universal truths not in scripture but in himself.

Serious Call, however, belongs to only one part of Law's life, and, for the spiritual seeker, not the most interesting part. His life, as orderly and logical as his prose, falls into three stages: a period of controversy when his lucid and witty pen was at the service of all morality; a period of reason and appraisal when he established his ideals and wrote *Serious Call*; and the mystical period which burst forth at last in divine fire after a lifetime of devotion.

Law was born at King's Cliffe in Northamptonshire, became a fellow of Emmanuel College, Cambridge, and an ordained minister of the Church of England. But upon the accession of George I as king and consequently head of the church, his conscience forbade him to take the oath of allegiance. This made him what was known in those days as a non-juror, and caused him to be deprived of his fellowship and of any opportunity for advancement in the church.

This fact, however, did not by any means cut him off from living the active life of a churchman and theologian, for he had a vigorous and interested mind and threw himself enthusiastically into all kinds of social, moral, and theological controversies. He defended the high church which had demoted him, he defended morality, he defended reason against superstition, and he even published a piece called "The Absolute Unlawfulness of Stage Entertainments," whose very fist-banging title reveals the vigor with which he thought and wrote.

At the age of thirty-seven he became tutor to Edward Gibbon and lived in the Gibbon household for fifteen years. It was in their home he wrote *Serious Call.*

This book was composed for a generation of people whom Law considered irreligious and hypocritical, to point out to them vigorously that the Christian life is more than lip-service, more than morality even, that true Christianity implies a new birth in spirit, a new principle of life, an entire change of disposition. He says that if all those who profess to be Christians, really were, "it would change the whole face of the world."

From his acquaintances and observations of people, he created synthetic characters to make his points: among the many was Flavian, the orthodox churchwoman who, despite her riches, thinks that charity consists in giving a few pennies to the church; Flatus, restlessly searching for peace in the world and never finding it; Succus, whose greatest happiness is a good meal and who praises the minister who sets the best table; Negotius, the honest businessman who gives to the church hoping for success in his business. And Miranda, the true pattern of piety, who lives a life of renunciation, humility, charity, devotion, and abstinence.

It is when he describes the ideal Christian life that Law is most pragmatic. He begins with a plea for all Christians to have the sincere intention to please God in all actions. He begs them not to waste time. He points out that worldly business is to be made holy unto the Lord by being done as a service to Him. He urges chanting the name of the Lord, and praying for others. He says, "There is nothing that makes us love a man so much as praying for him."

He even plans an ideal day for the devotee. "I take it for granted," he begins, "that every Christian is up early in the morning." At daybreak, he says, chant a psalm to the glory of the Lord. At nine o'clock meditate on humility. At noon pray for humanity. At three o'clock surrender to the will of God. At six o'clock make a careful examination of the day and of yourself resolving to correct wrongs and repent of mistakes. At bedtime think of death. Remember, he cautions, that "the greatness of those things which follow death makes all that goes before it sink into nothingness. Then commit yourself to sleep as into the hands of God."

That he practiced what he preached goes almost without saying. If the fact needs a witness, one is found in the autobiography of his pupil, Edward Gibbon, who draws an appealing picture of Law as "a wit and a scholar, who believed all that he professed and practiced all that he enjoined. The character of non-juror which he maintained to the last is sufficient evidence of his principles in state and church. The sacrifice of interest to conscience will always be respectable."

A Serious Call which appeared in 1728 made a sensational impact on the public. The book had a profound effect on Samuel Johnson who read it while a student at Oxford. Despite a certain roughness of character and outspokeness, Johnson wrote some of the most inspiring prayers which might never have been written except for the influence of Law's words. Johnson himself said, "I expected to find it a dull book (as such books generally are) and perhaps to laugh at it, but I found Law quite an overmatch for me; and this was the first occasion of my thinking in earnest of religion after I became capable of rational inquiry." Consequently he was convinced that it was possible to be a Christian without any loss of intellectual integrity. John Wesley, the Methodist, was impressed enough by the book to seek out Law at the Gibbon home and become his friend. And many churchmen and writers of the day praised the book for its sincerity and its fine style. Even an agnostic, Leslie Stephen, some time later wrote of it respectfully, "Its power can only be adequately felt by readers who can study it on their knees."

But then, when he was forty-eight, William Law chanced upon the writings of Jacob Boehme. Into his open and prepared soul flooded the radiance of Boehme's strange teachings, vibrant, altogether overwhelming. Ethics immediately broadened away into mysticism. Rationalism was at once set afire with passion. And we have the paradoxical spectacle of the austere, conforming, soberly dressed, Anglican churchman, in a supremely rational century, burning and glowing with the unreasoning, unrestrained fire of God's love. Even the titles of his writings from now on show the awakening that has taken place: *The Way to Divine*

Knowledge, The Spirit of Prayer, The Spirit of Love, Truths of Revelation, and the like.

WHEN a man becomes a mystic, he breaks with society and walks alone with God. He sets up revelation against orthodoxy and intuition against reason, and cares not for the consequences. Many of Law's admirers dropped away at this period, among them John Wesley who was too practical-minded to follow this new path. But there were others who recognized Law for what he was, became his true disciples, and followed him to the end. Two of them were women, Miss Hester Gibbon, sister of his former pupil, and a Mrs. Hutcheson, whose husband on his death-bed had urged her to put herself under the spiritual protection of Law. When Law's patron died and the Gibbon household dispersed, this interesting trio moved to King's Cliffe, his birthplace, where he had a house and small property, and set up housekeeping. There for the next twenty-one years, they lived the severely simple life set forth in *A Serious Call,* a life wholly given to devotion, study, and charity. About devotion Law writes:

> Devotion signifies a life given to God. It is neither public nor private prayer. He is the devout man who lives no longer to his own will, or the way and spirit of the world, but to the sole will of God. This is the common devotion which is to be made part of the common life of all Christians. If our common life is not a common course of humility, self-denial, renunciation of the world, poverty of spirit, and heavenly affection, we do not live the lives of Christians.

For nine years after moving to King's Cliffe, William Law's pen was silent. It must have been a period of deep study and meditation, of extremely active spiritual work, for out of it came his greatest mystical writings. One thing was quite evident, that he made an exhaustive study of the works of Jacob Boehme, who, he announced enthusiastically, was "a guide to the truth of all the mysteries of the kingdom of God." Law's rational mind was able to sift out the sugar from the sand. He lovingly set himself the task of interpreting and clarifying the difficult and often fantastic metaphorical writings of the "illumined shoemaker". But Boehme was not his only study. He was an assiduous reader. In his library at King's Cliffe today there are more than six hundred volumes by mystical writers, said to be only a fragment of those that he collected.

His life now was a dedicated one, strict and ascetic to the point of austerity. He rose at five every morning for several hours of devotion. Most of his day was spent in his study, which was a room fourteen feet square, furnished with a table, a chair, the Bible, and his mystical books. Here he had his highest moments and put them down on paper for us.

The first writing that came from this period was *The Spirit of Prayer,* and the very first line of it shows the spirit of the new man. It states unequivocally, "The greatest part of mankind — nay, of Christians — may be said to be asleep, and that particular way of life which takes up each man's mind, thought, and actions may very well be called his particular dream."

Law's treatises are completely ordered, planned to the last paragraph. There could be no greater contrast than between his writing and Boehme's. Boehme

struggles with obscurities. Law presents his points with
the greatest simplicity and clarity. Yet within this framework of reason, the mystic lifts up his voice and sings.
Witness this definition of God, this hymn to God, at
the beginning of *The Spirit of Prayer:*

This is the amiable nature of God. He is the
Good, the unchangeable, overflowing fountain
of good that sends forth nothing but good to all
eternity. He is the Love itself, the unmixed,
unmeasurable Love, doing nothing but from
love, giving nothing but gifts of love to everything He has made; requiring nothing of all His
creatures but the spirit and fruits of that love
which brought them into being. Oh how sweet
is this contemplation of the height and depth
of the riches of Divine Love!

After defining the object of contemplation, he tells
what results can be expected of spiritual exercise:

And for the man who lives in this spirit of
love, all his wants are satisfied, all disorders of
nature are removed, no life is any longer a
burden, every day is a day of peace, everything
you meet becomes a help to you because everything you see or do is all done in the sweet,
gentle element of love.

Then he goes on to practical advice:

Stop, therefore, all self-activity, listen not
to the suggestions of thy own reason, run not on

in thy own will, but be retired, silent, passive, and humbly attentive to this new risen light within thee. Open thy heart, thy eyes and ears to all its impressions. Let it enlighten, teach, frighten, torment, judge, and condemn thee as it pleases, turn not away from it, hear all it says, seek no relief from it, consult not with flesh and blood, but, with a heart full of faith and resignation to God, pray only this prayer, that God's Kingdom may come and His will be done in thy soul. Stand faithfully in this state of preparation thus given up to the Spirit of God, and then the work of thy repentance will be wrought in God and thou wilt soon find that He that is in thee is much greater than all that are against thee . . . Through all the whole nature of things nothing can do or be a real good to thy soul but the operation of God upon it.

In his spiritual advice, he shows himself to be an experienced *guru*. On the practice of mortifications, he cautions, "Their only worth consists in this, that they break down what stands between God and us. But many people mistake the whole nature and worth of them. They practice them for their own sake, as things good in themselves, and so rest in them and look no further, but grow full of self-admiration for their mortifications."

He has a most beautifully graphic way of making his points:

The evil seek wrong and the good seek right, but they are both seekers, and for the same reason, because their present state has not that which it wants to have. And this must be the state of human life and of every creature that has fallen from its first state or has something in it that it should not have.

Purification therefore is the one thing necessary, and nothing will do in the stead of it. It is the purity and perfection of the divine nature that must be brought again into him, because in that purity and perfection he came forth from God. For nothing impure or imperfect in its will and working can have any union with God.

You are to seek your salvation, not in taking up your traveling staff, or crossing the seas to find out a new Luther or a new Calvin to clothe yourself with their opinions. No. The oracle is at home that always and only speaks the truth to you because nothing is your truth but that good and that evil which is yours within you. What you are in yourself, what is doing in yourself, is all that can be either your salvation or damnation.

LAW'S energy and enthusiasm for the work of God did not abate as he grew old, rather grew stronger, until we have at the very end of his life, at age 74, a fiery attack in forceful language upon what was in that day considered Christianity. He gave this work the deceptive title of *An Humble, Earnest, and Affectionate Address to the Clergy*. True, it is all that, but much more. He rolls up his sleeves and efficiently applies his axe to the forest of deceptions, pretensions, and pride that he sees in the Christian community. Let the chips fall where they may! He had been independent since he left college, all his life careless of clerical standing or social esteem. At 74, just before his death, he was not likely to suppress truth out of any personal consideration. He strides right in and lays his axe at the roots of everything men held dear and important — learning, patriotism, comfort, social refinements, all self-deception.

In a way, this treatise is a summing up of all his conclusions of a life of spiritual practice. He begins in his usual straightforward manner by announcing the one thing needful for Christians:

> The Spirit of God brought again to His first power of life in us. Everything else, be it what it will, however glorious and divine in outward appearance, everything that angels, men, churches, or reformations can do for us is dead and helpless, but so far as it is the immediate work of the Spirit of God breathing and living in it.

Then he analyzes the problem and makes the simple point that all struggle is between self-pride and humility. On the one side, pride of learning, wealth, and power. On the other, love, goodness, and the perfection of the divine nature. Then someone may ask, is there no place for learning and erudition in the church?

And Law replies, leaving no room for argument, "He in whom the law, the prophets, and the Gospel are fulfilled is the only well-educated man and one of the first-rate scholars of the world." And he proceeds to thrust this sharp truth at the clergymen of the day:

> For until your heart is an altar in which the heavenly fire never goes out, you are dead in yourself and can only be a speaker of dead words about things that never had any life within you.

A fiery man indeed! This is the courage of one who knows he speaks the truth.

He concludes his address to the clergy by saying,

> All that Christ was, did, suffered, dying in the flesh and ascending into Heaven, was for this sole end, to purchase for all His followers a new birth, a new life, and new light in and by the Spirit of God, restored to them and living in them as their support, comforter, and guide into all truth. And this was His *'Lo, I am with you always, even unto the end of the world.'*

The paragraph was written a few days before Law died — was written, it is said, on the last occasion when his hand was able to hold a pen.

PLOTINUS
Clive Johnson

Our aim is . . . to be what God is.

- Plotinus

Even a cursory study of the religions of the world will reveal that among them there exist certain differences in dogma, ritual, and creed. But looking further, we discover a connecting unity, a common thread of truth, running through all faiths. This truth has been propagated through the ages by a small number of men and women who, building their wisdom on the rock of spiritual experience, have transcended these religious differences.

The Roman philosopher Plotinus was one of these. Born into a corrupt age, in an empire sick and tottering from excess, he rises like a shaft of pure light from a dark and troubled period in history. His influence was such that St. Augustine, a century later, praised him as instrumental in his own conversion, thereby infusing Plotinian ideals into many Christian thinkers to follow. Numerous lines of poetry by Dante, Spenser, Coleridge, Emerson, and Wordsworth echo Plotinus, and we can only wonder at his effect upon those who lacked their facility of pen.

In the third century, the western world was beset with internal discord, constant warring, and a rapid succession of emperors (twenty-nine in seventy years). Famine and plague were commonplace, impoverishing an empire once thought invincible. Philosophy, too, was at its lowest ebb. Stoicism, which had been the moral guide of the cultured for five centuries, was reduced to insignificance.

But a religious consciousness began to seize the minds of a few men. Drawn to the philosophy of Plato, they hoped to extract from his dialogues the nucleus of a spiritual life.

It was to this group that Plotinus belonged. Yet, Plotinus occupies a unique position among his contemporaries. For, above all, he was a philosopher who not only discoursed on God, but had experienced Him. Serene, joyful, and supremely responsive to the radiance of his own soul—these are his distinguishing traits. They mark him as a mystic. A member of that small fraternity of men who have fallen in love with Truth, and found it by the agency of truth itself.

Most of what we know of his life is to be learned from a short biographical treatise written by his principal disciple, Porphyry, who also compiled and edited the *Enneads*, the only written works of Plotinus. Porphyry's account, which he attached by way of introduction to the *Enneads*, is somewhat gossipy and meandering, and often contains blatant eulogizing. But his intimate comments on his master's life and his accuracy in matters of fact make it historically noteworthy.

Porphyry introduces us to Plotinus by curiously noting that his teacher had not the slightest desire himself for recognition. "Plotinus showed an unconquerable reluctance to sit to a painter or a sculptor," he begins. "Is it not enough to carry about this image in which nature has enclosed us? Do you really think I must also consent to leave, as a desirable spectacle to posterity, an image of an image?" Plotinas himself confirmed.

How close in thought is this following selection from the *Crest-Jewel of Discrimination,* written some six hundred years later by the Indian seer-philosopher Shankara: "You never identify yourself with the shadow cast by your body, or with its reflection, or with the body you see in a dream or in your imagination. Therefore you should not identify yourself with this living body, either."

There exists no record that Plotinus ever came into contact with Indian philosophy, but some historians have suggested that it was for that specific purpose he accompanied Emperor Gordian in an expedition to the East. The campaign failed, however, and the Emperor was murdered. Plotinus barely escaped with his life to Antioch the following year, A.D. 244.

PLOTINUS was then forty years of age. It was to be another ten years before he would begin writing the *Enneads.* Porphyry tells us his master soon after went to Rome, where he spent the remaining twenty-six years of his life teaching and expounding his philosophy among a growing number of students. Plotinus himself was educated in Alexandria, a seat of learning and culture in the western world. For a period of eleven years he studied under the neo-Platonist Ammonius Saccas. Little is known of Ammonius, except that he was born a Christian, but later converted to paganism.

Porphyry relates that Plotinus was consistently reluctant, even loathful, to disclose details about his past. "Plotinus . . . seemed ashamed of being in the body," he commented. "So deeply rooted was this feeling that he could never be induced to tell of his ancestry, his parentage, or his birthplace." However, this did not completely discourage his biographer, who somehow managed to determine the year of his birth (204). But, as he later wrote:

> . . . He never disclosed the month or day. This was because he did not desire any birthday sacrifice or feast; yet he himself sacrificed on the traditional birthdays of Plato and Socrates, afterwards giving a banquet at which every member of the circle was expected to deliver an address.

Throughout his life Plotinus remained a contemplative observer of the world around him, virtuous to a fault, and ascetic in his habits. He considered celibacy essential to growth of the spirit, insisting upon renunciation of sensual pleasures if one is to remove the dross of the world.

Shankara, too, clearly emphasized the importance of withdrawing the mind from the objects of sense pleasure if one is to attain the goal of liberation:

> A man should be continually occupied in trying to free himself from the bondage of ignorance . . . . He who neglects this duty and is passionately absorbed in feeding the cravings of the body, commits suicide thereby. For the body is merely a vehicle of experience for the human spirit.
>
> Attachment to body, objects and persons is considered fatal to a seeker for liberation. He

who has completely overcome attachment is ready for the state of liberation.

Again, much like Shankara, Plotinus stressed a continuing process of purification, and used the example of a sculptor and his marble to illustrate his point: "Withdraw into yourself," he tells us, "and if you do not find yourself beautiful yet, act as does the creator of a statue that is to be made beautiful . . . cut away all that is excessive, straighten all that is crooked . . . and never cease chiseling until . . . you shall see the perfect Goodness established in the stainless shrine."

THOUGH stern in renunciation, Plotinus did not lack sweetness of character. His warmth and gentleness of disposition drew a wide assortment of people to him, philosophers, statesmen, and children alike. "He is gentle," noted Porphyry, "and always at the call of those having the slightest acquaintance with him. After spending twenty-six entire years in Rome, and acting, too, as arbiter in many differences, he had never made an enemy of any citizen."

A strict vegetarian, he strongly condemned the killing of animals for any purpose. "Plotinus was often distressed by an intestinal complaint." Porphyry writes, "but . . . he refused such medicaments as contained any substances taken from wild beasts and reptiles; all the more, he remarked, since he could not approve of eating the flesh of animals reared for the table."

Plotinus' stainless character and contemplative life encouraged many to renounce the world for a higher purpose. The Senator Rogatianus, when on the point of assuming a position of City Magistrate, suddenly determined to forsake his position, property, and life of indulgence. Plotinus frequently praised the senator and considered him a model for others to follow who were drawn to philosophy.

There is a story that an Egyptian priest once visited Rome, and desiring to exhibit his powers, offered to call forth a visible manifestation of Plotinus' indwelling spirit. At the summons a divine being appeared, and the Egyptian exclaimed: "You are singularly graced; the guiding spirit within you is none of the lower degree, but a god."

"Thus Plotinus had for an indwelling spirit," Porphyry tells us, "a Being of the more divine degree, and he kept his own divine spirit unceasingly intent upon that inner presence." According to Porphyry, his master experienced ecstatic union with that "inner presence" four times. "His one aim in life was to rise to God and become one with Him. Four times during the time I was with him, he achieved this relation, not as mere passive mergence, but by the ineffable act." Porphyry also related that "I too was once admitted and entered into Union."

Although Plotinus professed a dislike for medical practitioners, he had among them one close friend, Eustochius. In the year 270, Plotinus fell seriously ill from a throat infection and left Rome to stay on an estate in Campania. He sent for Eustochius immediately, but the doctor was delayed and Plotinus, as it were, had to put off dying. When the physician arrived, Plotinus said: "I have been waiting for you; now I shall restore the Divine in me to the Divine that is all." He then abandoned the body. Thus passed away one of the most remarkable spiritual personalities of the Roman age.

SCHOLAR A.H. Armstrong comments on the scope of Plotinus' greatness:

> He is at once metaphysician and mystic, a hard and honest thinker who enjoyed intense spiritual experience and could describe it in the language of a great poet . . . a traditionalist who could think for himself and encouraged free discussion in others.

It must be mentioned that Plotinus was not a completely original thinker. He borrowed heavily, for instance, from Plato's *Timaeus* and the sixth book of the *Republic* to create his own interpretation of the One (or Good), Divine Intellect, and Soul — the Platonic trinity. According to this theory, Reality proceeds from its transcendent First Principle, or the One, in an unbroken chain of successive stages, through Divine Intellect — the highest knowable principle — and thence to the Soul, where it manifests itself in various levels of experience and activity. In its final stages, Reality assumes the forms of bodies. But, Plotinus emphasized, despite their variety, these bodily forms are not independent of one another, but create a homogenous "unity embracing all." Multiplicity is discovered in unity, and unity in multiplicity; for all things ultimately proceed from God, and, in turn, the Divine permeates everything.

The destiny of the soul, Plotinus stressed, is to become spirit, to flower into perfection through contemplation of its real nature. And though he was ready to admit that the true contemplative must divorce himself from the world's pleasures and pursuits, Plotinus looked upon this world as a "majestic" manifestation of beauty, reverberating with divinity. Thus began a continuing argument with the Christians, particularly the Gnostics, who were inclined to consider the world as the creation of "fallen gods and demons." We find for example, this dark outlook on life typified in the commentaries of a recluse such as Peter Damiani. He writes: "Whoever would search the summit of perfection should . . . shudder at traversing the world, as if he were to plunge into a sea of blood. For the world is so filthy with vices, that any holy mind is befouled even by thinking about it."

But the holy mind of Plotinus found it far different:

> It would be unsound to condemn this universe as less than beautiful, or as less than the noblest universe possible on the corporeal level. A majestic organism complete within itself, the minutest part related to the whole, a marvelous artistry shown not only in the stateliest parts but in those of such littleness you would not have thought Providence would bother about them . . . the exquisite design of fruits and leaves, the abundance and the delicacy and diversity of flowers . . . . The Divine Spirit, in Its unperturbed serenity, has brought this universe into being by communicating from Its own store to matter.

PLOTINUS held that the cosmos was without beginning, guided by Divine Intellect from which issue the visible manifestations of its supreme Intelligence. This cosmic Intellect serves, as it were, as a mediator between the Soul and the One. Under its orderly rule, Plotinus contended, there exists no estrangement of parts, no "feebleness of distinction." It is a universe, in the final analysis, directed by reason, consort of the Divine Intellect, in whose bosom all differences are absorbed. In the third *Ennead*, we find:

> The Divine Intellect, then, in Its unperturbed serenity has brought the universe into being by communicating from Its own store to matter; and this emanation of the Divine Intellect is Reason [or *Logos*]. This Logos within a seed contains all the parts and qualities concentrated in identity; there is no distinction, no internal hindering; then there comes a pushing into bulk, part rises in distinction from part, and at once the members of the organism stand in each other's way and begin to wear each other down. Yet while each utters its own voice, all is brought into an ordered system by the ruling Reason.

This concept of a primal "seed" from which the material universe springs and at the same time has its being is basic to Vedantic philosophy. It is impossible for the Vedantist to conceive any first chapter in the creation of the cosmos. It is beginningless and endless.

Swami Prabhavananda, in *The Spiritual Heritage of India*, writes:

> God, who contains within Himself the seed, the material cause, of the universe, first brings forth

the universe out of His own being, and then in due time takes it back again to Himself. This process of creation and dissolution goes on for ever and ever, for it is beginningless and endless.

The inhabitants of this world are all moving toward one goal — absorption in God. Eternity, the dimensionless ocean of joy and bliss, is the witness of our universe, a cycle only in an "infinite succession of universes." But in the lower planes of existence the creatures of the world, deluded by ignorance (or *maya*), remain fettered by the chain of cause and effect. Thus, to the Vedantist, human birth, the highest rung on the ladder of bodily existence, is extolled because only to man is final liberation from the round of birth and rebirth possible. "Only through God's grace," says Shankara, "may we obtain those three rarest advantages — human birth, the longing for liberation, and discipleship to an illumined teacher."

But the Divine Mystery still remains. How did man ever become separated from the Primal Cause, the nature of his true Self, in the first place? Vedanta says that in truth he is not separated, but because of the enigmatic workings of maya he remains ignorant of the Self — deluded. The majority of us wander in the world of appearances, mechanically responding to names and forms. It is only when we transcend name and form (by means of one or more or all of the four *yogas: bhakti, jnana, raja*, or *karma*), and finally perceive the spacial and temporal attributes of the world to be merely shadows of Reality, that the veil of ignorance is torn aside, and the Author of all reveals Himself.

Plotinus ascribes this ignorance of the Divine to self-will, the desire for "self-ownership." He writes in the Fifth Ennead: "All awe and admiration [by those ignorant] . . . is for the alien, and clinging to this they have broken away as far as a soul may; their regard for the mundane and their disregard of themselves bring about their utter ignoring of the Divine."

St. Augustine expressed much the same idea a century later: ". . . Men go abroad to admire the heights of mountains, the mighty waves of the sea, the broad tides of rivers, the compass of the oceans, and the circuits of the stars—and pass themselves by."

Still, Plotinus regarded the world as essentially good. Only its superficial temptations and allurements have led man away from God. Identified with the mortal body, he forgets his immortal Self.

> The soul by nature loves God and longs to be at one with Him in the noble love of a daughter for a noble father; but coming to human birth and lured by the courtships of this sphere, she takes up with another love, a mortal, leaves her father and falls. But one day coming to hate her shame, she puts off evil, once more seeks her father and finds peace.

This "straying away" from God to meander down the paths of the world, forgetfully immersed in its pleasures and enticements, is illustrated by a parable of Sri Ramakrishna:

> In a room away from their mother, little children play with dolls just as they like; but as

soon as the mother comes in, they throw aside the dolls and run to her, crying, "mamma, mamma." You also are now playing in this world, deeply absorbed in the dolls of wealth, honor and fame, without caring for anything else. But if you once see the Divine Mother in you, you will no more find pleasure in any of these, be it wealth, honor, or fame. Leaving them all away, you will run to her.

PLOTINUS refused to draw any hard and fast boundaries across the field of experience — worldly or spiritual. To him God was the container of all, the fountain through which all things flowed. God is not absent from the lower world of sensate experience, but His bliss remains hidden from us until we free ourselves from the bondage of sensual pleasure. Once released, we melt into Divine Union.

Like many of his contemporaries, Plotinus subscribed to the belief that through birth part of the soul attached itself to earthly things, although its real place was with God. For, he says, "not the whole of our soul sinks into our body; some part of her ever remains in the Divine Sphere." Thus, when the soul finally recognizes its true divinity — its oneness — will it repose triumphant, like a victorious huntsman, in joyful reunion with the Divine.

An anecdote related by a contemporary of Aristotle, Aristoxenos of Tarentum, illustrates the friendship that Plotinus unknowingly shared with Indian philosophy. At the same time it suggests his argument with some aspects of Platonic idealism. "Socrates," Aristoxenos relates, "met an Indian in Athens who asked him what philosophy he was practicing. When Socrates replied that his inquiries dealt with human life, the Indian began to laugh and said that one could not contemplate human things if one knew nothing about divine things."

These "divine things" were the ultimate concern of Plotinus. The dialectic groundwork performed by Plato seven centuries earlier provided him with a philosophic foundation, but he used the materials of his mystical experiences to complete the structure of his religious life.

With a remarkable clarity, he describes this experience:

> The one who has experienced understands what I mean: how the soul takes on another life as it approaches God. Having come into His presence, it rests in Him, it merges in Him. It knows Him as the Dispenser of the only true life. Everything earthly is stripped away; bonds that fetter us are loosened so that we may adhere to Him, no part remaining in us, but with it we may cleave to God. Then shall we be worthy to behold Him and ourselves in a single light; but it will be a self lifted into splendor, radiant with spiritual light, nay, itself become a light, pure, buoyant, incandescent, identical with Godhead.

Time and again he reminds us "the Supreme is near at hand . . . " and exhorts us to "seek God with assurance, for He is not far away and you will attain unto Him . . . " To Plotinus, union with God was the natural, ascending aspiration of the Soul, a momentary embrace of the Absolute. And how is this to be accomplished? His answer is terse and direct: "Let all else go!"

DANIEL CONSIDINE
F.C. Devas, S.J.

It is both inspiring and refreshing to confront in religious writings a simple, unaffected faith in God. All too often our tendency is to weigh down religion with a cloak of learning, forgetting that saints are rarely doctors of theology. If, indeed, the ultimate nature of Truth is unity, then complexity and diversity are of the nature of the world, not spirit. Therefore the seeker after God is enjoined to simplify and purify both his external and internal life.

In his own simple approach to God, Father Daniel Considine, an English Jesuit of this century, certainly reflected more of the saint than the theologian. He stressed religious life, surrender, love, and, above all, joy in the thought and service of God. "The spiritual life," he wrote, "is the easiest, sweetest, and happiest thing in the world." Although Father Considine was a member of a renowned teaching order, he had none of its intellectualism. Instead, he possessed something of the trusting faith of a Brother Lawrence, a spiritual quality much needed now, in an age when people are pressed by doubt and fear — and faith, tragically enough, has apparently become foreign to the temper of the times.

DANIEL HEFFERNAN CONSIDINE was born on January 1st, 1849, at Derk House, in Old Pallas, in the county of Limerick, Ireland. At the age of nineteen he entered the English Province of the Society of Jesus, and after spending fifty-four years as a Jesuit, he died on January 10th, 1922, having just completed his seventy-third year.

Being a normal, healthy-minded boy, Daniel kept his thoughts about God to himself. No one could know what spiritual development was taking place in his soul, but his attraction towards God and the things of God must have begun early. In his old age he confided to a friend that in his thirteenth year he had made a sort of vow of perfection, something more than a mere resolution, a promise to God always to do the more perfect thing. This promise, he said, had been a source of considerable worry and scruple to him for some time. The idea of a vocation to the Society of Jesus seems to have been suggested to him in a perfectly natural but rather curious manner.

During a journey home to Ireland for the holidays, one of his schoolfellows entertained the party by forecasting their future careers. "Of course, Dan," he said, "you will be a Jesuit." The remark was a joke and might have produced no effect had it not been overheard by a distant relative of the Considines, who took the earliest opportunity of calling Dan aside and warning him, if he had a vocation, not to fight against it. This warning, given by one whose own life was apparently devoted wholly to horse-racing and other forms of sport, made a deep impression on the boy's mind.

"I used to think of what he had said when I was back at school at Stonyhurst, and I would get out of bed in the night to pray," he told someone a few months before his death. But his prayer was not for a vocation. He did not want to be a Jesuit, and when he crept back into his bed it was, as often as not, to cry himself to sleep. Not only was the prospect distasteful to him personally, but he knew that the choice of such a career would be a grievous disappointment to his father. He kept his trouble to himself, not seeking counsel from any priest, or sympathy from any friend, determined to do God's will, and hoping against hope that he might be mistaken.

As the months passed conviction grew, and, however reluctantly, he had to admit that God was calling him from father and mother, and all ambition, and all other interest, to service difficult and obscure in the Society of Jesus.

At the end of his Stonyhurst course he successfully passed the London University matriculation, and then for the first time told his father of his vocation, and asked permission to offer himself to the English Provincial. His father, surprised and disconcerted, begged him to wait before coming to so momentous a decision until he had taken his degree at Oxford. But the boy, now that his mind was made up, dreaded delay, and was anxious to put his project into execution at once. Eventually a compromise was effected: he was to go to Oxford for one year, at the end of which period, if his determination still held, he was to be free to apply for admission into the Society of Jesus.

At Lincoln College, as previously at Stonyhurst, Daniel led a quiet, reserved life, in marked contrast to that of his elder brother, whose social and sporting qualities endeared him to so many friends. Catholic undergraduates in those days were few in number. They used to meet together for lunch on Fridays at the Mitre Hotel, but even on that small group the younger brother left no impression. His time for influencing others had not yet come. The year's delay not only served to confirm him in the certainty of his vocation, it also witnessed the change in his mind from reluctance to desire. He did not return to the University, but after a few months at home, entered the English novitiate at Manresa House, Roehampton, on February 14, 1868.

Never, from that day till the day of his death, was he troubled with the least doubt concerning the reality of his vocation, and in the grace of that vocation he found, throughout his life, an unfailing source of joyful gratitude.

One who was a novice with him has written: "His fellow-novices noticed, that though in outward demeanor he differed in nothing from others, yet, in a certain sense, he was hardly a novice at all; he seemed already to have reasoned out with himself the whole conception of religious life and pious practices, and so to have attained to a greater maturity in his pursuit of holiness than was to be found in their first experimental essays.

"Already, too, in those early days, we noticed beneath his calm exterior manner a common-sense way of speaking of religious subjects. More than once those kneeling beside him in the chapel noticed that his tears were flowing plentifully as he prayed, dropping on the bench in front of him, while he remained absorbed and motionless."

Until his arrival at St. Beuno's, where he was sent to pursue his theological studies in 1881 at the age of 32, he had never really come out of his shell. Whatever he had done had been well done, but in so quiet and un-ostentatious a way as to attract little attention from any except his superiors. In the community he had never been in any sense a leading spirit, nor had he exercised

over the boys at Beaumont, or the young Jesuit
scholastics at Manresa, where he had taught, any marked
influence. At St. Beuno's, on the contrary, he began
almost at once to make his presence felt and to be
appreciated at his true value by his fellow-theologians,
as well as by his professors and superiors.

Almost immediately after ordination, Father
Considine was placed in authority. As a Superior he
won from all his subjects an instant respect, and, as they
came to know him better, an increasing admiration. No
one could come in contact with him without realizing
that he was a man of prayer and mortification, and no
one could fail to appreciate the sincerity of his complete
unselfishness. But those knew him best who needed him
and had the courage to confide in him.

"Courage" may seem an unnecessarily strong word,
but—and especially in the case of his novices—no little
courage was needed to break through the barrier of his
precise, correct, but always courteous, manner. Father
Considine was a man who never seemed to be "off
duty." He could never be caught in an unconventional,
easy attitude. His private conversation was as formal as
his public. He did not seem to invite confidences. A
timid novice was inclined to think he was being spoken
to as a complete stranger by one who was always polite
to strangers. The result was that the relations between
the Master and his novices were too often distant, cold,
restrained.

Many who were novices under him have regretted
this. They would have wished for less formality, more
intimacy, more encouragement, more individual instruction, perhaps even more private admonition. Such,
however, was not his way. If there was to be any

advance towards intimacy, that advance must be made by others, not by himself. But, once the advance was made, his reception of it left nothing to be desired: he was kind, he was understanding, he was strong; above all, he was patient to a degree that could not fail of final success even with the most difficult of his subjects or penitents.

As Novice-master he was recognized by all his novices to be a man of extraordinary holiness. His regularity, his self-control, his zeal for the glory of God, the fervor of his public exhortations, the spiritual insight revealed in his points for meditation, and his instructions on religious life, all witnessed to his close union with God; and though his severe corporal austerities were surmised rather than known, these, and the many hours he spent in prayer before the Blessed Sacrament, confirmed the common opinion. And in this intense personal holiness lay the secret of his power. His influence over others was gained less by what he said or did than by what he was. From his example the novices were really able to derive that inspiration which so many of them sought in vain from words of encouragement, or consolation, or remonstrance, that he could not or would not utter.

This method of teaching has undeniable drawbacks, but it avoids the danger of "spoon-feeding," makes for independence and virility in the spiritual life, and, most important of all, does not tend to interfere unduly with the working of the Holy Ghost in the soul. If Father Considine did not exercise as much direct personal influence as some might have wished, at least he did not impose his own personality on anyone.

Father Considine came into contact with many

priests at Manresa at the monthly meetings of the Apostolic Union. His humble, unworldly manner, and anxious care for their comfort, encouraged them to seek for a closer acquaintance with him, and then to ask for spiritual advice and help. Several lifelong friendships were thus begun, and of course, besides these, he had priest friends whom he had met on other occasions, especially when giving clergy retreats.

The following tribute from Canon Edward Murnane, written at the time of Father Considine's death, may be taken as typical of the regard in which he was held by many priests:

". . . No words can express all that I owe to dear Father Considine. He was to me a father, as he was to many more: wise, patient and holy. He was my confessor for many years, and it is only in Heaven I shall know all that he did for me. What he was to me spiritually he was also as a guide in my work as a priest. I never left his presence without carrying away many useful lessons. Although always a very busy man, he never grudged the time he gave me. What he was to me he was to many souls . . ."

Another priest who had known Father Considine under different circumstances wrote also at this time:

". . . For some thirty years, I counted Father Considine as my best and dearest friend, from the time when I was a convert lad and he was Prefect of Studies at Beaumont till the time when I was a middle-aged priest on the mission and he was an old Father at Farm Street. It stands to reason that in all these years our relative positions varied very much, but no passage of years could alter his unfailing kindness, his sympathy, or his intuition.

"Whether as a lad with a vague wish to be a priest, or as a young man in business, or later as a clerical student, or as a priest, without hesitation I took all my real difficulties to Father Considine, and by his decision did I abide, and never once have I regretted my act.

"There was about him a sense of security, he was humble and unassuming, he was courteous and kind, his sensitiveness and almost feminine faculty of intuition made him somewhat of a prophet; but above all, he had the gift of sanctified common sense, and it was this last which gave him his power for good when dealing with ordinary souls such as mine.

"Step by step, and with infinite patience and forbearance, he guided me through many difficulties and dangers, never proposing more than he knew I could carry out, ever encouraging, practical, and uplifting."

THE last stage of Father Considine's apostolic life was the period of eight years spent at Farm Street. Here he devoted himself with untiring zeal to the care of souls, preaching, giving retreats, instructing converts, and acting as director and confessor to an ever-increasing number of people of every class who sought his aid.

Throughout the weary course of World War I his services to anxious and sorrowful women were enormous. His delicate sympathy, his strong and infectious confidence in God, the generosity with which he gave his time to those who leaned on him in their hour of need, drew a host of penitents to his confessional and of visitors to the Mount Street parlors. Many of these visits he knew to be unnecessary; but though occasionally he would refuse to see a too insistent visitor in the parlour, never would he refuse a call to his confessional. As a friend in real need or distress he was indefatigable. The call of illness brought him at once to the sufferer's house, nor could any personal inconvenience or indisposition keep him away. Throughout his life, in spite of his natural shyness (it cost him a great effort to overcome his nervousness on being summoned to the parlour to meet a stranger), he had shown marked attention to the sick and sacrificed himself in many ways for their sake.

While Father Charles Plater was at Manresa, his father, a man whose holiness allowed him to be witty and humorous about his own death, lay dying of a long and painful illness. Father Considine frequently visited him, and on one occasion the sick man fell asleep holding his visitor's hand. Though the position in which he was sitting was very uncomfortable, Father Considine insisted on remaining motionless for the space of nearly two hours rather than risk disturbing the patient's much-needed sleep.

His self-sacrifice for the healthy and normal was shown in the perfection of his practice of the natural virtue of punctuality. He never kept people waiting, never forgot an appointment, answered letters promptly, and was careful to write at once if any plans had, unavoidably, to be altered.

During the last three years of his life many stories were circulated about extraordinary favors he was supposed to have received from God. The evidence for these is not sufficiently decisive to lead us to enlarge on the subject or insert here any of the incidents which have been related. There can, however, be little doubt that while saying Mass he was often the recipient of very special graces. His emotion while offering the Holy Sacrifice was most noticeable. From after the Consecration till after the Communion he was seized with violent trembling, and at the Communion he seemed to have great difficulty in forcing the chalice from his lips.

Whatever be the real explanation of these and other occurrences, his intense love for our Lord was known to all who had the least knowledge of Father Considine.

With advancing age he seemed to become more and more absorbed in the simple contemplation of the wonderful goodness of God. His presentation of God was always of One waiting to heap favors upon us if we would but let Him.

He could, even to the end, be stern, and administer sharp snubs on occasion, but for the most part his direction was marked by quaint and gentle humor, as when he likened one of his penitents to a rabbit, because "whenever you see God coming towards you, you immediately bolt."

During the period of his last illness his mind was frequently clouded. In conversation he would pass from sheer nonsense to his old sound "sanctified common sense" with a suddenness that bewildered his visitors. He himself was conscious of this, and told the Brother who was nursing him that he felt the humiliation of not being able to talk rationally and piously of holy things.

The constant deep interior happiness and peace of his soul had manifested itself during his life, not only in his speech but in his whole appearance, especially in his blue eyes, bright and clear as those of a child, and no less innocent. In death the same happiness was his, and was apparent to those who prayed by his bedside. In peace and calm he gave back his soul to God.

NOTES OF SPIRITUAL DIRECTION
Daniel Considine

Distractions and tediousness in prayer do not matter at all so long as your heart is with the Lord. You must humble yourself as much as you can. God loves humble souls and gives his graces to them.

Do not worry about recalling the thought of the presence of God at special times. He lives in your heart; keep a calm liberty of spirit. Don't be narrow or straitlaced in any way.

God does not want our spiritual life to be a constant stress, uneasy, foggy, stormy. He loves peace and joy and spiritual gaity. We often offend other people without meaning to do so. But God knows us through and through and understands what we mean.

The more we abandon ourselves to God, the more He can make of us, and we are never so much under his government as when we trust least to ourselves. The spiritual life is the easiest, sweetest and happiest thing in the world—to love God and be loved by him.

There are few invariable rules in the spiritual life, but this is one: Pray in the way you like best.

Try to think more of Him, and less of the human element in things. He is really behind everything that happens to you. You must try to realize this, and it will make everything easier and happier.

Just love Him, trust Him, and be happy with Him, and your faults will fall away of themselves. If you have been unfaithful, don't have a fuss about it. Turn to Him lovingly and trustingly, and begin at once to be more faithful without further ado. Never be sad or dismal. It does not become one whom our Lord loves. Be quite simple, free, and happy in His love.

Sometimes the best prayer you can make is just to think that God reads your heart.

So many books give a wrong idea of mortification. They fix all the attention on the things that are given up instead of on God. When a mother goes to the nursery door and calls her child, do you think the child says to himself, "I will mortify myself by leaving all my toys and go to my mother"? Certainly not. In the joy of seeing her he forgets all about his toys, throws them down, and runs into her arms.

God shows such wonderful courtesy in dealing with us. Very often He asks some small sacrifice of us merely as an excuse to make it the occasion of giving us a magnificent grace.

It is a mistake to say that you would be better if some person or some circumstance in your life were removed. God arranges all these things with the greatest care, to bring out what is best in you. The fault is in you not in circumstances. When a person with weak lungs goes out in fine warm weather he often thinks that he is better. The improvement is in the weather, not in himself. The disease remains there though he does not feel it, and it will show itself again as soon as the weather is less favorable.

After all, what is a saint? Only one whose will is united to God's in all things, not one who does extraordinary things. You need not do anything more than you do now to be a saint. Ecstasies are not necessary. You have only to do His will all day long because it is His will. The first point is arranged for you by obedience; the second point lies with yourself, and is not difficult. It does not mean that you must think about God all the time. That is not possible, and He does not require it. He only wants your will to be fixed in His.

You often see on the bureau of a businessman or a doctor the photographs of his wife and children. He is not thinking of them— he could not do his work properly if he were— but his heart is with them and he is working for their sakes. That is a good illustration of the way we ought to do our work. God does not want us to be on our knees when we ought to be teaching children or cooking the dinner.

Sometimes kneel before our Lord in silence and ask Him to speak to you. That kind of prayer will transform you.

Forget whether you have been slack or not and give yourself up altogether to loving God.

God is always perfectly consistent. He is infinitely powerful, and He knows perfectly well the weaknesses and limitations of our nature. He will never ask us to do anything which He is not most ready to help us do. It is as easy for God to give us a thousand graces as it is for Him to give us one grace. Our trust is the only thing wanting.

Let your spiritual life be as simple as possible, and do away with any apparatus in it that does not help you to come easily and happily into communication with God. Say to Him quite simply whatever is in your heart. He does not wish you to stand on ceremony with Him. God himself is more simple than we can understand. He is more like a little child than a man of the world.

Fortunately, in the things of Eternity, time does not count. It is the intensity of our acts that counts, and it is possible, with God's grace, to make extraordinary progress in a very short time.

If God is your Lover, how foolish to worry about anything!

The best way to meet temptation is to ignore it and go quietly on with what you are doing. If you are doing God's work, your heart is in His hands. Just go on quietly and God will take care of you.

God means the spiritual life to be a life of great supernatural happiness, and so it is to those persons who are generous and refuse nothing to God. And, after all, what are the things that God asks you to give up? Are they not things that you are really ashamed of, that lower you even naturally in your own estimation?

No one ought to be able to offend you, because your one endeavor ought always to be to humble yourself in everything.

There is nothing small or narrow or rigid about God. Even our faults can make Him love us more tenderly, as He heals us, and the forgiveness makes another bond between us. God does not endure us. He loves us passionately — if I may use such a word — more than we can understand.

Give up schemes and regulations about the spiritual life, and abandon yourself to the guidance of God, living from moment to moment in His presence and trying each moment to give Him all He wants.

Little children are simple and direct. They say exactly what they think without pose or affectation. Do you say things exactly as they are to God? He loves straight-forwardness and simplicity.

Many books are fond of warning people about the higher graces of prayer, because [they say] there is great danger of pride. The truth is that these graces humble the soul. She understands that God is doing everything, not she herself. It is like a master guiding the hand of a little child to write. The child knows that she could not write by herself, and so she is not vain about it.

You are too jerky in spiritual life; you go by fits and starts. As you get nearer to God you will go as fast but more steadily. You have plenty of time — indeed, time does not count with God. He can give you in one moment enough graces to make you a saint. When you love a person, you don't go by starts, loving him in the morning and disliking him in the afternoon. You must have the same confidence in God always, and be sweet and loving to Him always.

If you have done wrong, go to Him and say, "Dear Lord, I am extremely sorry for having been such a naughty child. Now we must begin again." And then begin at once to love our Lord more than before, and don't be upset or worried. Very often such distress is really only wounded pride seeking to find some excuse for self.

It is not good for you to go with great detail into the causes of particular faults, or to set yourself to think much about them or give accounts of them. What you need is to love our Lord more and more, and keep near Him more and more, and get closer to Him, and run to Him for everything. His love is the great motive-power. That is what you need. Go to Him for comfort and help and strength and love, and ask Him to supply all your needs, and then, just as a mother loves her little child to depend upon her for everything, so He will gladly take care of and provide for you.

When a person of mere ordinary virtue makes a mistake, it takes him some time to feel the same towards God as he did before. When a saint makes a mistake, he runs to God at once like a little boy to its mother, without excuse, like a brave, honest, confiding son.

One of the great signs of progress in the spiritual life is this quick return and peace of soul after a fault.

The saint understands mistakes better than the ordinary person, but what is far more important, he understands God better.

We please Him and win His love in the same way as we please and win an earthly friend.

God does not love you as a community, but separately and individually. Every soul is like a separate world to Him.

Keep yourself pliable in God's hands. He will most certainly mold you in a way that you don't expect.

One of the best proofs of advance is the facility of finding God everywhere and in everything where, indeed, as we know, He always is and is always working.

Ask our Lord to impress upon your soul the thoughts of confidence that help you, and He will do so. When in trouble or temptation, realize that God is allowing this in His love, to train and prepare your soul for greater graces.

Whatever we ask of God trustfully, He will do for us if there is good reason for it. Go especially to God the Father. Call Him your Father and ask Him to help His child. That touches His heart.

Don't trust in your own strength or wisdom or judgement any more than a tiny child does, but say, "The Lord rules me, and I shall want for nothing."

Depend on Him, not on yourself. There are two things needed to make a saint: absolute confidence in God, and complete distrust of yourself. The more you confide in God, the more He will do for you. God wants us to feel that we can do nothing of ourselves . . . Then He can come to us, and then we trust to Him for everything.

You are consecrated to God, so your body is His and your soul is His. Look upon both as entrusted to you by God, and thus by taking care of your body you will be doing a service to God. You must treat it as a sick child.

You will not progress by your own action, but by God's action on your soul. So don't trouble about the distractions, but confide in God. In your relations with others, remember thoughts and feelings do not matter, but only actions and words.

Don't be guided by spiritual books in your intercourse with our Lord, if in any way they cramp your loving, reverent freedom of intercourse with Him, or tend to sow the least distrust of Him in your soul. Ask Him to teach you himself what He is like.

The call to religious life is a call to be a saint. You cannot abandon yourself too completely to His love. If you do so, He is bound to honor to take great care of you, and you may be sure He will do so.

SARADA DEVI

Ray Berry

SARADA DEVI was born in the small village of
Jayrambati in Bengal, India in December, 1853. She was
the oldest of seven children in a large family. She said of
her own parents, "My father was very orthodox and
would not accept gifts from other people. He liked
smoking and as he smoked he would accost passers-by
in a friendly way and say, 'sit down brother and have a
smoke', and he would prepare the pipe for them. And
how kind my mother was. She would feed people and
take care of them as if they were her own children."
From an early age she showed a marked desire to help
others — working around the home and in the fields and
helping with the younger children. The old people of the
village would reminisce that from her young days,
Sarada was as diligent in her work as she was intelligent,
quiet, and peaceful. She never had to be asked to do any
work. Of her own accord and with great resourcefulness
she always did what had to be done.

Even at a young age Sarada was devoted to the
Mother Goddess and at times could be found absorbed in
meditation while performing the worship of Kali or
Lakshmi. Once during a worship ceremony, a neighbor
found young Sarada lost in meditation before the deity.
He carefully observed her for a long time, but he could
not distinguish as to who was the deity and who was the
child. He left the place with some trepidation.

Later in life she said about herself, "As a young girl
I saw another girl of my age always accompanying me,

helping in my work, and frolicking with me, but she disappeared at the approach of other people. This continued till I was ten or eleven years old."

You may ask why one should dwell so much on her childhood. There is no question that there was a very potent manifestation of divinity during these early years. Her mother, in later years, remembering her daughter's growing up and the remarkable events that occurred then, asked Sarada, "My child, I wonder who you really are? How can I recognize you, my daughter!" The daughter brushed this respect aside with apparent dislike, "Who am I? Who can I be? Have I grown four arms like a goddess? If so, why should I have come to you?"

AT the age of five Sarada was married to Sri Ramakrishna who was then twenty-three years old, and who himself had suggested Sarada for his bride. She had very little contact with Sri Ramakrishna, who was engaged in intense spiritual practices at the Dakshineswar temple near Calcutta, until she herself travelled to Dakshineswar to be with him at the age of eighteen.

Sri Ramakrishna had already taken monastic vows from a Sannyasin who had told him, "That man is really established in God whose discrimination, detachment, and realization remain intact even in the presence of his wife."

Upon her arrival at the temple, Sri Ramakrishna's first words to Sarada were, "Ah! You are here at last! That's well done." Sarada, happy at last to be with her husband, was overjoyed to serve him and learn from him. Sri Ramakrishna proceeded to instruct her in practical matters ranging from worldly affairs, household duties, and relationships with others, to spiritual matters like religious music, worship, and meditation. It was not long before he asked Sarada, "Well, my dear, have you come to drag me down to the worldly level?" She replied, "No. Why should I drag you to worldly ways? I have come to help you in your chosen path." And one night she asked him while massaging his feet, "How do you regard me?" He replied, "The same Mother that is in this Kali temple, and who gave birth to this body, is now massaging my feet. Truly do I see you as a veritable form of the Blissful Mother!"

They were extremely close in mind and spirit. However, there was no sexual relationship. Husband and wife were also monk and nun. When a married couple lives in this way, something extremely remarkable happens. The highest realizations were being put into practice in their everyday life. Sri Ramakrishna saw the Divine Mother in all women. He actually performed the worship of the Mother in his wife. Sarada Devi experienced the mystical union of her *Self* with her husband's *Self*. They lived accordingly.

Sri Ramakrishna later said, "Would it have been possible to live side by side with her without her undemanding nature? If she had not been as pure as she really was, if she had lost self-control, then who can say if I too might not have lost my self-control? My prayer to the Divine Mother that she remove even a trace of lust from Sarada's mind was literally fulfilled."

Sarada's days at Dakshineswar were spent hidden away from the public gaze — cooking for visitors, taking care of her elderly mother-in-law, and performing her *japa* (repetition of the Lord's name) and meditation. The

manager of the temple, when asked about her said, "I
have heard that she is here, but I have never seen her."
One day she told her young niece, "What a lot of work I
did when I was your age! . . . And yet in spite of all
those chores, I repeated my *mantra* (the name of the
Lord) a hundred thousand times every day." Along with
this japa and meditation, she would pray to God with
tears in her eyes, "Even the moon has its stains — may
my mind have no stains at all."

And of course with all of this practice there came
deep spiritual experiences. Yet Sarada kept these hidden
from even her closest companions. One day she asked
her closest friend, Yogin-Ma, to intercede with Sri
Ramakrishna so that she could have a little of spiritual
ecstasy. In her innocence, Yogin-Ma broached the
subject with him, but he became grave and remained
silent. On returning to Sarada's room, she found the door
ajar. Sarada was meditating, and Yogin-Ma saw her by
turns laughing and then weeping — the tears streaming
down; and then the next moment she lost all
consciousness and was in *samadhi*. Yogin-Ma shut the
door and left. When she returned she accosted Sarada
with these words, "How so, Mother? You don't have
ecstasies?" Sarada smiled bashfully to cover up her
embarrassment. Of these times she later said, "I always
felt as if a pitcher of bliss were placed in my heart."

EVERY so often Sarada would return to her village
home. Many interesting and telling events happened
during these visits.

While returning on foot to Dakshineswar from her
village Sarada fell behind her companions who were
hurrying to cross a large plain that was notorious for its

fearsome robbers. Suddenly she was accosted by a tall, rough man with a cudgel on his shoulder who growled at her in a menacing tone, "Who is standing there and where are you going?"

She answered meekly, "I am heading east."

The robber replied, "You are going the wrong way." Sarada stood still as the robber approached. As he looked at her face his mood changed, and he said gently, "Don't be afraid, my wife is with me. She is coming now."

She spoke to the robber confidingly, "Father, my friends went ahead and I am lost. Your son-in-law lives at the Kali temple at Dakshineswar. I am going there. Please go with me to him." Then when the robber's wife arrived, she clasped her hand trustingly and said, "Mother, I am your daughter Sarada. I am terribly afraid. It is my good fortune that you have come."

The robber and his wife took her to the nearest village, bought her some simple food, and put her to bed at a country inn. The robber stood watch all night. The next day they caught up with Sarada's companions, and the party set off for Dakshineswar. When the robber and his wife finally parted from the group, Sarada and her adopted parents began to weep.

The robber and his wife visited Dakshineswar several times. Sarada said, "Though my adopted father was honest and good, I believe he was a highwayman." She asked them once why they were so kind to her. They replied, "You are no ordinary human being. We saw you as Mother Kali."

"How is that? What did you see?" she countered.

But they confidently said, "No, Mother, we saw you as Kali. You hide that form from us because we are sinners."

She indifferently replied, "You may say so, but really I know nothing about it."

Although Sarada was extremely shy, soft-spoken, and mild mannered, she could assume a very strong and stern aspect that proved itself effective. This incident occurred at Kamarpukur, Sri Ramakrishna's village, many years later. Harish, a disciple of his who was mentally deranged, was chasing Sarada around the courtyard. One cannot help but think that his intentions were not honorable. The Mother said, "I ran out of energy and breath. I was forced to assume my real nature [that of Bagala, the terrific aspect of the Divine Mother]. I stopped running and turned to face Harish. When he came up to me with that crazed look in his eyes, I threw him to the ground, put my knee on his chest, pulled out his tongue, and slapped his face till he came to his senses."

But some of the most revealing incidents of her village life centered around her relationship with some Muslim families that lived nearby Jayrambati. These Muslims had for years been involved with the silk trade. When the British introduced cheap cloth woven in English mills, the local silk industry declined and was virtually destroyed. These people fell on hard times, and in many cases they resorted to stealing and robbery to fend off their poverty and near-starvation. They were a terror to Jayrambati and other neighboring villages.

Some of these men were hired to do some work on Mother's house, to the consternation of the other villagers.

One day one of them brought some plantains for the worship. A local woman saw this and objected saying, "He's a thief, Mother. Should those things be offered for the worship?" The Mother undaunted by this interference, gave him some sweets and fried rice. When he had gone, she rebuked this woman with these words, "I know who is good and who is not. To err is human, but few know how to lift up a man."

Amzad, another of the brigands, was a recipient of Mother's unconditional grace. One day she invited him for a meal. A niece of her's was serving his food from a distance, throwing it at Amzad's plate from fear of losing her caste. Mother chided her, "How can one eat when the food is offered with such scorn? Let me serve him." And when Mother removed Amzad's plate and this niece called out, "Aunt, you have lost your caste!" The Mother scolded her, "Keep quiet. Amzad is my son just as Sarat is." Sarat was a monastic disciple of Sri Ramakrishna, much loved by Mother. She added, "I am the Mother of all, the good and the bad."

Once Mother was lying ill with fever and Amzad tottered into the compound. He was emaciated, his clothes in tatters, and he was supporting himself by a staff. He peered over the bamboo screen, and suddenly Mother turned and endearingly said, "Is that you Amzad my dear? Please come in." They immediately entered into an intimate conversation on mundane matters. Amzad stayed the day with Mother and had a bath and a full meal. He left in the evening with a bag of tidbits, some oil for his hair, and a vial of medicine to help him sleep. If anything had to be done for Mother, and word was sent to him, Amzad responded. As if by magic, he could procure difficult items for her. But he could not free himself from his thieving and robbery. Once after a long absence he showed up at Mother's with some gourds for offering. She was delighted to see him and asked, "Where have you been all these days?" Amzad explained that he had been arrested for cattle rustling and put in jail. Unperturbed by the answer Mother sighed, "Ah me! I was really worried about you."

Such was the unconditional love of the Mother, and because of this love, Jayrambati remained free of the depredations of these people. Gradually the villagers realized the situation, and one was heard to remark, "Even desperadoes become devotees through the grace of Mother."

THE march of events continued with Sarada living mainly at the temple garden at Dakshineswar, sharing her joy and work with her companions and the women devotees of Sri Ramakrishna. Occasionally she would visit Jayrambati. Sri Ramakrishna, who was approaching his fiftieth year, encouraged Sarada to help others along the spiritual path and minister to their inner needs. Once he said to her, "Well, my dear, won't you do anything? Must I do everything single-handedly?" To which she replied, "I am a woman, what can I do?" But the Master replied, "No, you will have much to do."

Sri Ramakrishna died in August of 1886. Sarada Devi was thirty-two years old. The grief of his passing was shattering to the mind and the senses. But Sarada had several visions of the Master who impressed upon her that he had, as it were, just passed from one room to another. This gave her the strength to overcome her grief and the will to plunge deeply into a period of intense spiritual practice.

The Master had told her that after his death she should retire to Kamarpukur, his village, ask no one for anything, depending on the Divine Mother for her wants, and to become absorbed in her spiritual practice, repeating the name of the Lord. This was a time of great physical privation, loneliness, and uncertainty. But it was also a time of great spiritual accomplishment and far reaching realizations.

Sarada emerged from this quiet period of *sadhana* to become a remarkable example of what the spiritual life can produce. And this spiritual nature shone warmly and brightly throughout her life.

In the year 1897 she shifted her country residence from Kamarpukar to her village, Jayrambati. In 1908 a house called the Udbodhan was built for her in Calcutta. It was at these two places that the role of teacher really manifested itself and where she ministered to her many devotees until her death in 1920.

At the Udbodhan hundreds of people would line up to see her everyday. The line would extend into the street and around the block, and on special days of worship to the Divine Mother, the flowers offered to her would have to be removed in heaps to make way for more that were yet to be offered. Yet through all this she remained the same simple, loving, self-effacing Mother.

How many could digest this open adulation and still maintain a cool head, warm heart, and humility that permeated her entire life? One day a disciple seeing her doing ordinary household tasks complained to her, "Mother, why do you work so hard here?" And she answered, "My child it is good to be active. Please bless me that I may serve others as long as I live."

SHORTLY after Sri Ramakrishna's death, his disciples, under the leadership of Swami Vivekananda, banded together and formed the Ramakrishna Order, an order of monks. In 1898 Belur Math, a piece of property on the Ganges north of Calcutta, was purchased as the order's headquarters. One day Mother was taken there to inspect and bless the grounds. She had previously hoped that these young men, whom she considered her own children, would have their own monastery. She was delighted with the place and said, "Now my children finally have a place to lay their heads." Although she never assumed the role of head of the order, these disciples of the Master deferred to her in all important matters, and her word was taken as final in these decisions. Swami Brahmananda, the president of the order, was asked by a junior monk, who was a disciple of Sarada Devi, a question about his spiritual practice. Brahmananda, who was a powerhouse of spirituality himself, deferred to her. He said, "Mother will be coming in a few days. It's better that you put this question to her directly. My solution may be different from hers."

She, herself, gave *sannyasa* (monastic initiation) to many young men. It was her firm conviction that one who renounced the world for God was really blessed. And yet to one, who found he had to leave the order and had come to say farewell, she said with tears in her eyes, "Never forget me, I know that you will not, but still I say so. Believe me I shall ever be with you, do not harbor any fear."

Then there were those whom she encouraged to marry and live the lives of devout householders. To one who said, "Mother I won't marry." She replied with a smile, "How so my son? All things in this world are arranged in pairs, and just so are husband and wife. Why be afraid?"

The Mother also gave her approval to women who

were ready to renounce the world. To a mother who tried to dissuade her daughter from the life of a nun she wrote, "How much does a woman suffer her whole life as a slave to her husband, always catering to his whims. Let her renounce!"

The giving of sannyasa was only a small part of her ministrations. Mother came into contact with an untold number of devotees, and many of them received initiation from her. These included men and women, monks and nuns, and children. It was a rare, unfortunate person who could not receive her grace. She herself said, "If anyone addresses me as Mother, I cannot turn him away."

Swami Premananda, who managed Belur Math, had this to say, "Who has understood Holy Mother? She does not reveal the slightest trace of her power. But what great power she possesses. The poison we dare not swallow, we pass on to her, and she gives shelter to all."

Mother carried on a constant mental japa. Her attendant who noticed that even in bed she was doing japa late one night asked her, "Are you not asleep?" The Mother replied, "What can I do my son? The children come and eagerly entreat me for initiation. They take the mantra and return home. But nobody does any japa regularly. Some don't do it at all. Should I not look after them? That is why I do japa. This world is full of troubles and tribulations. May they never have to come back again."

To people who came to her for guidance Mother reiterated again and again, "The aim of life is to realize God and remain immersed in contemplation of Him. God alone is real and everything else is false." To most of these she held up the ideal of Sri Ramakrishna's life.

She said, "He who prays to the Master has nothing to fear. Through this constant prayer one obtains ecstatic love. This love is the essence of spiritual life."

But she was never narrow or dogmatic. She said to a disciple, "God exists everywhere and at all times. Are people not realizing God in other countries? Holy men are born on earth to show people the way to God. They teach differently. There are many paths leading to the same goal. Therefore the teachings of all the saints are true. Realization of God does not mean anything peculiar or abnormal. It enables a man to discriminate between the real and the unreal, deepens a man's knowledge and consciousness, and enables him to pass beyond life and death. In the course of time God and His forms disappear after the awakening of knowledge. Then there remains only the Mother. One finally sees that Mother alone exists, pervading the whole universe."

One touching incident that reveals the Mother's compassionate nature is the story of Padmabinode. He was returning from the theater late at night. While passing by the Udbodhan, her Calcutta residence, he was under the influence of alcohol, and he called out for his friend Swami Saradananda, who was her caretaker. No one in the house responded to his call for fear of waking her. Finding that he was being ignored, he sang out in a plaintive voice:

Waken, Mother! Throw open your door.
I cannot find my way through the dark;
My heart is afraid.
How often I have called out your name,
Yet, kindly Mother,
How strangely you are acting today!

Soundly you are sleeping in your room,
Leaving your poor child alone outside.
I am all skin and bones from crying,
"Mother, O Mother!"
With proper tone, pitch, and mode, using
All the three gamuts,
I call so loud, and still you sleep on.

Is it because I was lost in play
That you shun me now?
Look on me kindly, and I shall not
Go playing again.
To whom can I run, leaving your side?
Who but my Mother will bear the load
Of this wretched child?

As he sang with all his soul, the Mother opened her window. Noticing this he called up to her, "Mother, so you have awakened. Have you heard your son's call? Please accept my salutation." He prostrated in the dust of the street and then sang:

Cherish my precious Mother Syama
Tenderly within O mind.
May you and I alone behold Her
Letting no one else intrude.

The next day Mother remarked, "Did you notice his firm conviction?" And when her attendant complained about the disturbance of the Mother's sleep she countered, "I cannot control myself when he calls on me in that way."

SISTER Nivedita, who was an English disciple of Swami Vivekananda, and did much educational work with women in India, and was closely associated with the Mother for many years, wrote these telling words about her:

> In her one sees realized that wisdom and sweetness to which the simplest of women may attain. And yet to myself the stateliness of her courtesy and her great open mind are almost as wonderful as her saintlihood. I have never known her to hesitate in giving utterance to large and generous judgment, however new and complex might be the question put before her. Her life is one long stillness of prayer . . . she rises to the height of every situation. Is she tortured by the perversity of any about her? The only sign is a strange and quiet intensity that comes upon her. Does one carry to her some perplexity beyond her ken? With unerring intuition she goes straight to the heart of the matter, and sets the questioner in the true attitude to the difficulty.

Swami Shivananda, a disciple of Sri Ramakrishna and the second president of the Ramakrishna Order, wrote in a letter in the early 1920's:

> Holy Mother is not an ordinary woman, not a spiritual aspirant, not just a perfect person. She is eternally perfect, a partial manifestation of the Primordial Energy. If that Mother of the Universe, through her love that knows no

reason, has touched a devotee with her blessed hand, his spiritual consciousness has either been awakened or will be so; this is my unshakeable conviction.

Holy Mother assumed a human body to awaken the womanhood of the entire world. Don't you see, since her advent, what an amazing awakening has set in among the women of the world? They are now resolved to build up their lives gracefully and advance in all directions. A very surprising renaissance is swaying women in the fields of spirituality, politics, science, literature, etc. And more will come. This is the play of the Divine Power. Ordinary mortals cannot understand this mystery.

Early in the morning of Tuesday, July 21, 1920 Holy Mother passed away. Her last words of instruction to a disciple sitting at her bedside were:

Let me tell you something. My child, if you want peace, then do not look into anybody's faults. Look into your own faults. Learn to make the world your own. No one is a stranger, my child; the whole world is your own.

TEACHINGS OF SARADA DEVI

The world is the Lord's. He created it for His own play. We are mere pawns in the game. We suffer as a result of our own actions; it is unfair to blame anybody for it.

Give up this dry discussion. Who has been able to know God by reasoning. Reasoning does not disappear as long as one has not attained to perfect knowledge.

If one can regard God as one's own and call on Him without seeing Him, that is God's grace.

If one calls upon Him repeatedly, He becomes compassionate; and so a devoted attachment comes into being. This love for love's sake should be hidden from all eyes.

The body means the existence of desire, otherwise it would not have existed. It all ends when one no longer has any desires.

In one word, one should desire of God desirelessness. For desire alone is at the root of all suffering. It is the cause of repeated births and deaths. It is the obstacle in the way of liberation.

However spiritual a man may be, he must pay the tax for the use of the body to the last farthing. But the difference between a great soul and an ordinary man is this: the latter weeps while leaving this body, whereas the former laughs. Death seems to him a mere play.

This attachment to the body, the identification of the self with the body, must go. What is this body, my darling? It is nothing but three pounds of ashes when it is cremated. Why so much vanity about it?

The happiness of the world is transitory. The less you become attached to the world, the more you enjoy peace of mind.

My child, this mind is just like a wild elephant. It races with the wind. Therefore one should discriminate all the time. One should work hard for the realization of God.

Disciple: "I have been practising religious disciplines, but it appears that the impurities of the mind are not growing less."
Mother: "You have rolled different threads on a reel — red, black, and white. While unrolling you will see them all exactly in the same way."

Can anyone altogether destroy lust? A little of it remains as long as one has the body. But it can be subdued, as a snake can be subdued by charmed dust.

He who has a pure mind sees everything pure.

The mind keeps well when engaged in work. And yet japa, meditation, and prayer are specially needed. You must at least sit down once in the morning and again in the evening. That acts as a rudder to a boat.

As wind removes the cloud, so the Name of God destroys the cloud of worldliness.

Do you know the significance of japa and other spiritual practices? By these, the power of the sense organs is subdued.

See what a tiny seed is the Name of God. From it in time come divine moods, devotion, love, and spiritual consummation.

In time the mind itself becomes the guru. To pray to God and meditate on Him for two minutes with full concentration is better than doing so for long hours without it.

Devotee: "Mother what is the secret?"

Mother, pointing to a small timepiece in a niche, said: "As that timepiece is ticking, so also go on repeating God's Name. That will bring you everything. Nothing more need be done."

Just see the power of habit. By the law of habit man attains realization by continuous practise of japa.

Without regular practice nothing can be attained.

Spiritual practices are meant to keep the mind steady at the feet of God; to keep it immersed in His thought, repeat His Name.

Spiritual progress becomes easier if husband and wife agree in their views regarding spiritual practices.

I cannot see others' faults. I am simply not made that way. There are enough people always ready to criticise others. Surely the world will not come to an end if I refrain from doing so.

I am the Mother of the wicked, as I am the Mother of the virtuous. Never fear. Whenever you are in distress, just say to yourself, "I have a Mother."

CONTRIBUTORS

ARNOLD TOYNBEE 1889-1975, noted historian.

SWAMI PRABHAVANANDA 1893-1976, Monk of the Ramakrishna Order, was founder and head of the Vedanta Society of Southern California from 1929 until his death in 1976.

C.H. MACLACHLAN 1901-1985, former editor of the Long Islander, a newspaper founded by Walt Whitman.

NANCY POPE MAYORGA 1905-1984, was a successful short story writer. Her final published work was *The Hunger of the Soul, A Spiritual Diary.*

RABBI ASHER BLOCK (now retired) has long been a student of Jewish mysticism and mysticism in general. He has authored articles of religious interest for publications here and abroad.

CHARLES ALEXANDER EASTMAN (Ohiyesa) 1858-1939 was a mixed-blood Sioux. He received a B.S. from Dartmouth and his M.D. from Boston University. He devoted his life to helping his fellow Indians adapt to the white world while preserving the best of their own culture. He wrote twelve other books on Indian life.

CLIVE JOHNSON, a former monk and editor of *Vedanta and the West* and other works, is a writer and communications consultant.

PHILLIP L. GRIGGS is now a monk of the Ramakrishna Order at the Vivekananda Monastery in Ganges, Michigan.

F.C. DEVAS, S.J. 1877-1951 was a novice under Fr. Daniel Considine and a life-long friend of his.

RAY BERRY, a carpenter, mason, and woodsman has been associated with Vedanta for almost thirty years.

NICLAS BERRY, the artist, is a senior at Haverford College, majoring in sculpture. He has already won several awards for his artwork in various media.

ACKNOWLEDGEMENTS AND BIBLIOGRAPHY

SRI RAMAKRISHNA: *Vedanta for East and West,* vol. VIII, no. 5 published by the Ramakrishna Vedanta Centre, Bourne End, Bucks SL8 5LG UK.

The Gospel of Sri Ramakrishna as translated into English by Swami Nikhilananda and published by the Ramakrishna-Vivekananda Center of New York, Copyright 1942 by Swami Nikhilananda.

SWAMI VIVEKANANDA: *Vedanta and the West* no.158, November-December 1962, copyright 1962 by Vedanta Society of Southern California.

HENRY DAVID THOREAU: *Prabuddha Bharata* Mayavati, U.P. India.

RABI'A': *Rabi'a' the Mystic A.D. 717-801 and Her Fellow Saints in Islam* by Margaret Smith, Cambridge University Press, 1928.

Muslim Saints and Mystics by Farid al-Din Attar translated by A.J. Arberry 1966 published by Arkana, a division of Penguin Books.

GERHART TERSTEEGEN: *Vedanta and the West* no. 185 May-June 1967.

The Quiet Way translated by Emily Chisholm. The Epworth Press, London 1950.

Hymns of Ter Steegen translated by Francis Bevan, Peckering and Inglis, London.

Great Saints by Walter Nigg, translated by William Sterling, Henry Regnery Co. Hinsdale, Illinois.

THE BAL SHEM TOV: *Vedanta Kesari* Annual 1989 Sri Ramakrishna Math Mylapore, Madras.

Tales of the Hasidim: The Early Masters by Martin Buber

Tales of the Hasidim: The Later Masters by Martin Buber copyright 1947, 1948, and 1975 by Schocken Books, Inc.

Souls on Fire by Elie Wiesel, 1972 Random House.

KABIR: *Vedanta and the West* no. 177 January-February, 1966

Songs of Kabir translated by Rabindranath Tagore.

SOJOURNER TRUTH: *Narrative of Sojourner Truth* by Olive Gilbert, Battle Creek, Michigan 1884.

Sojourner Truth, God's Faithful Pilgrim by Arthur Huff Fauset, The University of North Carolina Press 1938.

LAOTSE: *Vedanta and the West* no. 191 May-June, 1968.

ST. JOHN OF THE CROSS: *Vedanta and the West* no. 206 November-December, 1970.

THE SOUL OF THE INDIAN: *The Soul of the Indian* by Charles Alexander Eastman, University of Nebraska Press, 1911.

The Sacred Pipe, Black Elk's Account of the Seven Rites of the Oglala Sioux by Joseph Epes Brown, University of Oklahoma Press, 1953.

The Gospel of the Red Man by Ernest Thompson Seton, Doubleday, Doran, and Co., 1936.

Voices of Our Ancestors by Dhyani Ywahoo, Shambala, 1987.

The Sacred — Ways of Knowledge, Sources of Life by Peggy V. Beck and Anna L. Walters, Navajo Community College Press, 1980.

American Indian Prose and Poetry by Margot Astrov, Capricorn Books, New York, 1962.

Lame Deer: Seeker of Visions by John Fire/Lame Deer and Richard Erdoes, Simon and Schuster, 1976.

Native American Wisdom compiled by Kent Newburn and Louise Mengelkoch, New World Library, 1991.

RAMPRASAD: *Vedanta and the West* no. 180 July-August, 1966

The Gospel Of Ramakrishna, as translated by Swami Nikhilananda.

PEACE PILGRIM: *Peace Pilgrim* compiled by Friends of Peace Pilgrim, 43480 Cedar Ave. Hemet, Ca. 92344.

BROTHER LAWRENCE: *Vedanta and the West* no. 178 March-April, 1966.

KENKO: *Vedanta and the West* no. 186 July-August, 1967.

The Harvest of Leisure by Yoshida Kenko translated by Ryukichi Kerata, John Murray, London.

The Journal of Kenko by Herbert H. Gowen, University of Washington, Seattle, 1927.

ACKNOWLEDGEMENTS AND BIBLIOGRAPHY

THOMAS A KEMPIS: *Vedanta and the West* no. 196 March-April, 1968.

The Imitation of Christ by Thomas á Kempis, David McKay Co. Philadelphia.

The Following of Christ, The Spiritual Diary of Gerard Groote translated by Joseph Malaise, S.J, America Press, New York.

MIRA BAI: *Vedanta and the West* no. 169 September-October, 1964.

Mira:The Divine Lover by V.K. Sethi, Radha Soami Satsang Beas, Amritsar, Punjab, India, 1979.

MEISTER ECKHART: *Vedanta and the West* no. 115 September-October, 1955.

WILLIAM LAW: *Vedanta and the West* no. 187 September-October, 1967.

PLOTINUS: *Vedanta and the West* no. 179 May-June, 1966.

DANIEL CONSIDINE: *Vedanta and the West* no. 193 September-October, 1968. No. 195 January-February, 1969.

Delight in the Lord by Daniel Considine, S.J. Manresa House, 114, Mount Street, London.

The Virtues of the Divine Child by Daniel Considine Manresa House, London.

SARADA DEVI: *Holy Mother* by Swami Nikhilananda published by The Ramakrishna-Vivekananda Center of New York, Copyright 1982 by Swami Nikhilananda.

Holy Mother, Shri Sarada Devi by Swami Gambhirananda, Sri Ramakrishna Math, Mylapore, Madras, 1977.

Teachings of Sri Sarada Devi, The Holy Mother Sri Ramakrishna Math, Mylapore, Madras, 1983.

THANKS

Clive Johnson for the initial prodding to start the project.

Michael Sykes of Floating Island for guiding me in the first phases of publication.

David Gamble for suggesting the illustrations.

David Brast and Bramachari Sudhira Chaitanya, associate editors.

Gale Gregory, Gregory and Falk Lithographers.

Zea Morvitz, typesetting.

Robert Cooney, graphic design.

LeeLee Ammidon-Sutton, proofreading.

Gay and Stewart Schecter of Point Reyes Printing.

Wes Sokolosky, computer wars.

Robert Yarber, Karen Sexton, Sam and Elvira Graci, Michael Whitt, Carolyn Kenny, Heather Oakley, Ann Myron, Huston and Kendra Smith, John and Ann Rush and Richard Polese (friends of Peace Pilgrim), Nancy Hemingway, Chuck Eckhart and many other friends who commented on the manuscript and the artwork.

The brothers at Trabuco Monastery for their hospitality.

Mike Gallagher for the freedom to work in peace.

My wife Sonja for typing, proofreading, and editing.

My son Niclas for agreeing to do the artwork.

And particular thanks to Marion Weber who saw this project through from start to finish.

For more information concerning the ideas expressed in this book there are of course many sources. I am familiar with the different Vedanta Societies in this country, Canada, and Europe which are affiliated with the Ramakrishna Order of India.

For a complete listing of these centers and an extensive booklist of religious literature from all the major religious traditions, write to one of the following:

Vedanta Society of Southern California
1946 Vedanta Place
Hollywood, CA 90068
213-465-7114

Vedanta Society of Northern California
2323 Vallejo Street
San Francisco, CA 94123
415-922-2323

This book is available to the trade from:

Atrium Publishers Group
11270 Clayton Creek Road
Lower Lake, CA 95457
1-800-275-2606

Individual retail copies may be ordered directly from the publisher for $14.95 + $3.00 Shipping and handling; California residents add: $1.08 (7.25% Sales Tax).

Joshua Press
P.O. Box 21
Olema, Ca 94950